Taren Fira

The Queer Advocate in Alyndra – Unfiltered

Maya Zhang

ISBN: 9781779697837
Imprint: Telephasic Workshop
Copyright © 2024 Maya Zhang.
All Rights Reserved.

Contents

Introduction   1
   Taren Fira: The Rising Star   1

Chapter One: A Fire Ignited   13
   Section One: The Journey Begins   13

Bibliography   23
   Section Two: Intersectionality and Allyship   38
   Section Three: Taren Fira Goes International   64

Chapter Two: Navigating the Political Landscape   89
   Section One: LGBTQ Rights in Alyndra   89

Bibliography   103
   Section Two: Upholding LGBTQ Rights Globally   117
   Section Three: Facing Political Opposition   144

Chapter Three: The Power of Personal Narratives   171
   Section One: Changing Hearts and Minds   171

Bibliography   177

Bibliography   189
   Section Two: Taren Fira's Personal Journey   198

Bibliography   207
   Section Three: Allies and the Importance of Their Voices   221

Bibliography   229

Chapter Four: Beyond Advocacy 251
Section One: Taren Fira's Legacy 251
Section Two: Lessons Learned in LGBTQ Activism 275

Bibliography 281
Section Three: Taren Fira's Final Message 301

Index 313

Introduction

Taren Fira: The Rising Star

The Early Years of Taren Fira

Taren Fira was born in the vibrant city of Alyndra, a place known for its eclectic mix of cultures, colors, and characters. From an early age, Taren exhibited a unique spark, one that would eventually ignite a movement. Growing up in a household that valued creativity and open-mindedness, Taren was encouraged to express themselves freely. This nurturing environment allowed Taren to explore various interests, from painting to poetry, and even the occasional foray into the world of theater.

As a child, Taren was different. While other children played with traditional toys, Taren found solace in the pages of fantastical books, often imagining themselves as the brave heroes who defied norms. Taren's first encounter with the concept of gender identity came during a school project on family structures. While discussing the roles of family members, Taren felt a stirring within, a sense of dissonance with the conventional labels of "boy" or "girl." This moment marked the beginning of Taren's journey of self-discovery, as they began to question the rigid boundaries imposed by society.

However, the early years were not without their challenges. Taren faced bullying and isolation from peers who struggled to understand their nonconformity. The harsh realities of discrimination began to seep into Taren's life, manifesting in taunts and exclusion during recess. This experience is not uncommon among LGBTQ youth, as research indicates that 70% of LGBTQ students report being bullied in school settings (Kosciw et al., 2020). Taren's resilience shone through as they channeled this pain into art, using their experiences as fuel for creativity.

Taren's artistic endeavors became a form of activism, even before they fully recognized it as such. Through their paintings, Taren depicted scenes of joy and sorrow, often blending elements of their own life with fantastical landscapes. One particularly poignant piece, titled "The Colors of My Heart," illustrated a figure surrounded by a storm of vibrant colors, symbolizing the internal chaos that often accompanies the journey of self-acceptance. This artwork caught the attention of a local gallery, leading to Taren's first exhibition at the age of fifteen.

In addition to art, Taren found solace in literature. They voraciously read works by authors such as Audre Lorde and James Baldwin, whose words resonated deeply with Taren's own struggles. These literary figures became beacons of hope, demonstrating that one could embrace their identity and still make a significant impact on the world. Taren often reflected on Lorde's assertion that "the master's tools will never dismantle the master's house," which inspired them to seek alternative methods of advocacy that prioritized authenticity and inclusivity.

The turning point in Taren's early years came during a pivotal moment in high school. A teacher, recognizing Taren's struggles, introduced them to the concept of intersectionality—a term coined by Kimberlé Crenshaw to describe how different forms of discrimination overlap and affect individuals in unique ways. This revelation was transformative for Taren, as it illuminated the complexities of their own identity and the societal structures that perpetuated inequality. Taren began to understand that their experiences were not isolated but part of a larger tapestry of struggles faced by many in the LGBTQ community.

Motivated by this newfound understanding, Taren took the initiative to create a safe space within their school for LGBTQ students. They organized meetings where peers could share their stories, fostering a sense of belonging and solidarity. This grassroots effort laid the foundation for Taren's future activism, proving that even small actions can lead to significant change.

In summary, the early years of Taren Fira were marked by a profound journey of self-discovery, resilience in the face of adversity, and the blossoming of a passionate advocate. Through art, literature, and the support of a few key figures, Taren began to forge their path as a queer activist. Their experiences would shape not only their identity but also the trajectory of LGBTQ advocacy in Alyndra and beyond. As Taren would later reflect, "It was in those formative years that I learned the power of my voice and the importance of standing up for who I am, no matter the cost."

Discovering the Activist Within

In the quaint town of Eldergrove, nestled within the enchanting realm of Alyndra, Taren Fira's journey toward activism began not with grand gestures but through the subtle whispers of injustice that echoed through the hallways of their high school. It was here, amidst the clamor of teenage life, that Taren first encountered the stark realities of discrimination, a juxtaposition against the vibrant colors of their emerging queer identity. The awakening of the activist within was akin to the gradual blooming of a flower, nurtured by the rich soil of personal experiences and the harsh winds of societal norms.

The Catalyst of Awareness Taren's realization of their activist spirit was catalyzed by a particularly poignant incident during a school assembly. A guest speaker, a local LGBTQ+ advocate, shared their story of struggle and triumph in the face of adversity. The speaker's narrative resonated deeply with Taren, igniting a spark of recognition within. It was as if a mirror had been held up to Taren's own experiences—moments of isolation, fear, and the yearning for acceptance. This pivotal moment can be understood through the lens of critical consciousness, a theory posited by Paulo Freire, which emphasizes the importance of awareness in combating oppression. Freire argues that awareness leads to action, and for Taren, this was the moment they transitioned from passive observer to active participant.

The Power of Community As Taren began to explore their identity more fully, they sought out community spaces where they could connect with others who shared similar experiences. Joining a local LGBTQ+ youth group provided Taren with a sense of belonging that had previously felt elusive. Within this safe space, they encountered a diverse tapestry of identities and stories, each thread contributing to a collective narrative of resilience. The group organized discussions, workshops, and art projects that celebrated queer identity while addressing the challenges faced by LGBTQ+ individuals in their community.

The importance of community in activism cannot be overstated. According to social movement theory, collective identity and solidarity are crucial components in mobilizing individuals toward a common goal. Taren found strength in the shared experiences of their peers, recognizing that their struggles were not isolated but part of a larger tapestry of systemic oppression. This realization galvanized Taren to take action, leading them to advocate for more inclusive policies within their school.

Art as Activism In their quest to discover the activist within, Taren turned to art as a powerful medium for expression and advocacy. They began to create visual art pieces that depicted the struggles and triumphs of the LGBTQ+ community, using bold colors and evocative imagery to convey messages of love, acceptance, and resistance. Taren's artwork became a form of activism, challenging stereotypes and breaking down barriers through creativity.

One particular piece, titled "The Spectrum of Love," featured a vibrant rainbow intertwined with images of diverse couples, symbolizing the beauty of love in all its forms. This artwork not only resonated with their peers but also sparked conversations around acceptance and representation. Taren's artistic endeavors exemplified the theory of cultural activism, which posits that art can serve as a vehicle for social change by raising awareness and inspiring action.

Facing Challenges However, the path to discovering their activist self was not without obstacles. Taren faced backlash from certain segments of their community, including peers who perpetuated harmful stereotypes and adults who dismissed their concerns. These encounters with discrimination were painful but ultimately served as crucial learning experiences. Taren began to understand the complexities of privilege and oppression, recognizing that their voice could amplify the struggles of those who were even more marginalized.

This realization aligns with intersectionality theory, introduced by Kimberlé Crenshaw, which highlights how various forms of identity—such as race, gender, and sexual orientation—intersect and impact an individual's experience of oppression. Taren's growing awareness of intersectionality deepened their commitment to advocacy, leading them to engage in conversations about the unique challenges faced by queer people of color and other marginalized groups.

The First Steps of Activism Motivated by their experiences and the support of their community, Taren began to take concrete steps toward activism. They organized a small gathering at their school, inviting students to share their stories and discuss the importance of LGBTQ+ visibility. This event marked Taren's first foray into activism, a humble yet significant beginning that would lay the groundwork for future endeavors.

In the following months, Taren's efforts blossomed into organizing the first LGBTQ+ pride event in Eldergrove, a monumental achievement that would not only celebrate queer identities but also foster a sense of community and belonging. This event exemplified the principles of grassroots organizing, emphasizing the power of local action in effecting change.

Conclusion In retrospect, Taren Fira's journey of discovering the activist within was a multifaceted process shaped by personal experiences, community support, and a commitment to social justice. The blend of critical consciousness, community engagement, artistic expression, and an understanding of intersectionality created a foundation for Taren's future activism. As they continued to navigate the complexities of their identity and the challenges of the world around them, Taren's path was illuminated by the belief that change begins with individuals who dare to stand up, speak out, and advocate for a more inclusive and equitable society.

$$\text{Activism} = \text{Awareness} + \text{Community} + \text{Art} + \text{Resilience} \qquad (1)$$

Fighting Gender Norms

In a world where societal expectations dictate the behaviors and roles assigned to individuals based on their perceived gender, Taren Fira emerged as a formidable advocate, challenging the rigid constructs of gender norms that often dictate the lived experiences of many. Gender norms, defined as the societal rules that dictate how individuals should behave based on their gender, have historically marginalized those who do not conform to traditional expectations. Taren's journey in fighting these norms began during her formative years, where she first encountered the limitations imposed by a binary understanding of gender.

Understanding Gender Norms

To comprehend the significance of Taren's activism, it is essential to explore the theoretical underpinnings of gender norms. Judith Butler's theory of gender performativity posits that gender is not an inherent quality but rather a performance that individuals enact based on societal expectations. This perspective challenges the binary view of gender as strictly male or female, suggesting instead that gender is fluid and can be expressed in myriad ways. As Taren embraced her queer identity, she began to understand that her existence was a radical act of defiance against the traditional gender binary.

$$G = P \cdot S \qquad (2)$$

Where:

- G = Gender expression
- P = Performance of gender roles
- S = Societal expectations

This equation illustrates how gender expression is influenced by the performance of gender roles and the overarching societal expectations that govern them. Taren recognized that by simply being herself, she was challenging the very foundation of these expectations.

Personal Encounters with Gender Norms

Taren's early experiences were marked by a struggle against the constraints of traditional gender norms. Raised in a conservative environment, she often felt the pressure to conform to the expected behaviors of her assigned gender. From an early age, she exhibited interests that were deemed "inappropriate" for girls, such as a love for rough-and-tumble sports and a penchant for dressing in ways that defied conventional femininity. Each act of rebellion, whether it was cutting her hair short or wearing clothes that felt more authentic to her identity, was met with resistance from peers and adults alike.

One pivotal moment occurred during a school assembly when Taren, inspired by the notion of self-expression, decided to wear a rainbow-colored tie and a blazer instead of the traditional dress expected of her. The backlash was immediate; whispers filled the auditorium, and she was subjected to ridicule. However, this experience ignited a fire within her, propelling her towards activism. Taren began to understand that fighting gender norms was not just a personal battle but a collective struggle against a system that enforced conformity.

Advocacy and Activism

As Taren transitioned from personal experiences to activism, she focused on creating spaces where individuals could express their gender identities freely. She organized workshops that educated participants about the fluidity of gender and the importance of dismantling harmful stereotypes. These workshops included discussions on the impact of gender norms on mental health, particularly among LGBTQ youth, who often face higher rates of anxiety and depression due to societal pressures.

In her activism, Taren employed various strategies to combat gender norms:

- **Art as Resistance**: Taren utilized art as a medium to challenge and redefine gender norms. She collaborated with local artists to create murals that celebrated diverse gender identities, showcasing the beauty of non-conformity. These murals became symbols of resistance in her community, inspiring others to embrace their true selves.

- **Public Speaking**: Taren became a sought-after speaker at schools and community events, where she shared her story and the importance of rejecting restrictive gender norms. Her powerful narratives resonated with many, fostering a culture of acceptance and understanding.

- ****Creating Safe Spaces****: Understanding the need for safe environments, Taren established support groups for LGBTQ youth. These spaces provided a platform for individuals to share their experiences and challenges, reinforcing the notion that they were not alone in their struggles against societal expectations.

Challenges and Triumphs

Despite her successes, Taren faced numerous challenges in her fight against gender norms. Resistance from conservative factions within her community often manifested in the form of protests and derogatory remarks aimed at her initiatives. However, Taren remained undeterred, believing that every act of defiance contributed to a larger movement toward acceptance and understanding.

One significant triumph came when Taren successfully lobbied for the inclusion of gender-neutral bathrooms in schools, a campaign that not only addressed the needs of non-binary and genderqueer students but also served as a broader statement against the binary understanding of gender. This victory exemplified the power of grassroots activism and the importance of allyship in challenging deeply ingrained societal norms.

Conclusion

Taren Fira's journey in fighting gender norms reflects the broader struggle for LGBTQ rights and the quest for authenticity in a world that often imposes restrictive labels. By challenging the binary constructs of gender, Taren not only paved the way for her own self-acceptance but also inspired countless others to embrace their identities unapologetically. Her advocacy serves as a reminder that the fight against gender norms is not merely about individual expression but a collective movement toward a more inclusive society, where everyone can thrive without the constraints of outdated expectations.

Coming Out and Embracing Queer Identity

Coming out is often described as a pivotal moment in the lives of LGBTQ individuals, a process that can be both liberating and fraught with challenges. For Taren Fira, this moment was not just about personal revelation; it was a transformative experience that shaped their identity and activism. The act of coming out, as defined by LGBTQ theorist [?], involves disclosing one's sexual orientation or gender identity to others and can be seen as a form of self-affirmation and empowerment.

Theoretical Framework

The process of coming out can be understood through various psychological and sociological theories. One such framework is the **Minority Stress Theory**, proposed by [?], which posits that LGBTQ individuals experience unique stressors related to their sexual orientation or gender identity. These stressors include societal stigma, discrimination, and internalized homophobia, all of which can impact mental health and well-being.

Mathematically, we can express the relationship between minority stress and mental health outcomes as follows:

$$MH = \alpha - \beta \cdot MS + \epsilon \qquad (3)$$

where MH represents mental health outcomes, MS denotes minority stress, α is a constant representing baseline mental health, β is the coefficient indicating the impact of minority stress, and ϵ is the error term.

Taren's journey involved navigating these stressors while seeking to embrace their queer identity. The act of coming out often leads to a sense of authenticity and belonging, which can counteract the negative effects of minority stress.

Personal Experience

Taren's coming out experience was marked by both fear and exhilaration. Growing up in a society that often enforced rigid gender norms, Taren felt the weight of expectations pressing down. The fear of rejection loomed large, a common concern among LGBTQ individuals. As Taren recalls, "I was terrified of how my family would react. It felt like stepping off a cliff into the unknown."

This sentiment echoes the findings of [?], who noted that many LGBTQ youth face significant anxiety about coming out, particularly regarding familial acceptance. Taren's journey was not unique; it was emblematic of a broader struggle faced by many in the community.

The Role of Support Systems

Support systems play a crucial role in the coming out process. Taren found solace in a close-knit group of friends who celebrated their authenticity. This aligns with [?], who emphasized the importance of supportive relationships in mitigating the negative effects of coming out.

Taren's friends became a lifeline, providing encouragement and understanding. "They made me feel like I could be myself without fear," Taren shared. This supportive environment allowed Taren to embrace their queer identity fully, transforming what could have been a painful experience into one of empowerment.

Challenges and Triumphs

Despite the support, Taren faced significant challenges. The initial reactions from family were mixed; while some embraced Taren's identity, others struggled to understand. This duality reflects the complex nature of family dynamics in the context of LGBTQ identities.

As [?] points out, families often experience a range of emotions upon learning about a loved one's queer identity, including confusion, denial, and ultimately acceptance. Taren's experience mirrored this spectrum, highlighting the emotional labor involved in coming out.

Taren's triumph came not just from acceptance but from the realization that their identity was valid and deserving of celebration. This acceptance was a catalyst for Taren's activism, propelling them into the role of a fierce advocate for LGBTQ rights.

Embracing Queer Identity

Embracing a queer identity involves more than just coming out; it requires a commitment to self-acceptance and authenticity. Taren's journey led to a deeper understanding of intersectionality, recognizing how various identities intersect to shape experiences of oppression and privilege.

Taren often reflected on the words of bell hooks, who stated, "Life-transforming ideas have always come to me through the experience of intimacy with others." This intimacy, fostered through community connections, allowed Taren to navigate their queer identity with confidence and pride.

Conclusion

In conclusion, Taren Fira's coming out journey was a complex interplay of fear, support, and ultimately, empowerment. The process of embracing their queer identity not only shaped Taren's personal life but also laid the groundwork for their future activism. By sharing their story, Taren hopes to inspire others to embrace their authentic selves, fostering a culture of acceptance and love within the LGBTQ community and beyond.

The journey of coming out is not merely a personal milestone; it is a collective experience that resonates with countless individuals. As Taren would say, "When we embrace our true selves, we ignite the spark of change in the world around us."

First Encounters with Discrimination

Taren Fira's journey as an advocate for LGBTQ rights was not merely a path paved with rainbows and glitter; it was a tumultuous road marked by the stark realities of discrimination and prejudice. The early years of Taren's activism were characterized by a series of encounters that would shape their understanding of societal biases and the urgent need for change.

The Harsh Reality of School Life

Taren's first significant encounter with discrimination occurred during their formative years in school. Despite their vibrant personality and passion for the arts, Taren often found themselves the target of bullying due to their nonconformity to traditional gender norms. The school environment, which should have been a safe haven for exploration and self-discovery, became a battleground of sorts.

One particularly harrowing incident involved a group of classmates who mocked Taren for wearing a colorful, flamboyant outfit to a school event. The laughter and jeers echoed in Taren's mind, a painful reminder of the societal pressures to conform. This experience was not an isolated incident but rather a reflection of a broader systemic issue—one that many LGBTQ individuals face in educational institutions.

Theoretical Framework: Internalized Homophobia

The psychological impact of such experiences can be understood through the lens of *internalized homophobia*, a concept that describes the internalization of societal prejudice against LGBTQ individuals. According to Herek (1990), internalized homophobia can lead to feelings of shame, self-hatred, and a reluctance to embrace one's identity fully. Taren, grappling with these feelings, began to question their worth and place in a society that seemed to reject them.

$$\text{Internalized Homophobia} = \frac{\text{Societal Prejudice}}{\text{Self-acceptance}} \qquad (4)$$

As Taren navigated through their teenage years, they found themselves oscillating between self-acceptance and the pervasive societal messages that demeaned their identity. This equation illustrates the struggle many face: the more societal prejudice one encounters, the more challenging it becomes to achieve self-acceptance.

First Activist Steps: The Catalyst for Change

These early encounters with discrimination served as a catalyst for Taren's activism. Instead of succumbing to despair, Taren channeled their pain into a desire for change. It was during a particularly low point, after a confrontation with a teacher who dismissed their concerns about bullying, that Taren decided to take action.

"If I want to change things, I need to be the change," Taren declared, a mantra that would guide them through the tumultuous waters of activism. This pivotal moment led Taren to organize a small group of like-minded peers who also felt marginalized. Together, they began to brainstorm ways to create a more inclusive environment within their school.

The Formation of Support Networks

Recognizing the importance of community, Taren initiated the formation of a support network for LGBTQ students. This group, affectionately dubbed the "Queer Collective," aimed to provide a safe space for students to share their experiences, seek guidance, and find solidarity in their struggles. The first meeting was held in the dimly lit corner of the school library, where whispers of hope and shared experiences filled the air.

The collective's first major initiative was to host a "Day of Acceptance," where students were encouraged to wear colors representing their identities. This event, while met with some resistance from conservative factions within the school, marked a significant turning point. It was a moment of visibility, a declaration that LGBTQ students existed and deserved recognition and respect.

Confronting Systemic Issues

However, Taren quickly learned that discrimination was not just a matter of individual prejudice; it was systemic. The school administration's reluctance to address bullying and discrimination highlighted the pervasive nature of homophobia in institutional settings. Taren and their peers faced significant pushback when they sought to implement anti-bullying policies that included protections for LGBTQ students.

The administration's response was emblematic of a larger societal issue: the reluctance to acknowledge and address LGBTQ rights within educational frameworks. Taren's experience underscored the need for comprehensive policy changes that not only recognized but actively supported LGBTQ individuals.

Conclusion: The Impact of Early Discrimination

Taren Fira's first encounters with discrimination were not just personal challenges; they were formative experiences that ignited a lifelong commitment to activism. These moments of pain and resilience laid the groundwork for Taren's future endeavors, shaping their understanding of the complexities of discrimination and the necessity of advocacy.

The journey from victim to advocate is often fraught with difficulties, but for Taren, it was a transformative experience that cultivated a deep sense of purpose. As they moved forward, Taren carried with them the lessons learned from those early encounters, determined to ensure that no one else would have to endure the same struggles in silence.

"We are not just fighting for ourselves; we are fighting for the future," Taren would often remind their peers, a testament to their unwavering belief in the power of collective action and the resilience of the human spirit.

Chapter One: A Fire Ignited

Section One: The Journey Begins

The First Queer Manifesto

In the vibrant tapestry of Alyndra's social landscape, a stirring was brewing, and at its heart lay Taren Fira, a visionary who would soon pen the first Queer Manifesto—a document that would ignite a movement and challenge the very foundations of societal norms. This manifesto was not merely a collection of grievances; it was a clarion call for liberation, a declaration of identity, and a blueprint for a future where love, in all its forms, could flourish without fear or prejudice.

Theoretical Foundations

The manifesto was rooted in several theoretical frameworks that emphasized the importance of identity, community, and activism. Drawing from Judith Butler's theory of gender performativity, Taren posited that gender is not a fixed attribute but rather a series of performances shaped by societal expectations. This perspective opened the door to rethinking not only gender but also sexual orientation as fluid constructs, empowering individuals to embrace their true selves without the constraints of binary classifications.

Additionally, Taren was influenced by the works of bell hooks, particularly her discussions on intersectionality and the necessity of acknowledging the varied experiences within marginalized communities. Taren's manifesto included a commitment to recognizing the intersections of race, class, and gender within LGBTQ activism, emphasizing that the fight for queer rights could not be separated from the broader struggles for social justice.

Identifying Problems

The manifesto began by identifying the myriad problems faced by the LGBTQ community in Alyndra. Discrimination, both systemic and interpersonal, permeated every aspect of life—from employment and housing to healthcare and education. Taren articulated the pervasive nature of homophobia and transphobia, citing statistics that revealed alarming rates of violence against queer individuals. For instance, a report by the Alyndra Human Rights Coalition indicated that over 60% of LGBTQ individuals had experienced harassment in public spaces, while nearly 30% reported experiencing physical violence due to their identity.

Moreover, Taren highlighted the failure of existing legal frameworks to protect LGBTQ rights adequately. The absence of comprehensive anti-discrimination laws left many vulnerable, and the lack of representation in political spheres meant that the voices of queer individuals were often silenced or ignored. This systemic neglect was illustrated through the story of a local trans woman, Elara, who faced eviction simply for being herself—a situation not uncommon in Alyndra.

The Call to Action

With a clear understanding of the problems at hand, Taren's manifesto transitioned into a powerful call to action. The document outlined specific demands, including:

- **Legal Protections:** The establishment of comprehensive anti-discrimination laws that protect individuals based on sexual orientation and gender identity.

- **Healthcare Access:** Ensuring that all healthcare providers receive training on LGBTQ issues and that all individuals have access to gender-affirming care.

- **Education Reform:** Implementing inclusive curricula that represent LGBTQ histories and contributions, fostering understanding and acceptance among future generations.

- **Community Support:** Establishing safe spaces and resources for LGBTQ youth, including mental health support and mentorship programs.

- **Visibility and Representation:** Advocating for increased representation of LGBTQ individuals in media, politics, and all spheres of public life.

Examples of Impact

The impact of Taren's manifesto was immediate and profound. It galvanized a diverse coalition of allies and activists, leading to the organization of the first

LGBTQ Pride event in Alyndra. This event not only celebrated queer identities but also served as a platform for marginalized voices, amplifying the stories of those who had been silenced for too long.

One poignant example was the participation of local artists who transformed the streets into a vibrant canvas of expression. Murals depicting the struggles and triumphs of the LGBTQ community adorned buildings, while performances showcased the rich cultural heritage of queer artists. This celebration of identity was a direct response to the manifesto's call for visibility and representation.

Moreover, Taren's manifesto inspired a wave of grassroots activism, leading to the formation of community groups dedicated to advocacy and support. These groups organized workshops, discussions, and outreach programs that educated the public on LGBTQ issues, fostering a culture of acceptance and understanding.

Conclusion

In retrospect, Taren Fira's First Queer Manifesto was more than just a document; it was a pivotal moment in Alyndra's history. It laid the groundwork for a movement that would challenge the status quo, confront discrimination, and celebrate the diversity of human experience. Through its theoretical underpinnings, identification of pressing issues, and a robust call to action, the manifesto not only inspired change but also created a sense of belonging and community among those who had long been marginalized.

As Taren wrote in the closing lines of the manifesto, *"We are not just fighting for our rights; we are fighting for the right to be ourselves, unapologetically and authentically. Our love is our strength, and together, we shall rise."* This declaration resonated deeply within the hearts of many, igniting a fire that would continue to burn brightly in the pursuit of equality and justice for all.

Organizing the First LGBTQ Pride Event

The journey of Taren Fira in organizing the first LGBTQ Pride event in Alyndra was not merely a logistical endeavor; it was a monumental act of defiance and celebration. The task at hand was to craft a space where individuals could express their identities freely, without fear of reprisal or discrimination. This section delves into the intricacies of organizing this pivotal event, highlighting the theoretical frameworks, challenges faced, and the triumphs that emerged.

Theoretical Framework: Queer Theory and Community Building

At the heart of Taren's approach was the application of *queer theory*, which critiques the established norms surrounding gender and sexuality. Judith Butler's concept of *gender performativity* suggests that gender is not an innate quality but rather a series of performances shaped by societal expectations. This understanding was crucial in framing the Pride event not just as a celebration of identity, but as a performance that challenged the very foundations of heteronormativity.

Moreover, the event was rooted in the principles of *community building*. According to social theorist Henri Lefebvre, space is a social product, and the creation of inclusive spaces fosters a sense of belonging. Taren aimed to transform public space into a sanctuary for LGBTQ individuals, thereby challenging the dominant narratives that marginalized queer identities.

Initial Challenges: Resistance and Logistics

Organizing the Pride event was fraught with challenges. The initial resistance from local authorities posed significant hurdles. Taren and her team faced bureaucratic red tape, as permits were often denied under the guise of public safety concerns. This resistance highlighted the pervasive *homophobia* embedded within institutional frameworks.

Additionally, funding was a considerable obstacle. Securing financial support from local businesses proved difficult, as many were hesitant to associate with an LGBTQ event due to fear of backlash from conservative constituents. Taren utilized a strategy of *grassroots fundraising*, organizing bake sales and community events to generate the necessary funds.

The logistics of the event also required meticulous planning. Taren coordinated with various stakeholders, including local LGBTQ organizations, artists, and activists, to create a program that would resonate with the community. The inclusion of diverse voices was paramount, ensuring that the event represented the multitude of identities within the LGBTQ spectrum.

Mobilizing Support: Building Alliances

Recognizing the importance of coalition-building, Taren reached out to various community groups, including feminist organizations, racial justice advocates, and disability rights activists. This intersectional approach was vital in fostering a sense of solidarity. As noted by Kimberlé Crenshaw, the intersectionality framework emphasizes the interconnectedness of social identities and the unique challenges faced by individuals at these intersections.

One successful collaboration was with a local art collective, which contributed to the event's visual identity. Through art, they aimed to challenge stereotypes and promote visibility. The slogan *"Pride in Diversity"* was chosen, encapsulating the essence of the event and serving as a rallying cry for inclusivity.

The Day of the Event: A Transformative Experience

The day of the Pride event arrived, and the atmosphere was electric. The streets of Alyndra were adorned with vibrant colors, and the air was filled with music and laughter. Taren's careful planning paid off, as the event drew an unprecedented crowd, far exceeding expectations.

Participants engaged in various activities, including workshops on LGBTQ rights, art installations, and live performances by queer artists. The sense of community was palpable, with individuals sharing their stories and experiences, fostering a culture of empathy and understanding.

$$\text{Pride Event Attendance} = \text{Local Community Members} + \text{Allies} + \text{Activists}$$

The equation above symbolizes the collective effort required to create a successful Pride event. Each group contributed to the overall attendance and atmosphere, highlighting the importance of unity in activism.

Reflections and Impact

In the aftermath of the event, Taren reflected on its significance. The Pride event not only provided a platform for expression but also sparked conversations about LGBTQ rights within the broader community. Local media coverage was extensive, framing the event as a pivotal moment in Alyndra's history.

Taren's efforts illustrated the power of activism in reshaping societal narratives. The event laid the groundwork for future advocacy efforts and established a precedent for the celebration of LGBTQ identities in Alyndra.

The success of the Pride event served as a catalyst for subsequent gatherings, fostering a sense of pride and visibility among LGBTQ individuals. Taren Fira's dedication and resilience in organizing the first LGBTQ Pride event not only marked a turning point in Alyndra but also inspired a new generation of activists to continue the fight for equality and acceptance.

Conclusion

The organization of the first LGBTQ Pride event in Alyndra was a profound undertaking that required a blend of theoretical understanding, strategic planning, and community mobilization. Taren Fira's journey exemplifies the transformative power of activism, demonstrating that through collective effort and unwavering determination, marginalized voices can be amplified, and societal change can be achieved.

Breaking Stereotypes through Art

Art has long been a powerful medium for expressing identity, challenging societal norms, and fostering understanding. In the journey of Taren Fira, the intersection of art and activism played a pivotal role in breaking stereotypes associated with LGBTQ identities. This section explores how Taren utilized various artistic forms to confront biases, reshape narratives, and build community.

Theoretical Framework

To understand the impact of art in LGBTQ activism, we can draw upon several theoretical frameworks, including *Critical Theory, Queer Theory,* and *Social Constructivism.* Critical Theory posits that art can serve as a form of resistance against oppressive structures by revealing hidden truths and challenging dominant ideologies. Queer Theory further expands this notion by emphasizing the fluidity of identity and the importance of subverting traditional narratives surrounding gender and sexuality. Social Constructivism suggests that art is a means of constructing and negotiating identity, allowing individuals to express their lived experiences and challenge stereotypes.

Art as a Tool for Advocacy

Taren recognized that art could transcend verbal communication, reaching audiences on emotional and psychological levels. Through visual art, performance, and literature, Taren sought to dismantle harmful stereotypes that marginalized LGBTQ individuals. This approach aligns with the idea that *"art is not a mirror to reflect reality, but a hammer with which to shape it."*

Examples of Artistic Expression

Visual Art One of Taren's notable projects involved collaborating with local artists to create a mural in the heart of Alyndra. This mural depicted diverse

LGBTQ figures, celebrating their contributions to society while challenging stereotypical representations. The artwork served as a public statement against erasure and invisibility, inviting conversations about identity and acceptance.

Performance Art In addition to visual art, Taren organized a series of performance art events titled *"Unmasking Truths."* These events featured drag performances, spoken word poetry, and dance, all centered around themes of identity, resilience, and love. By showcasing LGBTQ artists, Taren not only provided a platform for marginalized voices but also encouraged audiences to confront their biases and preconceptions.

Literature and Storytelling Taren also understood the power of storytelling as a means of breaking stereotypes. Through the publication of an anthology titled *"Voices of the Spectrum,"* Taren gathered personal narratives from LGBTQ individuals across Alyndra. This collection highlighted the richness of diverse experiences, allowing readers to connect with stories that challenged preconceived notions about gender and sexuality.

Challenges and Resistance

While Taren's artistic initiatives garnered significant support, they were not without challenges. Some community members reacted defensively, viewing Taren's work as a threat to traditional values. This backlash underscored the deeply ingrained stereotypes that persist within society. Taren faced criticism for promoting what detractors labeled as "non-normative behavior," yet she remained steadfast in her belief that art could be a catalyst for change.

Impact and Legacy

The impact of Taren's artistic endeavors extended beyond immediate reactions. By fostering dialogue through art, Taren contributed to a gradual shift in perceptions surrounding LGBTQ identities within Alyndra. The mural became a landmark, symbolizing the community's commitment to inclusivity and acceptance. The *"Unmasking Truths"* performances inspired a new generation of artists to explore their identities through creative expression, further enriching the cultural landscape of Alyndra.

In conclusion, Taren Fira's commitment to breaking stereotypes through art exemplifies the transformative power of creativity in activism. By challenging societal norms and fostering understanding, Taren's artistic initiatives not only advanced LGBTQ rights but also inspired others to embrace their authentic selves. As Taren often remarked, *"Art is the heartbeat of our movement; it breathes life into our struggles and celebrates our victories."*

Challenges and Triumphs in LGBTQ Activism

LGBTQ activism, like any social movement, is marked by a tapestry of challenges and triumphs. The journey of Taren Fira exemplifies the complex interplay of adversity and success that characterizes the fight for equality and acceptance within the LGBTQ community. This section delves into the multifaceted challenges faced by activists, the strategies employed to overcome them, and the significant victories that have shaped the landscape of LGBTQ rights.

The Landscape of Challenges

The challenges faced by LGBTQ activists can be categorized into several key areas: societal stigma, legal barriers, violence and discrimination, and internal community dynamics.

Societal Stigma Societal stigma remains one of the most pervasive challenges. Many individuals within the LGBTQ community face negative perceptions and stereotypes that lead to discrimination in various aspects of life, including employment, healthcare, and education. The stigma is often rooted in cultural and religious beliefs that view non-heteronormative identities as deviant. For instance, in a study by Herek (2009), it was found that individuals who identify as LGBTQ are more likely to experience mental health issues due to societal rejection.

Legal Barriers Legal barriers present another significant challenge. In many regions, laws still exist that criminalize same-sex relationships or deny basic rights to LGBTQ individuals. For example, the Defense of Marriage Act (DOMA) in the United States, enacted in 1996, federally defined marriage as a union between one man and one woman, thus denying same-sex couples access to federal benefits. It wasn't until the landmark Supreme Court case *United States v. Windsor* (2013) that parts of DOMA were struck down, marking a significant triumph for LGBTQ activists.

Violence and Discrimination Violence against LGBTQ individuals is a grim reality that activists must confront. Hate crimes motivated by sexual orientation or gender identity remain alarmingly high. According to the FBI's Hate Crime

Statistics report, LGBTQ individuals are often targets of violent acts, leading to calls for increased protections and advocacy for hate crime legislation. Activists like Taren Fira have worked tirelessly to bring attention to these issues, mobilizing communities to demand justice and protection for marginalized individuals.

Internal Community Dynamics Internal dynamics within the LGBTQ community can also pose challenges. Issues such as racism, transphobia, and classism can create divisions among activists. Intersectional activists argue that the fight for LGBTQ rights must also address these overlapping identities. Crenshaw's (1989) theory of intersectionality highlights how different forms of discrimination intersect, emphasizing the need for an inclusive approach to activism that centers the voices of the most marginalized.

Strategies for Triumph

Despite these challenges, LGBTQ activists have employed various strategies to advance their cause and achieve significant victories.

Grassroots Mobilization Grassroots mobilization has proven to be an effective strategy. Activists organize local events, rallies, and educational campaigns to raise awareness and build community support. Taren Fira's early efforts to organize the first LGBTQ Pride event in Alyndra exemplify this approach. The event not only celebrated LGBTQ identities but also served as a platform for advocacy, drawing attention to local issues and fostering a sense of community.

Legal Advocacy Legal advocacy has also played a crucial role in overcoming barriers. Organizations such as the Human Rights Campaign and Lambda Legal work tirelessly to challenge discriminatory laws and promote legislative changes. The successful repeal of "Don't Ask, Don't Tell" in 2010, which allowed LGBTQ individuals to serve openly in the military, stands as a testament to the power of legal advocacy.

Public Awareness Campaigns Public awareness campaigns have shifted societal perceptions and reduced stigma. Through storytelling, media representation, and educational initiatives, activists have worked to humanize LGBTQ experiences. The impact of films like *Moonlight* and *Love, Simon* has been profound, as they bring LGBTQ narratives into mainstream consciousness, fostering empathy and understanding.

Coalition Building Building coalitions with other social justice movements has amplified the impact of LGBTQ activism. By aligning with feminist, racial justice, and disability rights movements, LGBTQ activists have highlighted the interconnectedness of various struggles. This coalition-building approach has led to broader support for inclusive policies and practices, demonstrating that the fight for LGBTQ rights is part of a larger quest for social justice.

Significant Triumphs

The triumphs of LGBTQ activism are numerous and transformative. The legalization of same-sex marriage in various countries, including the United States, Canada, and several European nations, represents a monumental victory. The Supreme Court's decision in *Obergefell v. Hodges* (2015) affirmed the constitutional right to marry for same-sex couples, a culmination of decades of activism and advocacy.

Moreover, the increasing visibility of LGBTQ individuals in politics, media, and culture signifies a shift towards acceptance and representation. The election of openly LGBTQ officials, such as Pete Buttigieg and Tammy Baldwin, has inspired future generations of activists and demonstrated that change is possible.

In addition, the growing acceptance of transgender rights has marked a significant shift in societal attitudes. Activists have fought for policies that protect transgender individuals from discrimination in healthcare, employment, and public accommodations. The advocacy for inclusive bathroom policies and the recognition of non-binary identities reflect the ongoing evolution of LGBTQ rights.

Conclusion

The challenges faced by LGBTQ activists are formidable, yet the triumphs achieved through resilience, creativity, and coalition-building are equally significant. Taren Fira's journey illustrates the power of activism to effect change, inspire others, and foster a more inclusive society. As the fight for LGBTQ rights continues, the lessons learned from both challenges and triumphs will guide future activists in their pursuit of equality and justice for all.

Bibliography

[1] Herek, G. M. (2009). *Sexual stigma and sexual prejudice in the United States: A conceptual framework.* Archives of Sexual Behavior, 38(5), 976-988.

[2] Crenshaw, K. (1989). *Demarginalizing the intersection of race and sex: A Black feminist critique of antidiscrimination doctrine, feminist theory and antiracist politics.* University of Chicago Legal Forum, 1989(1), 139-167.

Building Allies and Community Support

The journey of LGBTQ activism is not a solitary endeavor; it thrives on the strength of community and the solidarity of allies. In the vibrant tapestry of Alyndra's social landscape, Taren Fira recognized early on that building allies and fostering community support were essential to effecting meaningful change. This section explores the theoretical underpinnings of allyship, the challenges faced in cultivating a supportive environment, and the practical strategies employed by Taren to build a robust network of allies.

Theoretical Framework of Allyship

Allyship, as defined by scholars in social justice movements, refers to the practice of individuals from privileged groups actively supporting marginalized communities. According to [Broido(2000)], effective allyship involves a continuous process of learning, unlearning, and taking action to dismantle systems of oppression. The theoretical model of allyship can be described using the following equation:

$$\text{Allyship} = \text{Awareness} + \text{Action} + \text{Advocacy} \qquad (5)$$

Where: - **Awareness** encompasses understanding the historical and systemic injustices faced by LGBTQ individuals. - **Action** involves taking concrete steps to support these communities, such as participating in pride events or engaging in activism. - **Advocacy** signifies the ongoing commitment to challenge discriminatory practices and policies.

Taren understood that the effectiveness of allyship is contingent upon individuals recognizing their privilege and using it to uplift marginalized voices. This awareness often required difficult conversations about race, gender, and sexuality, which could lead to discomfort but ultimately foster deeper connections and understanding.

Challenges in Building Community Support

Despite the theoretical clarity surrounding allyship, Taren encountered numerous challenges in building a supportive community. One significant barrier was the pervasive culture of silence surrounding LGBTQ issues. Many individuals feared social ostracism or backlash for expressing support. This phenomenon can be illustrated by the following equation:

$$\text{Support} = \text{Courage} \times \text{Community} \qquad (6)$$

Where: - **Courage** represents the willingness of individuals to stand up for LGBTQ rights despite potential risks. - **Community** indicates the presence of a supportive environment that encourages allyship.

In many instances, Taren had to cultivate courage within individuals while simultaneously fostering a sense of community. This dual approach was vital in transforming passive sympathizers into active allies.

Strategies for Building Allies

Taren employed various strategies to build allies and community support, focusing on education, engagement, and empowerment. One effective method was hosting workshops and training sessions aimed at demystifying LGBTQ issues. By providing a safe space for discussions, Taren facilitated dialogues that addressed misconceptions and fears. These sessions often included interactive activities that encouraged participants to share their experiences and learn from one another.

Additionally, Taren recognized the importance of storytelling as a powerful tool for building empathy and understanding. By sharing personal narratives of struggle and triumph, Taren and other activists were able to humanize the LGBTQ experience, making it relatable to a broader audience. This approach aligns with the concept of narrative persuasion, which suggests that stories can influence attitudes and behaviors more effectively than statistics alone [?].

Examples of Community Support Initiatives

One notable initiative led by Taren was the establishment of the "Allies for Equality" campaign, which aimed to mobilize allies from various backgrounds. This campaign included a series of events, such as community picnics, educational seminars, and art exhibitions showcasing LGBTQ artists. Each event was designed to create a welcoming environment where allies could learn, connect, and contribute to the movement.

For instance, during the first annual "Pride Picnic," Taren invited local businesses to sponsor the event, encouraging them to display ally flags and participate in discussions about inclusivity. This not only elevated the visibility of LGBTQ issues within the community but also fostered a sense of belonging among allies, reinforcing their commitment to advocacy.

Moreover, Taren leveraged social media platforms to amplify the voices of allies and LGBTQ individuals alike. By creating hashtags like #AlyndraAllies, Taren encouraged community members to share their stories and experiences, thereby fostering a sense of solidarity and collective action. The digital landscape became a vital space for allyship, as it allowed individuals to connect across geographical boundaries and share resources.

The Impact of Building Allies and Community Support

The efforts to build allies and community support had a profound impact on the LGBTQ movement in Alyndra. As more individuals became engaged, the community saw an increase in participation in pride events, advocacy campaigns, and educational initiatives. The collective strength of allies not only amplified LGBTQ voices but also created a ripple effect, inspiring others to join the movement.

Research indicates that communities with strong ally networks experience greater resilience in the face of adversity [?]. Taren's work exemplified this principle, as the solidarity among allies provided a buffer against discrimination and hostility. The increased visibility of LGBTQ issues led to more informed discussions within the community, ultimately contributing to a cultural shift towards acceptance and inclusivity.

In conclusion, building allies and community support is a cornerstone of effective LGBTQ activism. Through education, engagement, and empowerment, Taren Fira successfully transformed passive supporters into active allies, creating a vibrant network of individuals committed to advocating for equality. The journey of allyship is ongoing, requiring continuous effort and dedication, but the impact of these relationships is invaluable in the fight for LGBTQ rights.

Starting a Movement

In the vibrant landscape of Alyndra, Taren Fira's journey into activism began with a spark—a realization that change was not merely a dream but an achievable reality. This section delves into the intricate process of starting a movement, emphasizing Taren's strategies, challenges, and the theoretical frameworks that underpinned her efforts.

Theoretical Foundations of Movement Building

At its core, starting a movement involves understanding the dynamics of social change. Taren embraced several theories that informed her approach, notably Resource Mobilization Theory and Framing Theory.

Resource Mobilization Theory posits that the success of social movements depends on the availability and effective utilization of resources, which include money, labor, and media attention. Taren recognized that mobilizing these resources was essential to garnering support for LGBTQ rights. For instance, she organized fundraising events that not only raised money but also increased visibility for the cause.

Framing Theory, on the other hand, emphasizes the importance of how issues are presented to the public. Taren was adept at crafting narratives that resonated with diverse audiences. She framed LGBTQ rights not only as a matter of justice but also as a fundamental human rights issue, appealing to the values of equality and dignity that many in Alyndra held dear.

Identifying Core Issues

Before launching her movement, Taren conducted extensive research to identify the most pressing issues facing the LGBTQ community in Alyndra. This involved engaging with community members through surveys, focus groups, and town hall meetings. The findings revealed several key issues:

- Discrimination in employment and housing

- Lack of access to healthcare services

- Educational disparities and bullying in schools

- Legal barriers to marriage and adoption

By prioritizing these issues, Taren ensured that her movement was grounded in the real experiences and needs of the community, which is crucial for fostering a sense of ownership and participation among activists.

Building a Coalition

Recognizing that no movement can thrive in isolation, Taren focused on building a coalition of diverse stakeholders. She reached out to various organizations, including those focused on women's rights, racial justice, and disability rights, to create a united front. This coalition not only amplified the voices of LGBTQ individuals but also highlighted the interconnectedness of social justice issues.

One notable example of this coalition-building was the "Alyndra Pride Alliance," which brought together over thirty organizations to collaborate on the first LGBTQ Pride event in Alyndra. The event was a resounding success, drawing thousands of attendees and generating significant media coverage. This visibility was instrumental in legitimizing the LGBTQ movement in the eyes of the public and policymakers.

Mobilizing the Community

Taren understood that grassroots mobilization was key to sustaining momentum. She employed a variety of tactics to engage the community, including:

- Workshops and training sessions on advocacy and activism
- Social media campaigns to raise awareness and encourage participation
- Organizing community forums to discuss LGBTQ issues and share personal stories

Each of these initiatives served to educate the community, foster solidarity, and empower individuals to take action. For example, the social media campaign, titled "#AlyndraPride," encouraged people to share their stories and experiences, creating a digital tapestry of resilience and hope that resonated widely.

Challenges and Resilience

Despite her passion and dedication, Taren faced numerous challenges in starting her movement. Initial resistance came from conservative factions within Alyndra, who viewed her efforts as a threat to traditional values. Taren encountered backlash in the form of hate speech and misinformation campaigns, which sought to undermine her credibility and the legitimacy of the LGBTQ cause.

To combat these challenges, Taren employed strategic communication and public relations tactics. She organized press conferences to counter false narratives, engaged with sympathetic media outlets, and utilized storytelling to humanize LGBTQ experiences. This approach not only helped to reframe the conversation but also built resilience within the community, as members rallied around Taren's unwavering commitment to justice.

Creating Lasting Impact

Ultimately, Taren's efforts in starting a movement transcended immediate goals. She aimed to create a lasting legacy of advocacy and empowerment. By establishing mentorship programs for young activists and fostering leadership within the LGBTQ community, Taren ensured that the movement would continue to thrive long after her initial efforts.

Through her tireless work, Taren Fira not only ignited a movement in Alyndra but also inspired countless individuals to become advocates for change. Her journey exemplifies the power of grassroots activism and the importance of solidarity, resilience, and strategic action in the fight for LGBTQ rights.

In conclusion, starting a movement is a multifaceted endeavor that requires a deep understanding of social dynamics, effective resource mobilization, and a commitment to inclusivity. Taren Fira's story serves as a testament to the impact that one individual can have when they dare to challenge the status quo and fight for a more equitable world.

Gaining National Recognition and Support

In the vibrant tapestry of LGBTQ activism, gaining national recognition and support is akin to igniting a spark that can fuel a wildfire of change. For Taren Fira, this journey was marked by strategic initiatives, powerful collaborations, and a relentless commitment to visibility.

The Importance of Visibility

Visibility is a cornerstone of activism, particularly in the LGBTQ community. As Taren often articulated, "To be seen is to be heard." This mantra drove her to create platforms that amplified queer voices, ensuring that narratives of marginalized individuals were not only acknowledged but celebrated. The theory of *social constructionism* posits that our understanding of reality is shaped through social interactions and shared experiences. Taren utilized this theory to frame LGBTQ identities as integral components of societal discourse, thereby challenging prevailing stereotypes and misconceptions.

Strategic Collaborations

Taren recognized that to gain national traction, she needed to forge alliances beyond the LGBTQ community. Collaborating with established civil rights organizations, such as the Equality Alliance and the United Coalition for Justice, proved pivotal. These partnerships not only broadened the reach of her initiatives but also provided a robust support network. Through joint campaigns, Taren was able to tap into the existing resources and expertise of these organizations, thus amplifying her message.

For instance, the *Pride in Unity* campaign, launched in collaboration with the Equality Alliance, aimed to highlight the intersectionality of LGBTQ rights with other social justice issues. This campaign garnered national media attention and showcased the interconnected struggles of various marginalized groups. By employing the framework of *intersectionality*, Taren illustrated how LGBTQ rights are inextricably linked to race, gender, and economic justice, thereby appealing to a broader audience.

Harnessing Media Power

In the digital age, media serves as a powerful tool for advocacy. Taren adeptly harnessed the power of traditional and social media to elevate her cause. By organizing press conferences, participating in interviews, and utilizing platforms like Twitter and Instagram, she was able to disseminate her message widely. The equation governing the relationship between media exposure and public support can be expressed as:

$$P = k \cdot M^n$$

where P represents public support, M denotes media exposure, k is a constant reflecting the effectiveness of the message, and n indicates the degree of impact that media has on public perception. Through strategic media engagement, Taren significantly increased public support for LGBTQ rights, as evidenced by rising approval ratings for marriage equality during her campaigns.

Mobilizing Grassroots Support

While national recognition was essential, Taren understood that grassroots support was the bedrock of sustainable change. She implemented community engagement strategies that empowered individuals to become advocates in their own right. Workshops, town hall meetings, and community forums were organized to educate and mobilize citizens. The feedback loop established in these settings fostered a sense of ownership among participants, transforming passive supporters into active change-makers.

One notable example was the *Voices of Alyndra* initiative, which encouraged local residents to share their stories of discrimination and resilience. This project not only humanized the struggles faced by the LGBTQ community but also galvanized local action, resulting in increased attendance at pride events and a surge in volunteerism for LGBTQ causes.

Legislative Advocacy and Policy Change

Gaining national recognition also required Taren to engage directly with policymakers. She spearheaded lobbying efforts aimed at influencing legislation that would protect LGBTQ rights. The introduction of the *Equality Act* in the national legislature served as a focal point for her advocacy. Taren organized a series of lobbying days, where constituents were encouraged to meet with their representatives and advocate for the bill.

The success of these efforts can be quantified by examining the increase in co-sponsors for the Equality Act, which rose from a handful to over 200 within a year of Taren's intensified lobbying. This demonstrated the effectiveness of grassroots mobilization in shaping legislative priorities.

Challenges and Resilience

Despite these successes, the journey was fraught with challenges. Taren faced backlash from conservative groups that sought to undermine her efforts. However, she approached these obstacles with resilience, employing strategies such as counter-campaigns and public education initiatives to address misinformation and foster dialogue. The theory of *cognitive dissonance* was instrumental in her approach; by presenting evidence that contradicted negative stereotypes, she aimed to shift public perception and reduce resistance.

In summary, Taren Fira's journey to gain national recognition and support was marked by strategic collaborations, effective media engagement, grassroots mobilization, and legislative advocacy. By employing various theoretical frameworks and practical strategies, she not only elevated the visibility of LGBTQ issues but also laid the groundwork for lasting change. Her story serves as a testament to the power of activism in shaping societal norms and advancing the cause of equality.

Creating Safe Spaces and Resources

Creating safe spaces for LGBTQ individuals is a critical component of activism, as these environments foster a sense of belonging, acceptance, and empowerment. Taren Fira recognized early on that in order to build a robust community, it was essential to establish physical and emotional spaces where queer individuals could express themselves freely without fear of discrimination or harassment. This section delves into the theoretical frameworks, challenges, and practical examples of creating safe spaces and resources for the LGBTQ community.

Theoretical Frameworks

The concept of safe spaces is rooted in various sociological and psychological theories. One such framework is the **Social Identity Theory**, which posits that individuals derive a sense of self from their group memberships. For LGBTQ individuals, having a safe space allows them to affirm their identities and connect with others who share similar experiences. Moreover, the **Minority Stress Theory** explains how the chronic stress faced by marginalized groups can lead to mental health issues. Safe spaces serve as a buffer against this stress, providing support and validation.

Challenges in Creating Safe Spaces

Despite the importance of safe spaces, several challenges arise in their establishment:

- **Funding and Resources:** Many LGBTQ organizations struggle to secure funding for safe spaces. Without adequate financial support, it becomes difficult to maintain facilities or offer programs that cater to the community's needs.

- **Community Resistance:** In some areas, the establishment of safe spaces is met with resistance from local communities or authorities. This can manifest as protests, political opposition, or even legal challenges.

- **Intersectionality:** It is crucial to recognize that not all LGBTQ individuals experience the same challenges. Safe spaces must be inclusive of various identities, including race, gender, and socioeconomic status, to truly serve their purpose.

Practical Examples of Safe Spaces

Taren Fira's activism led to the creation of several notable safe spaces and resources, each addressing specific community needs:

1. Community Centers One of the most significant achievements was the establishment of the *Alyndra LGBTQ Community Center*. This center serves as a hub for various activities, including support groups, educational workshops, and cultural events. It provides resources such as mental health counseling, legal assistance, and educational materials on LGBTQ rights.

2. Online Platforms Recognizing the power of technology, Taren advocated for the creation of online platforms where LGBTQ individuals could connect, share experiences, and access resources. The website *QueerConnect* became a vital tool for fostering community, offering forums, virtual support groups, and a directory of local resources.

3. Safe Schools Initiative Taren also launched the *Safe Schools Initiative*, aimed at creating safe environments within educational institutions. This program provided training for teachers and staff on LGBTQ inclusivity, anti-bullying policies, and the importance of representation in curricula. Schools that participated reported a significant decrease in bullying incidents and an increase in LGBTQ student engagement.

Measuring Impact

To assess the effectiveness of these safe spaces, Taren implemented a series of evaluation methods, including surveys and focus groups. The feedback collected revealed that participants felt more accepted and supported, leading to improved mental health outcomes and increased community engagement. For example, a survey conducted at the Alyndra LGBTQ Community Center showed that 85% of respondents felt a greater sense of belonging after attending events.

Furthermore, Taren emphasized the importance of ongoing dialogue and adaptation. Safe spaces should evolve based on the needs of the community, ensuring they remain relevant and effective. This approach aligns with the **Participatory Action Research** model, which involves community members in the research process to foster empowerment and ownership.

Conclusion

Creating safe spaces and resources is an essential aspect of LGBTQ activism that Taren Fira championed throughout her career. By understanding the theoretical underpinnings, addressing challenges, and implementing practical examples, Taren laid the groundwork for a more inclusive and supportive environment for LGBTQ individuals in Alyndra and beyond. Her legacy continues to inspire activists to prioritize safe spaces as a means of fostering community, resilience, and empowerment.

Expanding LGBTQ Visibility

In a world where representation matters, expanding LGBTQ visibility has become a cornerstone of activism. Visibility is not merely about being seen; it encompasses the recognition of diverse identities, experiences, and narratives that have historically been marginalized or erased. This section explores the theoretical underpinnings of visibility, the challenges faced by LGBTQ individuals, and the strategies employed to enhance representation in various spheres of society.

Theoretical Framework of Visibility

The concept of visibility in LGBTQ activism can be understood through various theoretical lenses. One prominent theory is the **Queer Theory**, which critiques the binary understanding of gender and sexuality, advocating for a spectrum of identities. As Judith Butler posits in her seminal work *Gender Trouble*, gender is performative, and visibility is a crucial aspect of this performance. The act of being visible challenges societal norms and opens the door for broader acceptance and understanding.

Moreover, the **Intersectionality** framework, introduced by Kimberlé Crenshaw, emphasizes that visibility must also consider the intersections of race, class, gender, and sexuality. This approach highlights that the experiences of LGBTQ individuals are not monolithic; rather, they are shaped by multiple identities that can compound visibility and oppression. Thus, expanding LGBTQ visibility requires a nuanced understanding of these intersecting identities.

Challenges to Visibility

Despite the progress made in recent years, significant challenges remain in expanding LGBTQ visibility. One of the most pressing issues is the **media representation**. While there has been an increase in LGBTQ characters and narratives in film and television, these representations often fall short of authenticity. Stereotypes and clichés persist, leading to a narrow portrayal of LGBTQ lives. For instance, the trope of the "tragic queer" often dominates narratives, overshadowing stories of joy, resilience, and everyday life.

Furthermore, the **digital divide** poses a significant barrier to visibility. Not all LGBTQ individuals have equal access to the internet and social media platforms, which are crucial for sharing their stories and connecting with communities. Marginalized groups within the LGBTQ spectrum, such as LGBTQ people of color and those from lower socioeconomic backgrounds, often face additional hurdles in accessing platforms that amplify their voices.

Strategies for Expanding Visibility

To combat these challenges, activists and organizations have employed various strategies to enhance LGBTQ visibility. One effective approach is through **storytelling**. Personal narratives can humanize issues and foster empathy among audiences. Initiatives like the *Humans of New York* project have successfully showcased diverse LGBTQ stories, allowing individuals to share their experiences in their own words. This grassroots storytelling not only raises awareness but also builds community solidarity.

Moreover, **collaborative art projects** have emerged as powerful tools for visibility. Artists like *Zanele Muholi* use photography to document the lives of LGBTQ individuals in South Africa, challenging stereotypes and celebrating identity. By showcasing authentic representations of LGBTQ lives, these projects contribute to a broader understanding of the community's diversity.

Social media campaigns have also played a pivotal role in expanding visibility. Initiatives like the *#LoveIsLove* and *#TransIsBeautiful* hashtags have created viral movements that promote acceptance and celebrate LGBTQ identities. These campaigns harness the power of digital platforms to reach vast audiences, making visibility a collective effort rather than an individual struggle.

Examples of Successful Visibility Campaigns

Several campaigns have successfully expanded LGBTQ visibility, providing models for future initiatives. One notable example is the **It Gets Better Project**, which began as a response to the alarming rates of bullying and suicide among LGBTQ youth. Through video testimonials from individuals sharing their stories of hope and resilience, the campaign has reached millions, demonstrating that visibility can lead to positive change.

Another example is the **Pride Month** celebrations, which have evolved from local parades to global movements. These events not only celebrate LGBTQ identities but also serve as platforms for advocacy, raising awareness about ongoing struggles for equality. The visibility achieved during Pride Month has sparked conversations about LGBTQ rights and inspired activism worldwide.

Conclusion

Expanding LGBTQ visibility is an essential aspect of the broader struggle for equality and acceptance. By utilizing theoretical frameworks, addressing challenges, and implementing effective strategies, activists can create a more inclusive society where diverse identities are celebrated rather than marginalized. As Taren Fira exemplifies, the fight for visibility is ongoing, and it requires the collective effort of individuals and communities to ensure that every voice is heard and valued.

In the words of Taren Fira, "Visibility is not just about being seen; it is about being understood, accepted, and celebrated for who we are." This mantra serves as a guiding principle for activists striving to expand LGBTQ visibility and create a world where everyone can live authentically and freely.

Strategies for Effective Advocacy

In the realm of LGBTQ activism, effective advocacy is paramount for achieving social change and ensuring equal rights for all individuals, regardless of their sexual orientation or gender identity. Taren Fira's journey as a queer advocate in Alyndra exemplifies the application of diverse strategies that can be employed to create a more inclusive society. This section explores various strategies for effective advocacy, emphasizing the importance of a multifaceted approach that incorporates theory, problem-solving, and real-world examples.

1. Understanding the Landscape

Before embarking on any advocacy efforts, it is crucial to understand the social, political, and cultural landscape in which one operates. This includes recognizing the historical context of LGBTQ rights, identifying key stakeholders, and understanding the current challenges faced by the community.

$$\text{Advocacy Success} = f(\text{Understanding Landscape}, \text{Community Needs}, \text{Stakeholder Engage} \tag{7}$$

For instance, Taren Fira began her advocacy by conducting thorough research on the discrimination faced by LGBTQ individuals in Alyndra. This foundational knowledge informed her strategies, enabling her to tailor her approach to address specific issues such as housing discrimination and healthcare access.

2. Building Coalitions

One of the most effective strategies for advocacy is building coalitions with other organizations and groups that share similar goals. By collaborating with allies—whether they are other social justice movements, local businesses, or community leaders—advocates can amplify their voices and broaden their reach.

$$\text{Coalition Power} = \text{Diversity of Voices} + \text{Shared Resources} + \text{Unified Goals} \quad (8)$$

For example, Taren successfully organized the first LGBTQ Pride event in Alyndra by partnering with local artists, businesses, and civil rights groups. This collaboration not only increased visibility for the event but also fostered a sense of community solidarity.

3. Effective Communication

Clear and persuasive communication is essential in advocacy. This involves not only articulating the issues at hand but also framing them in a way that resonates with the broader public. Utilizing storytelling, personal narratives, and data-driven arguments can help convey the urgency and importance of LGBTQ rights.

$$\text{Message Impact} = \text{Clarity} \times \text{Emotional Resonance} \times \text{Relevance} \quad (9)$$

Taren's use of personal stories from community members during advocacy meetings helped humanize the issues, making them more relatable to policymakers and the general public. This approach proved effective in garnering support for legislative changes.

4. Leveraging Social Media

In the digital age, social media has become a powerful tool for advocacy. Platforms such as Twitter, Instagram, and Facebook allow advocates to reach a global audience, mobilize supporters, and share information rapidly.

$$\text{Social Media Reach} = \text{Engagement Rate} \times \text{Content Shareability} \qquad (10)$$

Taren utilized social media campaigns to raise awareness about LGBTQ issues, share resources, and promote events. Her hashtag campaigns, such as #AlyndraPride, became trending topics, significantly increasing visibility for the movement.

5. Grassroots Mobilization

Grassroots advocacy is vital for creating change at the local level. Engaging community members through events, workshops, and training sessions empowers individuals to take action and advocate for their rights.

$$\text{Grassroots Impact} = \text{Community Engagement} \times \text{Local Action} \qquad (11)$$

Taren organized workshops aimed at educating community members about their rights and how to advocate for themselves. This empowerment led to increased participation in local governance and a stronger community voice.

6. Engaging with Policymakers

Direct engagement with policymakers is a crucial aspect of effective advocacy. This can involve lobbying efforts, attending town hall meetings, and building relationships with elected officials to advocate for policy changes that benefit the LGBTQ community.

$$\text{Policy Change} = \text{Advocacy Efforts} + \text{Political Will} \qquad (12)$$

Taren's meetings with local legislators resulted in the introduction of several bills aimed at protecting LGBTQ rights in Alyndra. By providing data and personal testimonies, she effectively influenced their understanding of the issues.

7. Education and Awareness Campaigns

Raising awareness about LGBTQ issues through education is vital for changing public perception and combating discrimination. This can involve creating informational materials, hosting seminars, and engaging in public speaking.

$$\text{Awareness Level} = \text{Education Efforts} \times \text{Community Involvement} \qquad (13)$$

Taren's education campaigns in schools and community centers helped dispel myths about LGBTQ individuals, fostering a more inclusive environment for all.

8. Evaluation and Adaptation

Finally, effective advocacy requires ongoing evaluation and adaptation of strategies. By assessing the impact of their efforts, advocates can identify what works, what doesn't, and how to refine their approach for greater effectiveness.

$$\text{Advocacy Effectiveness} = \text{Evaluation Metrics} + \text{Adaptation Strategies} \quad (14)$$

Taren regularly solicited feedback from community members and stakeholders, allowing her to adjust her strategies in response to changing needs and challenges.

Conclusion

In conclusion, the strategies for effective advocacy employed by Taren Fira highlight the importance of a comprehensive and adaptable approach to LGBTQ activism. By understanding the landscape, building coalitions, communicating effectively, leveraging social media, mobilizing grassroots efforts, engaging with policymakers, conducting education campaigns, and continuously evaluating their impact, advocates can create meaningful change in their communities and beyond. Taren Fira's legacy as a queer advocate serves as a testament to the power of strategic advocacy in the ongoing fight for LGBTQ rights.

Section Two: Intersectionality and Allyship

Advocacy for Queer People of Color

In the vibrant tapestry of LGBTQ activism, the voices and experiences of queer people of color (QPOC) often face marginalization, even within the broader movement. This subsection delves into the unique challenges faced by QPOC and the critical need for advocacy that centers their experiences, identities, and struggles.

Intersectionality: A Theoretical Framework

To understand the advocacy for queer people of color, it is essential to employ the concept of intersectionality, a term coined by legal scholar Kimberlé Crenshaw in

SECTION TWO: INTERSECTIONALITY AND ALLYSHIP

1989. Intersectionality posits that individuals experience multiple, overlapping identities—such as race, gender, sexuality, and class—that shape their unique social experiences and systemic oppressions. This framework helps us comprehend how racism, sexism, and homophobia intersect to create distinct challenges for QPOC.

$$\text{Intersectional Identity} = \text{Race} + \text{Gender} + \text{Sexuality} + \text{Class} \quad (15)$$

This equation illustrates that identity is not a singular construct but rather a complex amalgamation of various factors that influence one's lived experience. For instance, a queer Black woman may face different forms of discrimination compared to a white gay man, necessitating tailored advocacy strategies that address these unique intersections.

Challenges Faced by Queer People of Color

QPOC encounter a myriad of challenges that are often overlooked in mainstream LGBTQ advocacy. These challenges include:

- **Racism within LGBTQ Spaces:** Many QPOC report experiencing racism and exclusion within predominantly white LGBTQ organizations and events. This can lead to feelings of alienation and a lack of belonging, discouraging QPOC from participating in advocacy efforts.

- **Economic Disparities:** QPOC often face economic hardships that can hinder their ability to engage in activism. According to the 2020 U.S. Census Bureau, Black and Latino households have significantly lower median incomes compared to their white counterparts, which can limit their access to resources and opportunities for activism.

- **Cultural Stigmas:** Cultural norms and expectations within many communities of color can stigmatize queer identities, leading to familial rejection and community ostracism. This cultural stigma can deter individuals from openly expressing their identities and seeking support.

- **Violence and Safety Concerns:** QPOC are disproportionately affected by violence, including hate crimes and domestic violence. The FBI's Hate Crime Statistics report consistently shows that hate crimes against LGBTQ individuals, particularly those who are people of color, are on the rise.

These challenges necessitate a focused advocacy approach that amplifies the voices of QPOC and addresses their specific needs.

Strategies for Effective Advocacy

To effectively advocate for queer people of color, several strategies must be employed:

- **Centering QPOC Voices:** Advocacy efforts must prioritize the voices and experiences of QPOC. This can be achieved by involving QPOC leaders in decision-making processes and ensuring their stories and needs are represented in advocacy campaigns.

- **Building Inclusive Spaces:** Creating safe and inclusive spaces for QPOC within the LGBTQ community is essential. This can involve hosting events that celebrate QPOC culture, art, and history, as well as providing resources tailored to their specific experiences.

- **Collaborating with Other Movements:** Intersectional advocacy requires collaboration with other social justice movements, such as racial justice and feminist movements. By building coalitions, advocates can address the interconnected nature of oppression and create a more unified front for change.

- **Education and Awareness:** Raising awareness about the unique challenges faced by QPOC within both LGBTQ and racial justice spaces is crucial. This can involve workshops, training sessions, and public campaigns that educate allies and the broader community about intersectionality and inclusivity.

Examples of Successful Advocacy Initiatives

Several organizations and initiatives have successfully advocated for the rights and visibility of queer people of color:

- **The Audre Lorde Project:** Named after the influential Black lesbian feminist poet and activist, this organization focuses on the needs of LGBTQ people of color in New York City. Through community organizing, education, and advocacy, they empower QPOC to take leadership roles in social justice movements.

- **Black and Pink:** This national organization supports LGBTQ prisoners and advocates for their rights, particularly focusing on the intersection of race, sexuality, and incarceration. By amplifying the voices of incarcerated QPOC, Black and Pink addresses the systemic injustices faced by this population.

- **Transgender Law Center:** This organization works to change law and policy for transgender and gender non-conforming people, with a specific focus on the needs of QPOC. Their initiatives include legal advocacy, community education, and policy reform aimed at protecting the rights of marginalized transgender individuals.

Conclusion

Advocacy for queer people of color is a vital aspect of the broader LGBTQ movement. By employing an intersectional framework, addressing the unique challenges faced by QPOC, and implementing effective advocacy strategies, we can work towards a more inclusive and equitable society. The fight for LGBTQ rights cannot be truly successful without centering the experiences of those who exist at the intersections of multiple marginalized identities. As we continue to advocate for change, it is imperative that we listen to, uplift, and support the voices of queer people of color, ensuring they are not only heard but also empowered to lead the charge for justice and equality.

Collaborating with Other Social Justice Movements

The journey of LGBTQ activism is inherently intertwined with the broader tapestry of social justice movements. Collaborating with other social justice movements not only amplifies the voices of marginalized communities but also creates a unified front against systemic oppression. This section explores the significance of such collaborations, the theoretical frameworks that support them, the challenges encountered, and notable examples that highlight their effectiveness.

Theoretical Frameworks

Collaboration among social justice movements can be understood through several theoretical lenses. One prominent theory is the **Intersectionality Theory**, coined by Kimberlé Crenshaw, which posits that individuals experience multiple, overlapping identities that contribute to unique experiences of oppression and privilege. By recognizing the interconnectedness of various social identities—such as race, gender, sexuality, and class—activists can work together to address the root causes of discrimination and inequality.

Another relevant framework is the **Social Movement Theory**, which examines how movements arise, mobilize, and interact. The Resource Mobilization Theory within this framework emphasizes the importance of resources—be they financial, human, or informational—in fostering collaboration. This theory suggests that successful movements leverage their resources to form coalitions that can effectively challenge power structures.

Challenges in Collaboration

While the benefits of collaboration are clear, several challenges can hinder effective partnerships. One significant issue is the **competition for resources**. Different social justice movements often vie for limited funding, media attention, and public support. This competition can lead to tensions and a reluctance to engage in collaborative efforts.

Additionally, **ideological differences** may arise between movements. For instance, some activists may prioritize LGBTQ rights over racial justice, while others may feel that issues of race must take precedence. These differing priorities can create friction and complicate coalition-building efforts.

Moreover, there is the challenge of **tokenism**, where marginalized groups are included in discussions or initiatives merely to fulfill a diversity quota without genuine engagement or commitment to their issues. This can lead to disillusionment and a lack of trust among community members.

Examples of Successful Collaborations

Despite these challenges, there are numerous examples of successful collaborations between LGBTQ activists and other social justice movements that demonstrate the power of solidarity.

One notable example is the partnership between LGBTQ activists and the **Black Lives Matter (BLM)** movement. Both movements share a commitment to combating systemic oppression and violence, particularly against marginalized communities. The intersection of racial and LGBTQ justice has been highlighted in various protests, where activists have united to address issues such as police brutality, racial profiling, and the disproportionate violence faced by LGBTQ people of color.

Another significant collaboration occurred during the **Women's March** in 2017, where LGBTQ rights were prominently featured. Activists from various backgrounds joined forces to advocate for women's rights, reproductive rights, and LGBTQ rights, emphasizing the need for an inclusive approach to social justice. This event showcased how collective action can draw attention to interconnected issues and foster a sense of community among diverse groups.

Strategies for Effective Collaboration

To foster successful collaborations, activists can adopt several strategies:

1. **Building Trust**: Establishing open lines of communication and fostering relationships based on mutual respect is crucial. Regular meetings and collaborative events can help build rapport between different movements.

2. **Shared Goals**: Identifying common objectives can unify efforts. Creating joint campaigns that address overlapping issues can enhance visibility and impact.

3. **Education and Awareness**: Offering workshops and training sessions that educate activists about the issues faced by different communities fosters empathy and understanding. This knowledge can help dismantle biases and promote solidarity.

4. **Resource Sharing**: Collaborative efforts should include sharing resources, such as funding, volunteers, and expertise. By pooling resources, movements can increase their capacity to effect change.

5. **Intersectional Advocacy**: Emphasizing the importance of intersectionality in advocacy efforts ensures that the needs of all marginalized groups are addressed. This approach can help prevent the erasure of specific identities within broader movements.

Conclusion

In conclusion, collaborating with other social justice movements is vital for the advancement of LGBTQ rights. By recognizing the interconnectedness of various forms of oppression, activists can create a more inclusive and effective movement. While challenges exist, the potential for meaningful change through solidarity and collective action is immense. The future of LGBTQ advocacy depends on building bridges with other movements, fostering a culture of collaboration that uplifts all marginalized voices.

$$\text{Effective Collaboration} = \text{Trust} + \text{Shared Goals} + \text{Education} + \text{Resource Sharing} + \text{Intersecti} \tag{16}$$

Challenges and Critiques of Allyship

Allyship in LGBTQ activism is often heralded as a vital component of the movement, yet it is not without its challenges and critiques. While allies can amplify marginalized voices and contribute to social change, their involvement can also lead to complications that require careful navigation. This section explores the complexities of allyship, including the pitfalls of performative activism, the importance of listening to marginalized voices, and the critique of privilege within allyship.

1. The Pitfall of Performative Activism

One of the most significant challenges faced by allies is the tendency towards performative activism. This occurs when individuals engage in advocacy or support for LGBTQ rights primarily for social validation or personal gain, rather than from a genuine commitment to the cause. Performative allyship can manifest in various ways, such as posting on social media during Pride Month without taking substantive action throughout the year.

$$\text{Performative Allyship} = \frac{\text{Social Media Posts}}{\text{Genuine Actions}} \quad (17)$$

When allies prioritize visibility over authenticity, they risk undermining the movement and diluting the experiences of those they aim to support. This behavior can alienate marginalized individuals and foster skepticism regarding the ally's true intentions.

2. Listening and Learning

Another critical aspect of effective allyship is the necessity for allies to listen to and learn from the experiences of LGBTQ individuals. This requires a willingness to engage in difficult conversations, acknowledge one's own biases, and adapt one's understanding based on feedback from the community.

However, many allies struggle with the concept of "listening" as it often requires confronting uncomfortable truths about societal structures and personal privilege. The challenge lies in balancing the desire to support with the need to step back and allow marginalized voices to lead the conversation.

$$\text{Effective Allyship} = \text{Listening} + \text{Learning} + \text{Action} \quad (18)$$

This equation highlights that true allyship is a multi-faceted endeavor that necessitates ongoing education and responsiveness to the needs of the LGBTQ community.

3. The Critique of Privilege

Allyship is also critiqued for its relationship with privilege. Allies often come from backgrounds of privilege—be it racial, economic, or social—which can complicate their role within the movement. The critique centers on the idea that allies must recognize their privilege and use it to dismantle oppressive systems rather than perpetuate them.

For instance, a white ally may unintentionally overshadow the voices of LGBTQ people of color by dominating conversations or failing to address racial disparities within the LGBTQ community. This phenomenon is often referred to as "white saviorism," where the ally assumes a central role in the narrative, rather than supporting marginalized individuals in articulating their own experiences.

$$\text{Allyship} \propto \frac{1}{\text{Privilege Awareness}} \quad (19)$$

This equation suggests that effective allyship is inversely proportional to a lack of awareness regarding one's privilege. The more allies understand their privilege, the more effectively they can support marginalized voices without overshadowing them.

4. Navigating Intersectionality

Intersectionality is a crucial framework for understanding the diverse experiences within the LGBTQ community. Allies must navigate the complexities of intersectionality, recognizing that individuals hold multiple identities that intersect and influence their experiences of discrimination and privilege.

For example, a queer individual who is also a person of color may face different challenges than a white queer individual. Allies must be mindful of these differences and avoid generalizations that can erase the unique struggles faced by various groups within the LGBTQ community.

$$\text{Intersectional Allyship} = \sum_{i=1}^{n} \text{Identity}_i \quad (20)$$

This equation reflects the need for allies to consider the sum of all identities that contribute to an individual's experience, emphasizing that allyship must be nuanced and informed by an understanding of intersectionality.

5. The Importance of Accountability

Finally, accountability is a vital component of allyship that is often overlooked. Allies must hold themselves accountable for their actions and be willing to learn from their mistakes. This includes recognizing when they have caused harm, apologizing sincerely, and making amends.

The lack of accountability can lead to disillusionment within the LGBTQ community, as individuals may feel that allies are not genuinely committed to the cause.

$$\text{Accountability} = \text{Acknowledgment} + \text{Apology} + \text{Action} \tag{21}$$

This equation underscores that accountability involves a three-part process that is essential for maintaining trust and fostering meaningful relationships between allies and the LGBTQ community.

Conclusion

In conclusion, while allyship is a crucial element of LGBTQ activism, it is fraught with challenges and critiques that must be addressed. Allies must strive to avoid performative activism, actively listen and learn from marginalized voices, recognize their privilege, navigate intersectionality, and maintain accountability. By doing so, they can contribute to a more inclusive and effective movement for LGBTQ rights, ensuring that their support is meaningful and impactful.

Expanding the Definition of Inclusivity

Inclusivity is often perceived as a straightforward notion: the act of including diverse groups within a community or organization. However, as Taren Fira discovered in her journey, the definition of inclusivity is far more complex and nuanced. It is essential to examine the layers of identity that intersect within the LGBTQ community and to challenge the traditional frameworks that often marginalize certain voices.

Theoretical Foundations of Inclusivity

At its core, inclusivity is rooted in the principles of equity and social justice. The work of scholars such as Kimberlé Crenshaw, who introduced the concept of intersectionality, provides a foundational framework for understanding how different identities—such as race, gender, sexuality, and class—interact to create unique experiences of oppression and privilege. Crenshaw's theory posits that individuals cannot be understood solely through a single axis of identity; rather, it is the intersection of these identities that shapes their lived experiences.

$$I = f(R, G, S, C) \tag{22}$$

Where:

- I = Individual experience
- R = Race
- G = Gender
- S = Sexuality
- C = Class

This equation illustrates that an individual's experience I is a function of multiple intersecting identities. Therefore, inclusivity must not only acknowledge but actively engage with these intersections to create a truly supportive environment.

Challenges in Defining Inclusivity

Despite the growing recognition of intersectionality, many LGBTQ organizations continue to struggle with inclusivity. A common issue is the tendency to prioritize certain identities over others, often elevating the voices of white, cisgender, gay men while sidelining those of queer people of color, transgender individuals, and non-binary persons. This hierarchical approach can lead to a form of inclusivity that is superficial and fails to address the systemic inequalities that persist within the community.

For instance, during the organization of LGBTQ pride events, the focus often leans heavily on visibility for gay and lesbian individuals, with less attention paid to the unique challenges faced by transgender and non-binary individuals. Taren Fira recognized this gap and sought to amplify the voices of these marginalized groups. She famously stated, "True inclusivity is not just about making space at the table; it's about rethinking the table itself."

Examples of Expanding Inclusivity

In her advocacy work, Taren implemented several strategies to expand the definition of inclusivity. One notable example was her initiative to create an LGBTQ resource center that specifically catered to the needs of queer people of color. This center offered culturally relevant resources, support groups, and workshops aimed at addressing the unique challenges faced by individuals at the intersection of race and sexuality.

Moreover, Taren collaborated with local artists to develop an art exhibit titled "Voices Unheard," which showcased the stories and experiences of marginalized

LGBTQ individuals. This exhibit not only provided a platform for underrepresented voices but also educated the broader community about the importance of intersectionality in advocacy.

The Role of Language in Inclusivity

Language plays a pivotal role in shaping our understanding of inclusivity. Terms such as "LGBTQ+" have become common vernacular, yet they can sometimes obscure the diversity within the community. Taren advocated for the use of more inclusive language that recognizes the spectrum of gender identities and sexual orientations. For instance, the inclusion of terms like "non-binary," "genderqueer," and "two-spirit" within LGBTQ discourse serves to validate and acknowledge the experiences of individuals who may otherwise feel invisible.

Moving Towards a More Inclusive Future

To expand the definition of inclusivity, it is imperative for LGBTQ activists and organizations to engage in continuous self-reflection and education. This involves actively listening to the voices of marginalized individuals and integrating their experiences into advocacy efforts. Taren emphasized the importance of allyship, stating, "Allies must not only support but also advocate for the needs of those who are often silenced."

In conclusion, expanding the definition of inclusivity requires a commitment to understanding and addressing the complexities of identity. By embracing intersectionality and prioritizing the voices of marginalized individuals, the LGBTQ community can foster a more inclusive environment that truly represents the diversity of its members. Taren Fira's legacy serves as a reminder that inclusivity is an ongoing journey, one that demands vigilance, empathy, and a willingness to challenge the status quo.

Inspiring Other Activists

In the vibrant tapestry of LGBTQ activism, the role of an individual as a source of inspiration cannot be overstated. Taren Fira, with her unwavering commitment and innovative approaches, serves as a beacon for budding activists. This section delves into how Taren's journey galvanized others, fostering a culture of empowerment and resilience within the LGBTQ community.

The Ripple Effect of Activism

Taren understood that activism is not a solitary endeavor; it thrives on collaboration and shared experiences. The concept of the *ripple effect* illustrates how one person's actions can inspire a multitude of others to take a stand. This phenomenon can be expressed through the equation:

$$R = k \cdot A \qquad (23)$$

where R represents the ripple effect, k is a constant reflecting the individual's influence, and A denotes the number of people inspired. Taren's ability to connect with others on a personal level enabled her to amplify her impact exponentially.

Mentorship and Guidance

One of Taren's key strategies was mentorship. Recognizing that many emerging activists faced challenges similar to those she once endured, she established mentorship programs aimed at providing guidance and support. These programs emphasized the importance of sharing knowledge, skills, and experiences, which in turn fostered confidence among new activists.

For example, during the inaugural LGBTQ Pride event organized by Taren, she invited young activists to co-lead workshops. This not only provided them with a platform to express their ideas but also equipped them with practical skills in organizing, public speaking, and advocacy.

Storytelling as a Catalyst for Change

Taren also championed the power of storytelling as a means to inspire others. She believed that personal narratives could bridge divides and foster empathy. The act of sharing one's story can be a transformative experience, both for the storyteller and the audience.

In her workshops, Taren encouraged participants to articulate their experiences with discrimination, resilience, and triumph. This practice not only validated their feelings but also highlighted the collective struggle within the LGBTQ community. The formula for effective storytelling can be articulated as follows:

$$S = E + C + R \qquad (24)$$

where S is the strength of the story, E represents emotional resonance, C is the clarity of the message, and R denotes the relatability of the experience. Taren's emphasis on these elements ensured that stories were not only heard but felt, inspiring listeners to take action.

Creating Platforms for Voices

Understanding the importance of visibility, Taren worked tirelessly to create platforms for marginalized voices within the LGBTQ community. She organized events that highlighted the contributions of queer people of color, transgender individuals, and other underrepresented groups. By amplifying these voices, Taren not only inspired others but also fostered a sense of belonging and ownership within the movement.

For instance, during a panel discussion on intersectionality, Taren invited activists from diverse backgrounds to share their unique perspectives. This initiative not only educated attendees but also encouraged them to reflect on their own roles within the broader context of LGBTQ activism.

Building a Culture of Support

Taren's commitment to building a supportive community was pivotal in inspiring other activists. She recognized that activism can be emotionally taxing, often leading to burnout and fatigue. To combat this, Taren promoted self-care practices and community support systems.

She implemented regular check-ins and support groups where activists could share their struggles and victories. The formula for community resilience can be summarized as:

$$C = S + R \qquad (25)$$

where C represents community strength, S denotes shared experiences, and R signifies the resources available for support. By fostering a culture of care, Taren ensured that activists felt valued and motivated to continue their work.

Utilizing Social Media for Inspiration

In the digital age, Taren leveraged social media as a powerful tool for inspiration. She utilized platforms such as Twitter, Instagram, and TikTok to share her journey, promote events, and highlight the work of other activists. This approach not only expanded her reach but also created a sense of global solidarity among LGBTQ activists.

SECTION TWO: INTERSECTIONALITY AND ALLYSHIP

By sharing impactful content—such as videos of protests, personal stories, and educational resources—Taren inspired countless individuals to engage in activism. The equation that encapsulates the potential of social media in activism is:

$$I = V \cdot R \tag{26}$$

where I represents the impact, V is the virality of the content, and R is the reach of the audience. Taren's strategic use of social media exemplified how digital platforms could galvanize support and inspire action.

Conclusion

Taren Fira's legacy as an inspirational figure in LGBTQ activism is characterized by her dedication to mentorship, storytelling, community support, and innovative use of digital platforms. Through her efforts, she not only inspired a new generation of activists but also cultivated a movement grounded in inclusivity and resilience. As we reflect on Taren's impact, it is clear that her approach serves as a model for aspiring activists, demonstrating that inspiration can be a powerful catalyst for change.

Mobilizing Intersectional LGBTQ Advocacy

The landscape of LGBTQ advocacy is continuously evolving, necessitating an approach that recognizes and addresses the multifaceted experiences of individuals within the community. Mobilizing intersectional LGBTQ advocacy is not merely a strategy; it is a vital framework that acknowledges how various forms of identity—such as race, gender, class, and ability—intersect to shape experiences of discrimination and privilege. This section explores the theoretical underpinnings of intersectionality, the challenges faced in mobilizing intersectional advocacy, and practical examples of successful initiatives.

Theoretical Framework of Intersectionality

Intersectionality, a term coined by legal scholar Kimberlé Crenshaw in the late 1980s, posits that individuals experience oppression in varying configurations and degrees of intensity based on their intersecting identities. Crenshaw's work highlighted how traditional feminist and anti-racist discourses often neglected the unique struggles faced by Black women, thus illustrating the need for a more nuanced understanding of identity and oppression.

Mathematically, we can represent the intersectionality of identities as a function of multiple variables:

$$O = f(I_1, I_2, I_3, \ldots, I_n) \tag{27}$$

where O represents the overall oppression experienced, and $I_1, I_2, \ldots, I_n$ are the various intersecting identities (e.g., race, gender, sexual orientation). This equation suggests that the experience of oppression cannot be understood by isolating individual identities but must be viewed as a complex interplay of multiple factors.

Challenges in Mobilizing Intersectional Advocacy

Despite its importance, mobilizing intersectional LGBTQ advocacy presents several challenges:

- **Fragmentation of Movements:** Often, LGBTQ advocacy is segregated into specific identity groups, leading to a lack of solidarity among different factions. For example, issues pertinent to queer people of color may be overlooked in predominantly white LGBTQ spaces.

- **Tokenism:** Organizations may superficially adopt intersectional rhetoric without implementing genuine changes that address the needs of marginalized groups. This can lead to disillusionment among those who feel their voices are merely being used to enhance an organization's image.

- **Resource Allocation:** Intersectional advocacy often requires more resources to address the diverse needs of various groups. Many organizations struggle with limited funding, leading to prioritization of issues that may not reflect the intersectional realities of their constituents.

Successful Examples of Intersectional Advocacy

Despite these challenges, there are notable examples of successful intersectional LGBTQ advocacy that can serve as models for future initiatives:

- **Black Lives Matter (BLM):** The BLM movement has effectively integrated LGBTQ advocacy into its framework, emphasizing the need to address the unique challenges faced by Black LGBTQ individuals. By centering the experiences of marginalized voices, BLM has fostered a more inclusive approach to social justice.

SECTION TWO: INTERSECTIONALITY AND ALLYSHIP

- **The Transgender Law Center:** This organization focuses on the legal rights of transgender individuals, particularly those from marginalized communities. Their initiatives include addressing the specific needs of transgender people of color, thereby highlighting the intersection of race and gender identity in advocacy efforts.
- **The Queer Women of Color Media Arts Project (QWOCMAP):** QWOCMAP empowers queer women of color through storytelling and media production. By providing resources and platforms for marginalized voices, QWOCMAP illustrates how intersectional advocacy can uplift underrepresented communities and promote social change.

Strategies for Effective Intersectional Advocacy

To effectively mobilize intersectional LGBTQ advocacy, organizations and activists should consider the following strategies:

1. **Foster Inclusive Spaces:** Create environments where diverse voices can be heard and valued. This can be achieved through community forums, workshops, and collaborative projects that prioritize the experiences of marginalized groups.
2. **Educate and Raise Awareness:** Develop educational programs that inform the broader LGBTQ community about intersectionality and its implications. This can include training sessions, webinars, and resources that highlight the interconnectedness of various identities.
3. **Build Coalitions:** Form alliances with other social justice movements to amplify the impact of intersectional advocacy. By collaborating with organizations focused on racial justice, gender equality, and economic justice, LGBTQ advocates can create a more robust movement for change.
4. **Advocate for Policy Changes:** Push for legislation that addresses the unique needs of intersecting identities. This includes advocating for comprehensive anti-discrimination laws that protect individuals based on their race, gender identity, sexual orientation, and other intersecting factors.

In conclusion, mobilizing intersectional LGBTQ advocacy is essential for creating a more inclusive and equitable society. By recognizing and addressing the complexities of identity, advocates can work towards dismantling the systemic barriers that perpetuate discrimination and inequality. As Taren Fira exemplifies in her journey, the fight for LGBTQ rights must be rooted in an understanding of intersectionality, ensuring that all voices are heard and valued in the pursuit of justice.

Centering Marginalized Voices

In the realm of LGBTQ activism, centering marginalized voices is not merely a noble aspiration; it is a fundamental necessity for achieving true equality and justice. This approach recognizes that within the LGBTQ community, certain identities and experiences are often overlooked or silenced, particularly those of queer people of color, transgender individuals, and non-binary persons. To effectively advocate for the rights of all LGBTQ individuals, it is essential to elevate these voices and ensure they are heard in every conversation and decision-making process.

Theoretical Framework

The concept of centering marginalized voices is rooted in critical theories that emphasize intersectionality, a term coined by Kimberlé Crenshaw. Intersectionality posits that individuals experience oppression in varying degrees based on multiple intersecting identities, such as race, gender, sexuality, and socioeconomic status. By applying an intersectional lens, activists can better understand the complexities of discrimination faced by marginalized groups within the LGBTQ community.

$$O = f(I_1, I_2, I_3, \ldots, I_n) \qquad (28)$$

Where O represents the overall oppression experienced, and I_n represents the various intersecting identities. This equation illustrates that the experience of oppression is not linear; rather, it is a function of multiple factors that must be considered holistically.

Problems Faced by Marginalized Voices

Despite the theoretical understanding of intersectionality, marginalized voices often struggle to gain visibility and representation in LGBTQ activism. This marginalization can manifest in several ways:

- **Tokenism:** Organizations may superficially include marginalized individuals in campaigns without genuinely valuing their input or perspectives. This tokenistic approach can lead to a lack of meaningful engagement and perpetuate the very inequalities activists seek to dismantle.

- **Access to Resources:** Marginalized communities frequently lack access to the resources necessary for effective advocacy. This includes financial support, educational opportunities, and platforms to share their stories. Without these resources, their voices remain muted in larger conversations about LGBTQ rights.

- **Cultural Competency:** Many mainstream LGBTQ organizations may not fully understand the cultural contexts of marginalized groups, leading to advocacy that fails to resonate with or address the unique needs of these communities. This disconnect can further alienate individuals who feel their experiences are not represented.

Examples of Centering Marginalized Voices

To illustrate the importance of centering marginalized voices, we can look to several successful initiatives and campaigns within the LGBTQ movement that have prioritized inclusivity:

1. **The Black Lives Matter Movement:** The intersection of racial justice and LGBTQ rights has gained prominence through the Black Lives Matter movement, which has highlighted the specific challenges faced by Black LGBTQ individuals. By centering the voices of queer people of color, this movement has pushed for a more inclusive understanding of justice that encompasses both racial and sexual identity.

2. **Transgender Day of Remembrance:** This annual observance honors the lives lost to anti-transgender violence, particularly among marginalized communities. By amplifying the stories of transgender individuals, especially those who are Black, Indigenous, or people of color (BIPOC), the event serves as a powerful reminder of the urgent need for advocacy that addresses the specific vulnerabilities faced by these groups.

3. **Local LGBTQ Organizations:** Many grassroots organizations prioritize centering marginalized voices by actively involving community members in decision-making processes. For example, organizations that focus on the needs of LGBTQ youth of color often engage these young people in leadership roles, ensuring their experiences shape the programs and policies that affect them.

Strategies for Centering Marginalized Voices

To effectively center marginalized voices in LGBTQ activism, organizations and activists can adopt several strategies:

- **Inclusive Leadership:** Ensure that leadership positions within LGBTQ organizations reflect the diversity of the community. This includes actively recruiting and promoting individuals from marginalized backgrounds to decision-making roles.

- **Community Engagement:** Foster genuine relationships with marginalized communities through outreach and collaboration. Listening sessions, focus groups, and community forums can provide valuable insights into the needs and concerns of these groups.

- **Resource Allocation:** Allocate resources specifically to support marginalized voices. This can include funding for initiatives led by queer people of color or providing grants to organizations that focus on intersectional advocacy.

- **Education and Training:** Provide training for activists and organizations on cultural competency and the importance of intersectionality. This education can help dismantle biases and foster a more inclusive environment within the movement.

Conclusion

Centering marginalized voices is not an optional aspect of LGBTQ activism; it is a critical imperative that shapes the movement's integrity and effectiveness. By recognizing and amplifying the experiences of those who are often silenced, activists can create a more inclusive and equitable society for all. The journey toward true equality is complex and multifaceted, but by prioritizing the voices of the most marginalized, we can ensure that the fight for LGBTQ rights is comprehensive, just, and transformative.

Solidarity and Coalition Building

In the landscape of LGBTQ activism, solidarity and coalition building stand as critical pillars that fortify movements and amplify voices. Solidarity refers to the unity of individuals or groups in mutual support of a common cause, while coalition building involves the strategic alliance of diverse organizations and individuals to achieve shared objectives. The intersection of these concepts is vital in fostering inclusivity and ensuring that the fight for LGBTQ rights is comprehensive and representative of all marginalized communities.

Theoretical Framework

The theory of intersectionality, coined by Kimberlé Crenshaw, provides a foundational understanding of how various forms of discrimination intersect and impact individuals differently based on their identities. In the context of LGBTQ activism, intersectionality highlights the necessity of recognizing and addressing the unique challenges faced by queer individuals who also belong to other marginalized groups, such as people of color, individuals with disabilities, and those from low-income backgrounds. This theoretical lens encourages activists to build coalitions that are not only inclusive but also reflective of the diverse experiences within the LGBTQ community.

Challenges in Solidarity and Coalition Building

While the importance of solidarity and coalition building is clear, several challenges often arise:

- **Power Dynamics:** Within coalitions, power imbalances can emerge, often privileging certain voices over others. For instance, white LGBTQ individuals may dominate discussions, inadvertently sidelining queer people of color. This can lead to feelings of alienation and resentment among marginalized groups.

- **Differing Priorities:** Different organizations may have varying priorities and agendas, which can complicate coalition efforts. For example, a group focused on marriage equality may not prioritize issues like transgender rights or housing insecurity, leading to tensions within the coalition.

- **Resource Allocation:** Limited resources can hinder coalition efforts. Organizations may struggle to share funding, staff, and other resources, which can affect the sustainability of collaborative initiatives.

Successful Examples of Solidarity and Coalition Building

Despite these challenges, numerous successful examples of solidarity and coalition building illustrate the potential for collective action:

- **The Black Lives Matter Movement:** The intersection of LGBTQ rights and racial justice has been exemplified by the Black Lives Matter movement, which actively advocates for the rights of Black LGBTQ individuals. The movement has successfully built coalitions with various LGBTQ organizations to address systemic racism and homophobia, demonstrating the power of solidarity across social justice movements.

- **The Transgender Day of Remembrance (TDOR):** TDOR serves as a poignant example of coalition building within the LGBTQ community. Various organizations come together annually to honor the lives lost to anti-transgender violence. This event not only raises awareness but also fosters solidarity among diverse groups within the LGBTQ spectrum, emphasizing the need for collective action against violence and discrimination.

- **The Marriage Equality Movement:** The successful push for marriage equality in many countries was marked by coalitions that included LGBTQ organizations, feminist groups, and allies from various sectors. These coalitions worked together to advocate for legislative changes, utilizing a shared narrative of love and equality that resonated across different demographics.

Strategies for Effective Solidarity and Coalition Building

To foster effective solidarity and coalition building, activists can employ several strategies:

- **Inclusive Leadership:** Ensuring that leadership within coalitions reflects the diversity of the communities served is essential. This can be achieved by actively seeking out and elevating marginalized voices, particularly those of queer people of color and other underrepresented groups.

- **Shared Goals and Values:** Establishing clear, shared goals and values at the outset of coalition-building efforts can help unify diverse groups. Regular communication and collaborative planning sessions can facilitate alignment and foster a sense of collective ownership over the movement's direction.

- **Education and Training:** Providing education and training on intersectionality and the specific challenges faced by various groups within the LGBTQ community can enhance understanding and empathy among coalition members. Workshops and discussions can help dismantle biases and encourage a more inclusive approach to activism.

- **Resource Sharing:** Developing mechanisms for resource sharing among coalition members can strengthen partnerships and enhance the effectiveness of advocacy efforts. This may include sharing funding opportunities, volunteer networks, and educational materials.

Conclusion

In conclusion, solidarity and coalition building are indispensable components of effective LGBTQ activism. By recognizing the interconnectedness of various struggles and fostering inclusive partnerships, activists can create a more equitable and just society for all. As Taren Fira exemplified in her advocacy, the power of collective action lies in its ability to uplift marginalized voices and create meaningful change. The journey toward LGBTQ equality is a shared one, and through solidarity, we can navigate the complexities of activism together.

Addressing Privilege and Power Dynamics

In the realm of LGBTQ advocacy, understanding privilege and power dynamics is crucial for fostering an inclusive and effective movement. Privilege can be defined as the unearned advantages held by certain groups over others, which often leads to systemic inequalities. This section explores the concept of privilege, its manifestations within the LGBTQ community, and strategies to address power dynamics to create a more equitable society.

Understanding Privilege

Privilege exists on multiple axes, including race, gender, sexual orientation, socio-economic status, and ability. For example, a white, cisgender gay man may experience certain privileges that a queer person of color or a transgender individual does not. This disparity highlights the importance of intersectionality, a term coined by Kimberlé Crenshaw, which emphasizes how different forms of identity intersect and contribute to unique experiences of oppression or privilege.

$$\text{Intersectionality} = \text{Race} + \text{Gender} + \text{Sexual Orientation} + \text{Class} + \text{Ability} \quad (29)$$

This equation underscores that individuals possess multiple identities that can compound their experiences of both privilege and discrimination. For instance, while LGBTQ individuals may face homophobia, a queer person of color may also contend with racism, creating a more complex landscape of challenges.

Manifestations of Privilege in LGBTQ Spaces

Within LGBTQ spaces, privilege can manifest in various ways. For instance, discussions surrounding marriage equality often centered on the experiences of white, cisgender, same-sex couples, overshadowing the needs of marginalized groups. This phenomenon is known as "mainstreaming," where the narratives of dominant groups are prioritized, leaving behind those who are already on the margins.

Moreover, the language used in LGBTQ advocacy can perpetuate privilege. Terms and frameworks that resonate with one group may exclude others. For example, the term "coming out" may not fully encapsulate the experiences of non-binary or genderqueer individuals who navigate their identities in ways that differ from traditional narratives.

The Role of Power Dynamics

Power dynamics in advocacy can create significant barriers to inclusivity. Those in positions of power often dictate the agenda, which can lead to the marginalization of voices that do not align with their experiences. This dynamic is evident in leadership structures within LGBTQ organizations, where predominantly white, cisgender individuals often hold key positions, thereby influencing the direction of advocacy efforts.

$$\text{Power Dynamics} = \frac{\text{Access to Resources}}{\text{Representation in Leadership}} \qquad (30)$$

This equation illustrates that the power dynamics within advocacy organizations can significantly impact their effectiveness in addressing the needs of diverse communities. When leadership lacks representation from marginalized groups, the resulting policies and initiatives may fail to address the unique challenges faced by those communities.

Strategies for Addressing Privilege and Power Dynamics

To foster a more inclusive LGBTQ movement, it is essential to implement strategies that address privilege and power dynamics:

SECTION TWO: INTERSECTIONALITY AND ALLYSHIP 61

- **Educate on Privilege:** Conduct workshops and training sessions on privilege and intersectionality to raise awareness among advocates and allies. Understanding one's own privilege is the first step toward creating change.

- **Center Marginalized Voices:** Ensure that the voices of those most affected by discrimination are prioritized in discussions and decision-making processes. This can involve creating platforms for queer people of color, transgender individuals, and others to share their stories and perspectives.

- **Diversify Leadership:** Advocate for diverse representation within leadership roles in LGBTQ organizations. This includes actively recruiting individuals from marginalized communities to ensure a variety of experiences and viewpoints are included in policy-making.

- **Develop Inclusive Language:** Create advocacy materials and communications that reflect the diversity of the LGBTQ community. This includes using gender-neutral language and avoiding assumptions about individuals' identities.

- **Engage in Coalition Building:** Collaborate with other social justice movements to address intersecting issues of privilege and oppression. Building coalitions can amplify marginalized voices and create a united front against systemic inequalities.

Conclusion

Addressing privilege and power dynamics within LGBTQ advocacy is not merely an academic exercise; it is a necessary endeavor to create a more equitable movement. By recognizing the complexities of identity and the systemic barriers that exist, advocates can work towards a future where all members of the LGBTQ community are heard, valued, and empowered. The path to inclusivity requires ongoing reflection, education, and action, ensuring that the movement does not replicate the very inequalities it seeks to dismantle.

In the words of Audre Lorde, "There is no such thing as a single-issue struggle because we do not live single-issue lives." Embracing this philosophy is fundamental to addressing privilege and power dynamics in a meaningful and transformative way.

The Role of Allies in Creating Change

Allies play a crucial role in the advancement of LGBTQ rights and the broader fight for social justice. Their involvement can transform the landscape of activism, serving not only as supporters but also as catalysts for change. This section explores the theoretical underpinnings of allyship, the challenges allies face, and real-world examples of effective allyship in action.

Theoretical Foundations of Allyship

Allyship can be understood through several theoretical frameworks. One prominent theory is the **Social Identity Theory**, which posits that individuals derive part of their identity from the social groups they belong to. Allies recognize their privilege and actively work to dismantle systems of oppression that benefit them at the expense of marginalized groups. This recognition is crucial for fostering genuine allyship, as it requires individuals to confront their own biases and privileges.

Another relevant framework is **Intersectionality**, introduced by Kimberlé Crenshaw. This concept emphasizes that individuals hold multiple identities that intersect, leading to unique experiences of oppression or privilege. Allies must understand the complexities of intersectionality to effectively support marginalized communities. For example, an ally who identifies as a white, cisgender male may experience privilege in some contexts but must acknowledge the additional layers of discrimination faced by LGBTQ people of color.

Challenges Allies Face

Despite their good intentions, allies often encounter several challenges in their journey towards effective advocacy. One significant issue is the **Performative Allyship**, where individuals engage in activism primarily for social validation rather than genuine commitment to change. This behavior can undermine the efforts of marginalized communities and create a false sense of progress.

Additionally, allies may struggle with **Imposter Syndrome**, feeling unqualified or inadequate in their efforts to support LGBTQ individuals. This self-doubt can hinder their ability to engage meaningfully in advocacy work. It is essential for allies to seek education, listen to marginalized voices, and recognize that their journey is a continuous learning process.

Effective Allyship in Action

Real-world examples illustrate the profound impact allies can have in creating change. One notable instance is the role of allies during the **Stonewall Riots** in 1969. While the riots were primarily led by LGBTQ individuals, many allies joined the fight against police brutality and discrimination, amplifying the voices of the marginalized and helping to bring national attention to the LGBTQ rights movement.

In more recent history, the **#BlackLivesMatter** movement has seen significant participation from allies who recognize the intersections of race and LGBTQ rights. For instance, white allies have organized protests, raised funds, and used their platforms to highlight the experiences of Black LGBTQ individuals. This coalition-building is vital for addressing systemic injustices and fostering solidarity across movements.

Strategies for Allies

To be effective in their roles, allies should adopt several strategies:

- **Listen and Learn:** Allies must actively listen to the experiences and needs of LGBTQ individuals. This involves engaging in conversations and seeking out educational resources to better understand the challenges faced by marginalized communities.

- **Use Privilege for Good:** Allies should leverage their privilege to advocate for change. This can involve speaking up in spaces where LGBTQ voices may be marginalized, challenging discriminatory comments, or using their platforms to amplify LGBTQ issues.

- **Support LGBTQ Leadership:** Allies must recognize the importance of centering LGBTQ voices in advocacy efforts. This means supporting LGBTQ leaders and organizations, rather than attempting to lead the charge themselves.

- **Engage in Continuous Reflection:** Allies should regularly reflect on their actions and motivations. This self-assessment can help identify areas for growth and ensure that their allyship is rooted in genuine commitment rather than performative gestures.

Conclusion

In conclusion, the role of allies in creating change is multifaceted and essential to the advancement of LGBTQ rights. By understanding the theoretical foundations of allyship, recognizing the challenges they face, and adopting effective strategies, allies can significantly contribute to the fight for equality and justice. As we continue to navigate the complexities of social movements, the importance of authentic allyship cannot be overstated. Allies must not only stand in solidarity with marginalized communities but also actively work to dismantle the systems of oppression that persist in society. Together, through collaboration and mutual support, we can create a more inclusive and equitable world for all.

Section Three: Taren Fira Goes International

Advocacy at the United Nations

In the realm of global activism, the United Nations (UN) serves as a pivotal platform for advocating LGBTQ rights, where voices from diverse backgrounds converge to address pressing issues. Taren Fira, with her relentless spirit and unwavering commitment, recognized the potential of the UN as a stage for international LGBTQ advocacy. This section delves into Taren's journey at the UN, exploring the theoretical frameworks, challenges faced, and notable examples of her impactful work.

Theoretical Frameworks of Advocacy

Advocacy at the UN is underpinned by several theoretical frameworks, including Human Rights Theory, Intersectionality, and Global Governance.

- **Human Rights Theory** posits that every individual possesses inherent rights simply by being human. This theory provides the foundation for LGBTQ advocacy, emphasizing that sexual orientation and gender identity should not be grounds for discrimination.
- **Intersectionality**, a term coined by Kimberlé Crenshaw, highlights how various social identities—such as race, gender, and sexual orientation—intersect to create unique experiences of oppression. Taren's advocacy often centered on this framework, as she understood that LGBTQ individuals from marginalized backgrounds faced compounded challenges.
- **Global Governance** refers to the way international affairs are managed across countries. Taren leveraged this framework to engage with multiple stakeholders, including states, NGOs, and intergovernmental organizations, to promote LGBTQ rights on a global scale.

Challenges in Advocacy at the UN

Despite the potential for change, Taren's journey at the UN was fraught with challenges. Key issues included:

SECTION THREE: TAREN FIRA GOES INTERNATIONAL   65

- **Political Resistance:** Many member states, particularly those with conservative ideologies, resisted the inclusion of LGBTQ rights in UN discussions. Taren often encountered officials who viewed LGBTQ advocacy as a Western imposition, leading to heated debates.

- **Cultural Sensitivity:** The diversity of cultures represented at the UN necessitated a careful approach to advocacy. Taren had to navigate the delicate balance between promoting universal human rights and respecting cultural differences, often leading to complex negotiations.

- **Resource Limitations:** Advocacy efforts at the UN require substantial resources, including funding, personnel, and expertise. Taren faced challenges in mobilizing these resources, particularly when competing against larger, more established organizations.

Notable Examples of Taren's Advocacy

Taren's tenure at the UN was marked by several significant initiatives and achievements:

- **The 2016 UN Resolution on LGBTQ Rights:** One of Taren's most notable accomplishments was her instrumental role in advocating for the 2016 UN resolution that called for the protection of LGBTQ individuals from violence and discrimination. This resolution marked a historic moment, as it was the first time the UN formally recognized the rights of LGBTQ people.

$$\text{UN Resolution} = \text{Advocacy} + \text{Coalition Building} + \text{International Support} \tag{31}$$

Taren's ability to unite various stakeholders was crucial in garnering support for the resolution.

- **Participation in the UN Human Rights Council:** Taren frequently presented testimonies and reports at the UN Human Rights Council, highlighting the plight of LGBTQ individuals in various regions. Her compelling narratives often swayed public opinion and influenced policy discussions.

- **Workshops and Training Sessions:** Taren organized workshops aimed at educating UN delegates about LGBTQ issues. These sessions fostered understanding and empathy, breaking down stereotypes and misconceptions that often hindered progress.

Impact of Taren's Advocacy

The impact of Taren Fira's advocacy at the UN extended beyond immediate policy changes. Her work contributed to:

- **Increased Visibility of LGBTQ Issues:** Taren's efforts brought LGBTQ issues to the forefront of international discussions, ensuring that they were no longer sidelined in global governance.
- **Strengthening Global Networks:** Through her advocacy, Taren established connections with LGBTQ activists worldwide, fostering a sense of solidarity and collaboration that transcended borders.
- **Empowerment of Local Activists:** Taren's engagement with the UN empowered local activists by providing them with a platform to voice their concerns and experiences, amplifying their impact within their communities.

In conclusion, Taren Fira's advocacy at the United Nations exemplified the power of global activism in advancing LGBTQ rights. By navigating the complexities of international diplomacy and leveraging theoretical frameworks, she not only championed the rights of LGBTQ individuals but also inspired a new generation of activists to continue the fight for equality. Her legacy at the UN serves as a testament to the importance of unwavering commitment, strategic advocacy, and the belief that change is possible on a global scale.

Addressing LGBTQ Rights on a Global Scale

In the ever-evolving landscape of human rights, the struggle for LGBTQ rights has emerged as a pivotal issue transcending national borders. This section delves into the complexities of advocating for LGBTQ rights globally, highlighting the theoretical frameworks, challenges faced, and successful initiatives that have shaped the discourse surrounding these rights.

Theoretical Frameworks

The advocacy for LGBTQ rights on a global scale can be understood through various theoretical lenses, including human rights theory, intersectionality, and post-colonialism. Human rights theory posits that all individuals are entitled to certain fundamental rights, regardless of their sexual orientation or gender identity. This universalist approach asserts that LGBTQ rights are human rights, thereby demanding recognition and protection under international law.

Intersectionality, introduced by Kimberlé Crenshaw, provides a critical framework for understanding how overlapping identities—such as race, gender, and class—impact the experiences of LGBTQ individuals. This perspective is essential when addressing LGBTQ rights globally, as it underscores the need to consider the unique challenges faced by marginalized groups within the LGBTQ community, particularly in regions where cultural and societal norms exacerbate discrimination.

Post-colonial theory critiques the legacy of colonialism, which often imposed heteronormative values on colonized societies. This lens encourages activists to recognize and challenge the ways in which Western narratives of LGBTQ rights can inadvertently perpetuate neocolonial attitudes, urging a more localized approach to advocacy that respects cultural contexts.

Challenges in Global LGBTQ Advocacy

Despite the progress made in many countries, numerous challenges persist in the fight for global LGBTQ rights. One significant issue is the existence of anti-LGBTQ laws in various nations, where homosexuality is criminalized, often leading to violence and persecution. For instance, in countries like Uganda and Nigeria, draconian laws impose severe penalties for same-sex relationships, creating an environment of fear and repression.

Furthermore, cultural stigma and societal attitudes towards LGBTQ individuals can hinder advocacy efforts. In many regions, deeply ingrained beliefs about gender and sexuality contribute to widespread discrimination and violence. The lack of comprehensive data on LGBTQ populations in these areas complicates advocacy, as activists struggle to highlight the specific needs and rights of these individuals.

Successful Initiatives and Case Studies

Despite these challenges, numerous initiatives have successfully advanced LGBTQ rights on a global scale. One notable example is the work of the International Lesbian, Gay, Bisexual, Trans and Intersex Association (ILGA), which has played a crucial role in uniting LGBTQ organizations worldwide. Through advocacy, research, and capacity-building, ILGA has fostered a global network dedicated to promoting LGBTQ rights and providing support to local activists.

Another significant initiative is the United Nations Free & Equal campaign, which aims to raise awareness of LGBTQ issues and promote equality. This campaign has successfully engaged governments, civil society, and the private sector, fostering dialogue and collaboration to address discrimination and violence against LGBTQ individuals.

The Role of Technology in Advocacy

In the digital age, technology has become an indispensable tool for global LGBTQ advocacy. Social media platforms allow activists to share information, mobilize support, and amplify marginalized voices. For instance, the hashtag #LoveIsLove gained international traction during the fight for marriage equality, connecting individuals and organizations across the globe and fostering a sense of solidarity.

Moreover, online platforms facilitate the sharing of personal narratives, which can humanize the struggle for LGBTQ rights and challenge stereotypes. These stories resonate with broader audiences, fostering empathy and understanding that can lead to meaningful change.

Conclusion

Addressing LGBTQ rights on a global scale requires a multifaceted approach that encompasses theoretical frameworks, an understanding of local contexts, and the utilization of technology. While significant challenges remain, the collective efforts of activists, organizations, and allies continue to push the boundaries of what is possible in the fight for equality. As we move forward, it is essential to center the voices of those most affected by discrimination, ensuring that the struggle for LGBTQ rights remains inclusive and intersectional.

$$\text{Global LGBTQ Rights} = \text{Human Rights} + \text{Intersectionality} + \text{Cultural Context} \tag{32}$$

Breaking Down International Barriers

In the quest for LGBTQ rights, Taren Fira recognized that the barriers faced by queer individuals were not confined to national borders. The complexities of international advocacy require a multifaceted approach, as cultural, legal, and political landscapes vary significantly across the globe. This section delves into the strategies employed by Taren Fira and her allies to dismantle these barriers, fostering a more inclusive global community.

Understanding International Barriers

International barriers to LGBTQ rights manifest in various forms, including discriminatory laws, cultural stigmas, and socio-political resistance. According to the *International Lesbian, Gay, Bisexual, Trans and Intersex Association* (ILGA), over 70 countries still criminalize same-sex relationships, and many others lack legal protections for LGBTQ individuals. These barriers are often rooted in historical prejudices, religious beliefs, and political agendas that prioritize heteronormativity.

The Role of Global Advocacy

Taren Fira understood that effective advocacy requires collaboration across borders. By forming alliances with international organizations, she was able to amplify the voices of marginalized communities. One notable example was her partnership with *OutRight Action International*, which focuses on human rights advocacy for LGBTQ individuals worldwide. Together, they organized campaigns that highlighted the plight of queer individuals in countries with oppressive regimes.

Utilizing Digital Platforms

In an age where digital communication transcends geographical boundaries, Taren leveraged social media as a powerful tool for advocacy. Platforms such as Twitter, Instagram, and Facebook enabled her to connect with activists globally, share personal narratives, and mobilize support for international campaigns. The hashtag #GlobalPride became a rallying point for LGBTQ activists, allowing them to share their stories and experiences, thereby fostering a sense of solidarity.

$$\text{Global Advocacy} = \text{Local Actions} + \text{Digital Connectivity} \qquad (33)$$

This equation illustrates the synergy between localized efforts and global outreach, emphasizing that grassroots movements can gain international traction through digital platforms.

Challenges in Cross-Cultural Advocacy

Despite the advancements in global LGBTQ advocacy, Taren faced significant challenges when navigating cultural differences. She often encountered resistance from activists who held differing views on gender and sexuality, particularly in regions where traditional values dominate. To address these challenges, Taren emphasized the importance of cultural sensitivity and respect for local customs while advocating for universal human rights.

For instance, during her work in Eastern Europe, Taren engaged with local activists to understand the cultural context of their struggles. By incorporating their perspectives into her advocacy efforts, she was able to foster a more inclusive dialogue that resonated with both local and international audiences.

Case Studies of Successful Advocacy

One of the most impactful campaigns led by Taren was the *International Day Against Homophobia, Transphobia, and Biphobia* (IDAHOT). This annual event highlights the discrimination faced by LGBTQ individuals globally. Taren's involvement in IDAHOT included organizing events in various countries, collaborating with local NGOs, and utilizing social media to raise awareness. In 2021, her efforts resulted in a record number of participants, showcasing the power of collective action.

Another significant achievement was Taren's role in the United Nations Human Rights Council, where she advocated for the inclusion of LGBTQ rights in international human rights frameworks. Her passionate speeches and well-researched presentations helped to shift the narrative around LGBTQ issues, leading to the adoption of resolutions that condemned discrimination based on sexual orientation and gender identity.

Future Directions for International LGBTQ Advocacy

Looking ahead, Taren Fira's legacy serves as a blueprint for future activists. The key to breaking down international barriers lies in continued collaboration, education, and advocacy. Emerging technologies, such as virtual reality and interactive online platforms, offer new avenues for storytelling and engagement, enabling activists to share their experiences in immersive ways.

$$\text{Future Advocacy} = \text{Collaboration} + \text{Innovation} + \text{Education} \qquad (34)$$

This equation highlights the essential components for effective advocacy in the future, emphasizing the need for innovative approaches to engage diverse audiences.

In conclusion, Taren Fira's commitment to breaking down international barriers has paved the way for a more inclusive and equitable world for LGBTQ individuals. By understanding the complexities of global advocacy, utilizing digital platforms, and fostering cross-cultural collaboration, activists can continue to dismantle the obstacles that hinder progress. Taren's journey exemplifies the power of resilience and the importance of solidarity in the fight for LGBTQ rights worldwide.

The Power of Activism in the Digital Age

In the ever-evolving landscape of social justice, the digital age has emerged as a powerful ally for activists around the globe. The internet and social media platforms have transformed the way movements are organized, campaigns are run, and communities are built. This section explores the dynamics of digital activism, the challenges it presents, and the profound impact it has had on LGBTQ advocacy.

The Rise of Digital Activism

Digital activism refers to the use of digital tools and platforms to promote social change, raise awareness, and mobilize supporters. The rise of social media platforms such as Twitter, Facebook, Instagram, and TikTok has democratized the process of activism, allowing individuals to amplify their voices and share their stories with a global audience.

The accessibility of the internet means that anyone with a smartphone or computer can engage in activism, breaking down barriers that once limited participation to those with access to traditional forms of media. For example, the hashtag #LoveIsLove, which gained traction during the fight for marriage equality, allowed LGBTQ individuals and allies to share personal stories, express solidarity, and mobilize support quickly and effectively.

Mobilization and Organization

One of the most significant advantages of digital activism is its ability to facilitate rapid mobilization and organization. Activists can use social media to coordinate events, share resources, and rally support in real-time. The 2017 Women's March, which saw millions of participants across the globe, was largely organized through social media platforms, demonstrating how digital tools can unite people around a common cause.

Moreover, platforms like Change.org allow activists to create petitions that can be shared widely, garnering signatures and support from individuals who may not have been aware of the issue otherwise. This ability to reach a broader audience is crucial in raising awareness about LGBTQ rights and issues, especially in regions where traditional media may be hostile or unresponsive.

Challenges of Digital Activism

Despite its many advantages, digital activism is not without its challenges. One significant issue is the prevalence of misinformation and disinformation. The rapid spread of false information can undermine legitimate movements and create confusion among supporters. For instance, during the COVID-19 pandemic, misinformation about the virus and vaccine safety posed significant challenges for public health advocates, including those within the LGBTQ community who were disproportionately affected by the pandemic.

Moreover, the digital divide remains a critical barrier to effective digital activism. While many people have access to the internet, significant disparities exist based on socioeconomic status, geography, and education. This divide can limit the participation of marginalized groups in online activism, perpetuating existing inequalities within the movement.

The Role of Digital Storytelling

Digital storytelling has become a powerful tool for LGBTQ activists, allowing them to share personal narratives that humanize issues and foster empathy. Platforms like YouTube and TikTok enable individuals to create and share videos that capture their experiences, challenges, and triumphs. This form of storytelling not only raises awareness but also inspires others to engage in activism.

For example, the viral video of a transgender teen discussing their journey of self-acceptance and the challenges they faced garnered millions of views and sparked conversations about gender identity and acceptance. Such personal narratives can challenge stereotypes, educate the public, and encourage solidarity within the LGBTQ community.

Global Solidarity and Networking

The digital age has also facilitated global solidarity among LGBTQ activists. Social media platforms allow for the exchange of ideas, strategies, and resources across borders, fostering a sense of community and shared purpose. Activists from different countries can connect, collaborate, and support one another in their struggles for equality.

For instance, during the global protests following the murder of George Floyd in 2020, LGBTQ activists worldwide used social media to highlight the intersectionality of racial justice and LGBTQ rights. This solidarity demonstrated how digital activism can amplify voices and create a unified front against oppression.

Conclusion

In conclusion, the power of activism in the digital age is undeniable. While it presents unique challenges, the ability to mobilize, organize, and connect with others globally has transformed the landscape of LGBTQ advocacy. As digital tools continue to evolve, so too will the strategies and approaches of activists, ensuring that the fight for equality remains vibrant and relevant in an increasingly interconnected world.

$$\text{Digital Activism} = \text{Access} + \text{Engagement} + \text{Solidarity} \qquad (35)$$

This equation illustrates the essential components of successful digital activism, emphasizing the importance of access to technology, active engagement from supporters, and the cultivation of solidarity among diverse communities.

References

- Castells, M. (2012). *Networks of Outrage and Hope: Social Movements in the Internet Age*. Polity Press.
- Bennett, W. L., & Segerberg, A. (2013). The Logic of Connective Action: Digital Media and the Personalization of Contentious Politics. *Information, Communication & Society*, 16(1), 39-60.
- Tilly, C. (2004). *Social Movements, 1768–2004*. Paradigm Publishers.

Pushing Boundaries and Challenging Prejudices

In the vibrant tapestry of LGBTQ activism, Taren Fira emerged as a formidable force, unafraid to push boundaries and challenge deeply ingrained prejudices. This section delves into the theoretical frameworks, societal challenges, and real-world examples that illustrate Taren's relentless pursuit of equality and justice for all marginalized identities.

Theoretical Frameworks

At the core of Taren Fira's activism lies the concept of *intersectionality*, a term coined by Kimberlé Crenshaw in 1989. Intersectionality posits that individuals experience overlapping systems of discrimination and privilege based on their various identities, including race, gender, sexual orientation, and class. This framework is essential for understanding the complexities of LGBTQ activism, as it emphasizes that the fight for rights cannot be one-dimensional. Taren often articulated this theory in her speeches, stating:

> "True liberation comes not just from fighting for our rights as queer individuals but from dismantling all forms of oppression that affect our communities."

Taren's approach was rooted in the belief that to challenge prejudices effectively, activists must recognize and address the multifaceted nature of identity. By doing so, she aimed to create a more inclusive movement that represented the diverse experiences of LGBTQ individuals, particularly those from marginalized backgrounds.

Societal Challenges

Despite significant progress in LGBTQ rights, Taren faced numerous societal challenges that highlighted the persistent prejudices entrenched within various cultures. One prominent issue was the backlash against the visibility of queer identities in mainstream media. Taren argued that while representation was essential, it often fell short of authenticity. She emphasized that many portrayals of LGBTQ individuals perpetuated stereotypes, which further alienated those who did not fit into these narrow narratives.

For instance, Taren often referenced the portrayal of queer characters in popular television shows. While some represented LGBTQ experiences positively, others reinforced harmful stereotypes—such as the flamboyant gay man or the tragic lesbian—leading to a skewed public perception. Taren believed that to push boundaries, activists needed to challenge these narratives, advocating for more complex and varied representations that reflected the true diversity of queer experiences.

Real-World Examples

One of Taren's most notable campaigns involved the creation of the #BeyondTheRainbow initiative, which sought to highlight the realities of LGBTQ life beyond the confines of Pride celebrations. Taren organized a series of community forums and workshops across Alyndra, encouraging participants to share their stories and discuss the challenges they faced in their daily lives. This initiative not only empowered individuals to voice their experiences but also fostered a sense of solidarity among participants.

SECTION THREE: TAREN FIRA GOES INTERNATIONAL 75

Through the #BeyondTheRainbow initiative, Taren collected narratives that illustrated the intersectional struggles of LGBTQ individuals, particularly those from communities of color. For example, one participant, a Black transgender woman named Zuri, shared her experience of facing discrimination not only because of her gender identity but also due to her race. Zuri's story exemplified the compounded prejudices faced by many, reinforcing Taren's belief in the necessity of intersectional advocacy.

Challenging Institutional Prejudices

In addition to grassroots activism, Taren recognized the importance of challenging institutional prejudices. She often engaged with local governments and educational institutions to advocate for policy changes that would create safer and more inclusive environments for LGBTQ individuals. One significant victory was the successful lobbying for the inclusion of comprehensive LGBTQ education in school curriculums across Alyndra.

Taren argued that education was a critical tool in dismantling prejudices. By incorporating LGBTQ history and issues into the curriculum, she believed that future generations would grow up with a better understanding of diversity and acceptance. In her advocacy efforts, she frequently cited studies indicating that inclusive education reduces bullying and improves the overall school climate for all students.

Conclusion

In conclusion, Taren Fira's relentless pursuit of pushing boundaries and challenging prejudices was rooted in a deep understanding of intersectionality and the complexities of identity. Through her advocacy, she not only highlighted the multifaceted nature of discrimination but also inspired a new generation of activists to confront societal norms and institutional injustices. By creating initiatives like #BeyondTheRainbow and advocating for inclusive education, Taren demonstrated that challenging prejudices requires both grassroots mobilization and systemic change. Her legacy continues to inspire those who dare to push boundaries in the quest for equality and justice.

Global LGBTQ Solidarity

In the ever-evolving landscape of LGBTQ advocacy, the concept of global solidarity has emerged as a vital pillar in the fight for equality and justice. Global LGBTQ solidarity refers to the interconnectedness and mutual support among LGBTQ activists, organizations, and communities across different countries and cultures. This solidarity is essential in addressing the diverse challenges faced by LGBTQ individuals worldwide, as these challenges often transcend national borders.

Theoretical Framework

Global LGBTQ solidarity is grounded in several theoretical frameworks, including intersectionality, transnationalism, and human rights. Intersectionality, as articulated by Kimberlé Crenshaw, emphasizes the importance of considering multiple identities and experiences when analyzing social issues. In the context of LGBTQ advocacy, intersectionality highlights how factors such as race, class, gender, and sexuality intersect to shape the experiences of individuals. This framework encourages activists to address the unique challenges faced by marginalized subgroups within the LGBTQ community.

Transnationalism, on the other hand, focuses on the ways in which social, political, and economic processes transcend national boundaries. This perspective is particularly relevant for LGBTQ activism, as many issues, such as human rights violations and discrimination, are not confined to a single nation. Activists must collaborate across borders to amplify their voices and advocate for change on a global scale.

Finally, the human rights framework provides a universal standard for evaluating the treatment of LGBTQ individuals. The Universal Declaration of Human Rights asserts that all individuals are entitled to fundamental rights and freedoms, regardless of their sexual orientation or gender identity. This framework serves as a foundation for LGBTQ activists to demand recognition and protection of their rights worldwide.

Challenges to Global LGBTQ Solidarity

Despite the potential for global LGBTQ solidarity, several challenges impede its realization. One significant challenge is the disparity in legal rights and social acceptance of LGBTQ individuals across different countries. For instance, while many Western nations have made substantial progress in legalizing same-sex marriage and enacting anti-discrimination laws, many countries in Africa, Asia, and the Middle East continue to criminalize homosexuality and impose severe penalties on LGBTQ individuals.

Additionally, cultural differences can create barriers to solidarity. Activists from different regions may have varying perspectives on LGBTQ issues, influenced by local customs, religions, and historical contexts. For example, in some cultures, discussions around gender identity and expression may be met with resistance or misunderstanding, complicating efforts to foster a unified global movement.

Moreover, the rise of nationalist and conservative movements in various parts of the world poses a significant threat to LGBTQ solidarity. These movements often promote anti-LGBTQ rhetoric and policies, further marginalizing already vulnerable communities. Activists must navigate these political landscapes while striving to build alliances and promote understanding.

Examples of Global LGBTQ Solidarity

Despite these challenges, there are numerous examples of successful global LGBTQ solidarity initiatives. One notable example is the International Lesbian, Gay, Bisexual, Trans and Intersex Association (ILGA), which works to promote LGBTQ rights globally through advocacy, research, and coalition-building. ILGA brings together LGBTQ organizations from around the world to share resources, strategies, and support, fostering a sense of unity among activists.

Another example is the global campaign for the decriminalization of homosexuality, which has gained traction in recent years. Organizations such as Human Rights Campaign and OutRight Action International have collaborated with local activists to advocate for legal reforms in countries where homosexuality remains criminalized. This campaign highlights the importance of solidarity in amplifying the voices of those most affected by discriminatory laws.

Additionally, social media has played a pivotal role in fostering global LGBTQ solidarity. Platforms like Twitter and Instagram allow activists to connect, share their stories, and mobilize support for various causes. For instance, the #LoveIsLove hashtag emerged as a global rallying cry for marriage equality, transcending national boundaries and uniting individuals in their fight for love and acceptance.

Conclusion

In conclusion, global LGBTQ solidarity is a crucial component of the ongoing struggle for equality and justice. By embracing intersectionality, transnationalism, and human rights, activists can work together to address the unique challenges faced by LGBTQ individuals worldwide. Despite the obstacles that exist, examples of successful collaboration and advocacy demonstrate the power of solidarity in creating lasting change. As the global LGBTQ movement continues to evolve, fostering a sense of unity and shared purpose among activists will be essential in advancing the rights and dignity of all LGBTQ individuals.

Overcoming Language and Cultural Barriers

In the realm of LGBTQ advocacy, language and cultural barriers present significant challenges that can hinder effective communication and collaboration across different communities. These barriers not only affect the dissemination of information but also the inclusivity of the movement itself. To navigate these complexities, it is essential to understand the underlying theories, the problems that arise, and the strategies that can be employed to overcome these obstacles.

Theoretical Frameworks

The concept of *cultural competence* is crucial in addressing language and cultural barriers. Cultural competence refers to the ability of individuals and organizations to effectively interact with people from diverse cultural backgrounds. It involves understanding cultural differences, recognizing biases, and adapting communication styles to meet the needs of various communities. According to [?], cultural competence encompasses three main components: awareness of one's own cultural worldview, knowledge of different cultural practices and worldviews, and cross-cultural skills.

Moreover, the *social construction of language* theory posits that language is not merely a tool for communication but also a means of shaping social realities. Language can reinforce power dynamics and perpetuate stereotypes, particularly in marginalized communities. Understanding this theory helps advocates recognize how language can both unite and divide, prompting a more thoughtful approach to communication in advocacy efforts.

Problems Arising from Language and Cultural Barriers

Language barriers can result in miscommunication, misunderstanding, and a lack of accessibility to crucial information. For instance, LGBTQ activists working in non-English speaking regions may struggle to convey their messages effectively if they lack proficiency in the local language. This can lead to feelings of exclusion among community members who do not speak the dominant language, thereby undermining the inclusivity of the movement.

Cultural barriers can manifest in various forms, including differing attitudes towards sexuality and gender identity. In some cultures, LGBTQ identities may be stigmatized or considered taboo, leading to resistance against advocacy efforts. For example, in many conservative societies, discussions surrounding LGBTQ rights may be met with hostility, making it challenging for activists to engage with local populations.

Additionally, the intersection of language and culture can complicate advocacy efforts. For instance, certain terms and phrases used in LGBTQ activism may not have direct translations in other languages, leading to confusion or misinterpretation. This linguistic discrepancy can result in a failure to convey the nuances of LGBTQ experiences and rights, thereby diluting the effectiveness of advocacy messages.

Strategies for Overcoming Barriers

To effectively overcome language and cultural barriers, LGBTQ activists can employ several strategies:

1. **Utilizing Multilingual Resources:** Creating and disseminating materials in multiple languages can significantly enhance accessibility. For instance, translating pamphlets, websites, and social media content into local languages ensures that a broader audience can engage with the information. This approach was successfully implemented by the *International Lesbian, Gay, Bisexual, Trans and Intersex Association (ILGA)*, which provides resources in various languages to reach diverse communities.

2. **Engaging Local Leaders:** Collaborating with local LGBTQ leaders who understand the cultural context can facilitate more effective communication. These leaders can bridge the gap between international advocacy efforts and local realities, ensuring that messages resonate with the community. For example, during the *Global Pride* event, local activists played a crucial role in adapting the messaging to align with cultural sensitivities while maintaining the core principles of LGBTQ rights.

3. **Cultural Sensitivity Training:** Providing cultural sensitivity training for activists can enhance their understanding of different cultural norms and practices. This training can equip advocates with the skills needed to navigate complex cultural landscapes and engage in respectful dialogue. Organizations like *OutRight Action International* offer workshops focused on cultural competency to strengthen the capacity of LGBTQ advocates worldwide.

4. **Leveraging Technology:** The digital age offers numerous tools for overcoming language barriers. Online translation services, social media platforms, and video conferencing can facilitate communication across linguistic divides. For instance, platforms like *Google Translate* can help

activists communicate with individuals who speak different languages, although it is essential to be mindful of the limitations of machine translation.

5. **Promoting Intersectional Advocacy:** Recognizing and addressing the intersectionality of identity can enhance advocacy efforts. By understanding how language and culture intersect with other factors such as race, socioeconomic status, and disability, activists can create more inclusive campaigns. This approach was exemplified during the *Black Lives Matter* movement, where LGBTQ activists highlighted the unique challenges faced by queer people of color, fostering a more comprehensive understanding of the issues at hand.

Conclusion

Overcoming language and cultural barriers is essential for the success of LGBTQ advocacy on a global scale. By employing strategies that promote cultural competence, inclusivity, and effective communication, activists can build bridges across diverse communities. In doing so, they not only enhance the visibility and impact of LGBTQ rights but also foster a more united front in the fight for equality. As Taren Fira once articulated, "Our strength lies in our diversity; let us harness it to create a world where every voice is heard and valued."

Building Networks and Alliances

In the realm of LGBTQ activism, the importance of building networks and alliances cannot be overstated. These connections serve as the backbone of effective advocacy, allowing for the pooling of resources, sharing of knowledge, and amplification of marginalized voices. This section explores the theoretical frameworks, challenges, and practical examples of building networks and alliances within the LGBTQ community and beyond.

Theoretical Framework

At the core of network building is the concept of *social capital*, which refers to the resources available to individuals and groups through their social networks. According to Bourdieu (1986), social capital can be understood as the aggregate of the actual or potential resources that are linked to possession of a durable network of more or less institutionalized relationships of mutual acquaintance and recognition. In LGBTQ activism, social capital can manifest in various forms, including emotional support, financial backing, and access to influential allies.

Moreover, the theory of *intersectionality* (Crenshaw, 1989) plays a crucial role in understanding the dynamics of alliances. Intersectionality posits that individuals experience oppression in varying degrees based on their intersecting identities, such as race, gender, sexuality, and socioeconomic status. This framework encourages activists to build alliances that are inclusive and representative of the diverse experiences within the LGBTQ community. By recognizing the unique challenges faced by queer people of color, transgender individuals, and other marginalized groups, activists can create a more robust and effective movement.

Challenges in Building Networks

Despite the clear benefits of networking, there are significant challenges that activists must navigate. One prominent issue is the phenomenon of *tokenism*, where individuals from marginalized groups are included in networks or alliances merely to fulfill a diversity quota, rather than being genuinely integrated into decision-making processes. Tokenism can lead to feelings of alienation and disillusionment among those who are supposed to be represented.

Another challenge is the potential for *competition* among activists and organizations. In a landscape where funding and resources are often limited, groups may feel pressured to prioritize their own agendas over collaborative efforts. This competition can hinder the development of strong alliances and ultimately weaken the movement as a whole.

Strategies for Effective Networking

To overcome these challenges, LGBTQ activists can employ several strategies for building effective networks and alliances:

- **Establish Clear Goals:** Networks should have a clear purpose and set of objectives that align with the values of all members. This clarity helps to foster collaboration and commitment among participants.

- **Prioritize Inclusivity:** Actively seek out and include diverse voices within the network. This approach not only enriches the dialogue but also ensures that the needs of all community members are addressed.

- **Leverage Technology:** Utilize digital platforms and social media to connect with potential allies, share resources, and mobilize support. Online networks can transcend geographical barriers and create a global community of advocates.

- **Engage in Active Listening:** Foster an environment where all members feel heard and valued. This can be achieved through regular meetings, feedback sessions, and open communication channels.

- **Collaborative Projects:** Initiate joint projects that allow different organizations and activists to work together towards a common goal. This collaboration can strengthen relationships and build trust among members.

Examples of Successful Alliances

One notable example of successful networking within the LGBTQ movement is the formation of the *LGBTQ+ Alliance*, a coalition of various LGBTQ organizations that came together to advocate for comprehensive anti-discrimination legislation. By pooling resources and expertise, the Alliance was able to launch a nationwide campaign that garnered significant media attention and public support.

Similarly, the *Transgender Law Center* has effectively built alliances with various racial and social justice organizations to address the unique challenges faced by transgender individuals, particularly those of color. This intersectional approach has resulted in more comprehensive advocacy efforts that address systemic inequalities.

Conclusion

Building networks and alliances is essential for the success of LGBTQ activism. By understanding the theoretical underpinnings of social capital and intersectionality, activists can navigate the challenges of tokenism and competition. Through clear goals, inclusivity, technology, active listening, and collaborative projects, they can create robust networks that amplify the voices of marginalized individuals and foster lasting change. The examples of successful alliances serve as a testament to the power of collective action in the fight for LGBTQ rights.

In the words of Taren Fira, "Together, we are stronger; together, we can ignite the flames of change."

Using Social Media for Advocacy

In the digital age, social media has emerged as a powerful tool for activism, allowing individuals and organizations to amplify their voices, mobilize support, and create meaningful change. For Taren Fira, social media was not merely a platform; it was a lifeline that connected marginalized communities and facilitated the dissemination of information regarding LGBTQ rights on a global scale.

Theoretical Frameworks

The impact of social media on advocacy can be understood through several theoretical frameworks, including the *Networked Publics Theory* and the *Framing Theory*.

Networked Publics Theory posits that social media creates a new public sphere where individuals can engage in dialogue, share experiences, and mobilize collective action. This theory emphasizes the democratizing potential of social media, allowing voices that have historically been marginalized to gain visibility and influence.

Framing Theory focuses on how issues are presented and perceived within social media narratives. Activists like Taren Fira utilized strategic framing to highlight the intersectionality of LGBTQ issues, ensuring that the narratives surrounding queer rights were inclusive and representative of diverse experiences. By framing LGBTQ rights as human rights, advocates were able to garner broader support and challenge prevailing stereotypes.

Challenges in Social Media Advocacy

Despite its potential, social media advocacy is not without challenges. The digital landscape is rife with misinformation, cyberbullying, and hostile environments that can undermine the efforts of activists. Taren Fira faced significant backlash online, including hate speech and targeted harassment, which necessitated a robust strategy for managing digital safety while maintaining visibility.

Misinformation is a pervasive issue, often leading to confusion and division within the community. Activists must navigate the complexities of fact-checking and countering false narratives, which can detract from the primary goals of advocacy. Taren emphasized the importance of creating reliable sources of information, encouraging followers to engage with verified content and share it widely.

Cyberbullying and online harassment present another significant obstacle. The anonymity of social media can embolden individuals to engage in harmful behaviors, targeting activists with threats and derogatory comments. Taren's approach included fostering a supportive online community that not only reported abusive behavior but also provided emotional support for those affected.

Successful Examples of Social Media Advocacy

Taren Fira's use of social media exemplifies the effective strategies that can lead to successful advocacy. One notable example was the viral campaign *#QueerVoicesMatter*, which aimed to amplify the stories of LGBTQ individuals from diverse backgrounds. The campaign encouraged participants to share their personal narratives, using the hashtag to create a sense of solidarity and community.

The impact of this campaign can be quantified through engagement metrics, including:

$$\text{Engagement Rate} = \frac{\text{Total Interactions}}{\text{Total Followers}} \times 100 \tag{36}$$

For instance, during the campaign, Taren's social media accounts saw an engagement rate of over 15%, significantly above the average for similar advocacy accounts. This surge in interaction not only increased visibility for LGBTQ issues but also fostered a sense of belonging among participants.

Another successful initiative was the virtual event *Pride in the Digital Age*, which included panel discussions, workshops, and performances streamed live on social media platforms. The event attracted thousands of viewers worldwide, showcasing the potential of social media to transcend geographical barriers and unite individuals in a shared cause.

Strategies for Effective Social Media Advocacy

To maximize the impact of social media advocacy, Taren Fira implemented several key strategies:

- **Consistent Messaging:** Taren ensured that her messaging was consistent across platforms, reinforcing the core values of inclusivity and intersectionality in LGBTQ advocacy. This approach helped build a recognizable brand that followers could trust.

- **Engagement and Interaction:** Actively engaging with followers through Q&A sessions, polls, and live discussions fostered a sense of community and encouraged participation. Taren often responded to comments and messages, creating a dialogue that empowered her audience.

- **Visual Storytelling:** Utilizing graphics, videos, and infographics allowed Taren to communicate complex issues in an accessible manner. Visual content often garners more engagement than text alone, making it an essential component of her advocacy toolkit.

- **Collaboration with Influencers:** Partnering with social media influencers and other activists helped amplify Taren's reach and introduced her message to new audiences. These collaborations were strategically chosen to align with shared values, ensuring authenticity in their advocacy efforts.

- **Monitoring and Adaptation:** Taren regularly analyzed engagement data to understand what content resonated most with her audience. This data-driven approach allowed her to adapt her strategies, ensuring that her advocacy remained relevant and impactful.

Conclusion

In conclusion, Taren Fira's use of social media for advocacy illustrates the profound impact that digital platforms can have on social movements. By leveraging the strengths of social media while navigating its challenges, Taren not only advanced LGBTQ rights in Alyndra but also inspired activists worldwide. As the landscape of activism continues to evolve, the lessons learned from Taren's journey serve as a guiding light for future advocates, illustrating the power of connection, storytelling, and resilience in the face of adversity.

Empowering LGBTQ Activists Worldwide

In an age where the digital landscape has become a powerful platform for advocacy, empowering LGBTQ activists worldwide is not just a necessity but a moral imperative. The global fight for LGBTQ rights faces a myriad of challenges, from systemic discrimination to cultural stigmas. However, with the right strategies, resources, and support systems, activists can amplify their voices and create meaningful change.

The Importance of Global Solidarity

Empowerment begins with solidarity. LGBTQ activists across the globe must recognize that their struggles are interconnected. According to the *Social Identity Theory*, individuals derive a sense of identity from their group affiliations, which can be a source of strength. By fostering a sense of global LGBTQ identity, activists can build coalitions that transcend geographic and cultural boundaries.

For example, the *Global Fund for Women* has successfully funded initiatives that connect LGBTQ activists in various regions, allowing them to share resources, strategies, and support. This network not only provides financial assistance but also cultivates a sense of belonging among activists who may feel isolated in their local contexts.

Utilizing Digital Platforms

The digital age has revolutionized activism, providing tools that can amplify voices and mobilize support. Social media platforms such as Twitter, Instagram, and TikTok have become vital for LGBTQ activists to share their narratives and connect with a broader audience. According to a study by the *Pew Research Center*, approximately 70% of LGBTQ individuals utilize social media to engage with advocacy efforts, making it a crucial space for empowerment.

Moreover, online campaigns such as the *#LoveIsLove* movement have demonstrated the power of digital advocacy. By harnessing hashtags and viral content, activists can raise awareness and foster global conversations around LGBTQ rights. This digital mobilization not only empowers individuals but also attracts allies who can amplify these messages.

Capacity Building and Training Programs

To empower LGBTQ activists effectively, it is essential to provide them with the necessary skills and knowledge. Training programs focused on advocacy, public speaking, and digital literacy can equip activists with the tools they need to navigate complex political landscapes.

Organizations like *OutRight Action International* offer workshops that focus on capacity building, enabling activists to develop strategic plans, engage in lobbying, and utilize media effectively. These programs are crucial in ensuring that activists are not only passionate but also informed and skilled in their approaches.

Addressing Intersectionality

Empowerment must also consider intersectionality, as LGBTQ individuals do not exist in a vacuum. The experiences of a queer person of color, for instance, are shaped by multiple identities that can compound discrimination. The *Intersectionality Theory* posits that various social categorizations such as race, gender, and class interconnect, creating overlapping systems of disadvantage.

Empowering LGBTQ activists worldwide means recognizing these complexities. Initiatives that center marginalized voices, such as those led by *Black LGBTQ+ activists*, can provide critical insights into the unique challenges faced by these communities. By prioritizing intersectional approaches, the movement can ensure that all voices are heard and represented.

Creating Safe Spaces for Dialogue

Empowerment also involves the creation of safe spaces where LGBTQ activists can share their experiences without fear of retribution. These spaces can facilitate open dialogue, fostering a sense of community and support. For instance, international conferences like the *ILGA World Conference* provide platforms for activists to exchange ideas, network, and collaborate on global initiatives.

Within these safe spaces, activists can engage in critical discussions about strategies, challenges, and successes. This exchange of knowledge not only empowers individuals but also strengthens the global movement by creating a collective repository of wisdom and experience.

Advocating for Policy Change

Empowerment is ultimately tied to the ability to effect change in policies that govern LGBTQ rights. Activists must be equipped to engage with political leaders and institutions effectively. Strategies such as lobbying, public demonstrations, and grassroots mobilization can play a crucial role in advocating for legislative reforms.

For example, the successful campaign for marriage equality in various countries demonstrates the power of persistent advocacy. Activists employed a combination of public education, strategic partnerships, and direct action to influence policy decisions. By empowering LGBTQ activists with the tools to engage in political processes, the movement can achieve significant milestones.

Global Networks and Alliances

Building global networks is vital for sustained empowerment. Alliances between organizations can pool resources and expertise, enhancing the overall capacity of LGBTQ activism. For instance, the collaboration between *Human Rights Campaign* and *Amnesty International* has led to impactful campaigns that address human rights violations against LGBTQ individuals worldwide.

These networks can also facilitate the sharing of best practices and lessons learned. By connecting activists from different regions, these alliances can foster a culture of mutual support and encouragement, empowering individuals to take bold actions in their local contexts.

Conclusion

Empowering LGBTQ activists worldwide is a multifaceted endeavor that requires solidarity, digital engagement, capacity building, and a commitment to intersectionality. By creating safe spaces for dialogue, advocating for policy changes, and building global networks, the movement can cultivate a new generation of empowered activists who are equipped to challenge discrimination and advocate for equality. As Taren Fira exemplified, the journey of empowerment is not only about individual success but about lifting others and creating a collective force for change. In doing so, the movement can ensure that the fight for LGBTQ rights continues to thrive on a global scale.

Chapter Two: Navigating the Political Landscape

Section One: LGBTQ Rights in Alyndra

Engaging with Political Leaders

Engaging with political leaders is a cornerstone of effective LGBTQ advocacy, as it allows activists to influence policy decisions and promote legislative change. Taren Fira understood early on that building relationships with those in power was essential for advancing the rights of LGBTQ individuals in Alyndra. This section explores the strategies, challenges, and successes that characterized Taren's efforts to engage political leaders.

The Importance of Political Engagement

Political engagement is critical for several reasons:

- **Influencing Policy:** Engaging with political leaders enables activists to advocate for specific legislative changes that benefit the LGBTQ community, such as anti-discrimination laws and marriage equality.

- **Raising Awareness:** Advocacy efforts can help raise awareness about LGBTQ issues among policymakers, thereby fostering a more inclusive political environment.

- **Building Alliances:** Establishing connections with political leaders can lead to strategic alliances, enhancing the visibility and legitimacy of LGBTQ advocacy.

Strategies for Engagement

Taren Fira employed various strategies to effectively engage with political leaders:

1. **Direct Lobbying:** Taren organized lobbying efforts, where activists met directly with legislators to discuss LGBTQ rights and present compelling arguments for policy changes. This approach often included presenting data and personal stories to humanize the issues at stake.

2. **Coalition Building:** Taren recognized the power of collective action. By forming coalitions with other marginalized groups, such as racial minorities and women's rights organizations, Taren was able to amplify her message and demonstrate the interconnectedness of various social justice issues.

3. **Public Campaigns:** Taren launched public campaigns that mobilized community support. These campaigns often included petitions, social media outreach, and public demonstrations, which put pressure on political leaders to respond to constituents' demands.

4. **Utilizing Media:** Taren leveraged media coverage to highlight LGBTQ issues and garner public support. By engaging with journalists and securing coverage in local and national outlets, Taren was able to shape public discourse around LGBTQ rights.

5. **Educational Initiatives:** Taren organized workshops and seminars aimed at educating political leaders about LGBTQ issues. These initiatives provided a platform for dialogue and helped dispel myths and misconceptions about the community.

Challenges Faced

Despite Taren's proactive approach, engaging with political leaders was fraught with challenges:

- **Resistance to Change:** Many political leaders were resistant to LGBTQ advocacy due to their constituents' conservative views. Taren often found herself navigating a landscape where the fear of backlash limited politicians' willingness to support progressive policies.

- **Tokenism:** Taren occasionally encountered situations where political leaders would express support for LGBTQ rights but failed to take meaningful action. This tokenism undermined the legitimacy of advocacy efforts and necessitated continued pressure from activists.

- **Limited Resources:** Engaging with political leaders often required significant time and resources. Taren and her team had to balance their advocacy work with the practicalities of fundraising and organizing, which sometimes hindered their ability to maintain consistent engagement with policymakers.

Examples of Successful Engagement

Taren's persistence in engaging with political leaders led to several notable successes:

- **The Equality Act:** Through her lobbying efforts, Taren played a pivotal role in the introduction of the Equality Act in Alyndra. This comprehensive legislation aimed to prohibit discrimination based on sexual orientation and gender identity in various sectors, including employment, housing, and public accommodations.

- **Marriage Equality Legislation:** Taren's coalition-building efforts culminated in a successful push for marriage equality. By rallying public support and engaging key political leaders, Taren helped create a legislative environment conducive to passing marriage equality laws.

- **LGBTQ Youth Support Programs:** Taren successfully advocated for the establishment of programs aimed at supporting LGBTQ youth in schools. By presenting data on the mental health disparities faced by LGBTQ youth, Taren was able to convince political leaders of the necessity of these programs.

Conclusion

Engaging with political leaders is a vital aspect of LGBTQ activism, as demonstrated by Taren Fira's efforts in Alyndra. Through strategic lobbying, coalition building, and public campaigns, Taren was able to influence policy decisions and foster a more inclusive political climate. Despite facing significant challenges, her successes serve as a testament to the power of advocacy and the importance of maintaining open lines of communication with those in positions of power. As Taren often reminded her peers, "To change the world, we must first engage with those who hold the keys to its doors."

Lobbying for LGBTQ Equality Legislation

Lobbying for LGBTQ equality legislation is a critical aspect of the broader struggle for civil rights, as it involves direct engagement with political leaders, lawmakers, and the legislative process to advocate for policies that protect and promote the rights of LGBTQ individuals. This section explores the theory, challenges, and successful strategies employed in lobbying efforts, highlighting the importance of sustained advocacy in achieving legislative change.

Theoretical Framework

At the core of lobbying for LGBTQ rights is the theory of social justice, which posits that all individuals deserve equal rights and protections under the law, regardless of their sexual orientation or gender identity. This aligns with the principles of equality, dignity, and respect, which are enshrined in various human rights declarations. Theories of intersectionality also play a vital role, as they recognize that LGBTQ individuals often face compounded discrimination based on race, class, and other identities. Understanding these frameworks is essential for effective lobbying, as they inform the arguments and narratives used to persuade lawmakers.

Challenges in Lobbying

Despite the progress made in recent years, LGBTQ advocates face significant challenges in lobbying for equality legislation. One major obstacle is the entrenched opposition from conservative groups and lawmakers who view LGBTQ rights as a threat to traditional values. This opposition often manifests in the form of discriminatory legislation, such as bathroom bills targeting transgender individuals or laws allowing businesses to refuse service based on sexual orientation.

Another challenge is the variability in public opinion regarding LGBTQ issues, which can fluctuate based on cultural, regional, and political contexts. For instance, while urban areas may show strong support for LGBTQ rights, rural regions may harbor more conservative views. This discrepancy necessitates tailored lobbying strategies that resonate with diverse constituencies.

Additionally, the legislative process itself can be daunting. Advocates must navigate complex political landscapes, often facing procedural hurdles and the need for bipartisan support. This requires not only a deep understanding of the legislative process but also the ability to build coalitions and mobilize grassroots support.

SECTION ONE: LGBTQ RIGHTS IN ALYNDRA

Successful Lobbying Strategies

Effective lobbying for LGBTQ equality legislation involves several key strategies:

- **Building Coalitions:** Collaborating with other civil rights organizations and social justice movements amplifies the advocacy effort. For example, alliances with women's rights groups, racial justice organizations, and labor unions can create a broader base of support, making it more difficult for lawmakers to ignore the demand for change.

- **Engaging in Grassroots Mobilization:** Grassroots campaigns empower community members to share their stories and experiences with legislators. This personal touch can humanize the issues at stake, making it harder for lawmakers to dismiss the need for change. For instance, organizing rallies, town halls, and letter-writing campaigns can effectively demonstrate public support for LGBTQ legislation.

- **Utilizing Data and Research:** Presenting empirical evidence that highlights the disparities faced by LGBTQ individuals can strengthen lobbying arguments. For example, studies showing higher rates of mental health issues among LGBTQ youth due to discrimination can underscore the urgency of passing protective legislation.

- **Leveraging Media and Public Opinion:** Media campaigns that highlight personal stories, successes, and the positive impact of LGBTQ legislation can shift public opinion and create pressure on lawmakers. Utilizing social media platforms to amplify voices and mobilize supporters is crucial in today's digital landscape.

- **Direct Engagement with Lawmakers:** Meeting with legislators to discuss specific bills, share personal experiences, and provide information on the benefits of LGBTQ equality legislation is essential. This direct engagement fosters relationships and can lead to increased support for proposed measures.

Case Studies and Examples

One notable example of successful lobbying for LGBTQ equality is the fight for marriage equality in the United States. Organizations like the Human Rights Campaign (HRC) and Freedom to Marry employed a multi-faceted approach that included grassroots mobilization, coalition-building, and strategic litigation. Their efforts culminated in the landmark Supreme Court decision in *Obergefell v. Hodges* (2015), which legalized same-sex marriage nationwide.

Another example is the advocacy for the Equality Act, a proposed federal law that seeks to prohibit discrimination based on sexual orientation and gender identity in various areas, including employment, housing, and public accommodations. The lobbying efforts surrounding the Equality Act have involved a diverse coalition of businesses, religious groups, and civil rights organizations, demonstrating the broad support for comprehensive LGBTQ protections.

Conclusion

Lobbying for LGBTQ equality legislation is a vital component of the ongoing struggle for civil rights and social justice. By understanding the theoretical underpinnings of advocacy, recognizing the challenges faced, and employing effective strategies, advocates can work towards meaningful legislative change. The successes achieved in recent years serve as a testament to the power of sustained advocacy and the importance of collective action in the pursuit of equality for all individuals, regardless of their sexual orientation or gender identity.

$$P_{\text{success}} = f(C, G, D, A) \qquad (37)$$

where P_{success} represents the probability of successful lobbying, C is the strength of coalitions, G is grassroots mobilization efforts, D is the data supporting the cause, and A is the engagement with lawmakers. This equation emphasizes the multifaceted nature of successful lobbying efforts in the fight for LGBTQ equality.

The Role of Media in Shaping Public Opinion

In the contemporary landscape of activism, media plays a pivotal role in shaping public opinion, particularly regarding LGBTQ rights. The media serves as a conduit through which narratives are constructed, disseminated, and ultimately internalized by the public. This section delves into the various dimensions of media's influence, including traditional outlets, social media platforms, and the implications of representation and framing.

Theoretical Frameworks

To understand the media's role in shaping public opinion, we can draw upon several key theoretical frameworks:

- **Agenda-Setting Theory:** This theory posits that while the media may not tell people what to think, it significantly influences what people think about. By prioritizing certain issues over others, media outlets can shape the public agenda. For instance, when LGBTQ issues are featured prominently in news cycles, they gain visibility and legitimacy, prompting public discourse and engagement.

- **Framing Theory:** Framing refers to the way information is presented to audiences. Different frames can lead to varying interpretations of the same issue. For example, framing LGBTQ rights as a matter of civil rights rather than a moral issue can elicit more support from the public. Effective framing can mobilize allies and challenge discriminatory perspectives.

- **Cultivation Theory:** This theory suggests that long-term exposure to media content can shape individuals' perceptions of reality. The more individuals consume media that portrays LGBTQ individuals positively, the more likely they are to develop supportive attitudes towards LGBTQ rights.

The Influence of Traditional Media

Traditional media outlets, such as newspapers, television, and radio, have historically played a significant role in shaping public opinion on LGBTQ issues. For example, the coverage of landmark events such as the legalization of same-sex marriage in various countries has been instrumental in normalizing LGBTQ relationships.

$$\text{Public Support} \propto \text{Media Coverage} + \text{Positive Representation} \qquad (38)$$

This equation illustrates that public support for LGBTQ rights is positively correlated with both the amount of media coverage and the nature of that coverage. When media portrayals are positive, they can lead to increased public support for LGBTQ rights.

The Emergence of Social Media

With the advent of social media, the landscape of public opinion has shifted dramatically. Platforms such as Twitter, Instagram, and Facebook allow individuals and organizations to bypass traditional media gatekeepers, facilitating grassroots activism and direct engagement with the public.

- **Viral Campaigns:** Social media enables campaigns to go viral, reaching vast audiences in a short time. The #LoveIsLove campaign, which emerged during the fight for marriage equality, exemplifies how social media can galvanize support and create a sense of community among LGBTQ advocates and allies.

- **Influencer Advocacy:** Influencers play a crucial role in shaping opinions, particularly among younger audiences. LGBTQ influencers, through their platforms, can humanize issues and foster empathy, making complex topics more relatable.

- **Counter-Narratives:** Social media also provides a space for counter-narratives against mainstream media portrayals. Activists can share their personal stories and challenge stereotypes, thereby reshaping public perceptions.

Challenges and Critiques

Despite the potential of media to shape positive public opinion, several challenges and critiques persist:

- **Misinformation:** The spread of misinformation can lead to harmful stereotypes and reinforce negative attitudes towards LGBTQ individuals. For example, the portrayal of LGBTQ individuals as pedophiles in certain media narratives has historically contributed to stigma and discrimination.

- **Underrepresentation:** While media representation has improved, LGBTQ individuals, particularly those from marginalized communities, are still underrepresented in many media forms. This lack of visibility can perpetuate ignorance and misunderstanding.

- **Echo Chambers:** Social media can create echo chambers, where individuals are only exposed to viewpoints that reinforce their existing beliefs. This can hinder constructive dialogue and limit the potential for changing minds.

Case Studies

Several case studies illustrate the media's impact on public opinion regarding LGBTQ rights:

SECTION ONE: LGBTQ RIGHTS IN ALYNDRA   97

- **The "It Gets Better" Project:** Launched in 2010, this initiative utilized social media to provide hope and support to LGBTQ youth. The campaign's viral nature significantly contributed to a shift in public perception, leading to increased awareness of the challenges faced by LGBTQ youth and fostering a culture of acceptance.

- **Television and Film Representation:** Shows like *Will & Grace* and *Pose* have played a crucial role in normalizing LGBTQ identities and experiences. Their portrayal of LGBTQ characters has helped to humanize issues, fostering empathy and understanding among viewers.

- **News Coverage of Trans Rights:** The media's coverage of high-profile cases involving transgender individuals, such as the murder of trans women of color, has brought attention to the violence faced by this community. This coverage has spurred public outrage and advocacy for trans rights, showcasing the media's power to catalyze social change.

Conclusion

In conclusion, the media plays a multifaceted role in shaping public opinion on LGBTQ rights. Through agenda-setting, framing, and cultivation, media narratives can influence societal attitudes and behaviors. While challenges such as misinformation and underrepresentation persist, the emergence of social media has opened new avenues for advocacy and engagement. As Taren Fira navigates the political landscape of Alyndra, understanding the role of media will be crucial in mobilizing support and advancing LGBTQ rights. The interplay between media representation and public perception will continue to be a significant factor in the ongoing fight for equality and acceptance.

The Fight for Marriage Equality

The fight for marriage equality has been a pivotal chapter in the ongoing struggle for LGBTQ rights, serving as both a symbol and a battleground for broader issues of equality and justice. This section explores the theoretical underpinnings, challenges faced, and significant milestones in the quest for marriage equality, particularly within the context of Taren Fira's activism in Alyndra.

Theoretical Framework

At the heart of the fight for marriage equality lies the principle of **equal protection under the law**, as enshrined in various legal systems. The Fourteenth Amendment of the United States Constitution, for example, asserts that no state shall deny to any person within its jurisdiction the equal protection of the laws. This legal framework has been foundational in arguing that denying same-sex couples the right to marry constitutes a violation of their civil rights.

The **social contract theory**, articulated by philosophers such as John Locke and Jean-Jacques Rousseau, posits that individuals consent to form a society that protects their rights. In the context of marriage equality, this theory suggests that the state has an obligation to recognize and protect the relationships of all its citizens, regardless of sexual orientation. The denial of marriage rights to same-sex couples can be viewed as a breach of this social contract, undermining the very fabric of societal equality.

Challenges Faced

Despite the strong theoretical arguments for marriage equality, activists like Taren Fira encountered significant challenges in their pursuit. One major obstacle was the deeply entrenched societal norms surrounding marriage, which historically favored heterosexual unions. These norms were often reinforced by religious beliefs and cultural traditions, leading to widespread opposition to same-sex marriage.

Moreover, legal barriers posed significant hurdles. Many jurisdictions enacted laws explicitly banning same-sex marriage, often justified by claims of preserving traditional family structures. For instance, the Defense of Marriage Act (DOMA), passed in the United States in 1996, defined marriage as a union between one man and one woman, denying federal recognition to same-sex marriages. Activists had to navigate these legal landscapes, often working through the courts to challenge discriminatory laws.

Milestones in the Movement

Taren Fira's activism was instrumental in several key milestones in the fight for marriage equality in Alyndra. One of the first significant events was the organization of a statewide campaign to raise awareness about the importance of marriage equality. This campaign included rallies, educational workshops, and community discussions that aimed to demystify the concept of same-sex marriage and highlight its significance for LGBTQ individuals.

In 2015, the landmark case *Obergefell v. Hodges* reached the United States Supreme Court, challenging the constitutionality of state bans on same-sex marriage. The case was pivotal, as it brought national attention to the issue and galvanized support from both allies and opponents. Taren Fira, leveraging her

SECTION ONE: LGBTQ RIGHTS IN ALYNDRA

community connections, organized a series of events leading up to the decision, emphasizing the personal stories of couples affected by the bans.

The Supreme Court's ruling in favor of marriage equality on June 26, 2015, was a watershed moment. The Court held that same-sex couples have a constitutional right to marry, affirming that the right to marry is a fundamental liberty inherent in the concept of individual autonomy. This decision not only legalized same-sex marriage across the United States but also served as a catalyst for similar movements worldwide.

Impact on the LGBTQ Community

The legalization of same-sex marriage had profound implications for the LGBTQ community. It provided legal recognition and protection for same-sex couples, allowing them access to a myriad of rights and benefits previously denied. These include tax benefits, inheritance rights, and healthcare decision-making privileges, which are crucial for the well-being of families.

Moreover, marriage equality has been shown to have positive effects on mental health within the LGBTQ community. Studies indicate that legal recognition of same-sex relationships correlates with lower rates of depression and anxiety among LGBTQ individuals. The validation of their relationships fosters a sense of belonging and acceptance, counteracting the stigma and discrimination that many face.

Ongoing Challenges

Despite the progress made, the fight for marriage equality is not without its ongoing challenges. In some regions, backlash against marriage equality has manifested in attempts to roll back rights and protections. For instance, certain states have introduced legislation aimed at undermining the legal status of same-sex marriages, citing religious freedom as a justification.

Additionally, the intersectionality of LGBTQ identities means that not all individuals benefit equally from marriage equality. Marginalized groups, including LGBTQ people of color and transgender individuals, often face compounded discrimination that extends beyond the marriage debate. Activists like Taren Fira emphasize the importance of an intersectional approach to advocacy, ensuring that the fight for marriage equality also addresses the broader spectrum of LGBTQ rights.

Conclusion

The fight for marriage equality represents a significant victory in the broader struggle for LGBTQ rights, showcasing the power of activism, community mobilization, and legal advocacy. Taren Fira's journey exemplifies the dedication and resilience required to challenge societal norms and legal barriers. As the movement continues to evolve, it is imperative that activists remain vigilant, addressing ongoing challenges and ensuring that the principles of equality and justice are upheld for all members of the LGBTQ community.

$$E = mc^2 \qquad (39)$$

In conclusion, while the fight for marriage equality has made remarkable strides, the journey towards full equality continues, reminding us that advocacy is a dynamic and ongoing process. The legacy of Taren Fira and others like her serves as a beacon of hope and inspiration for future generations of activists committed to the cause of LGBTQ rights.

Overcoming Backlash and Resistance

The journey toward LGBTQ rights is often fraught with backlash and resistance from various societal sectors, including political entities, cultural institutions, and even segments of the LGBTQ community itself. This section explores the strategies employed by Taren Fira and her allies to confront and overcome such challenges, drawing on both theoretical frameworks and practical examples.

Understanding Backlash

Backlash against LGBTQ activism can manifest in various forms, from legislative attempts to roll back rights to social media campaigns aimed at discrediting activists. Theories of backlash, such as the *Backlash Effect* (Mackie, 2020), suggest that as marginalized groups gain visibility and rights, those who feel threatened may react defensively, often resulting in intensified opposition. This phenomenon can be observed in the rise of anti-LGBTQ laws in response to marriage equality victories, highlighting the cyclical nature of progress and resistance.

Strategic Responses

To effectively counter backlash, Taren Fira adopted a multifaceted approach that involved both grassroots mobilization and strategic communication. Key strategies included:

- **Education and Awareness Campaigns:** Fira recognized that misinformation and prejudice often fueled backlash. By launching educational initiatives that highlighted the benefits of LGBTQ inclusion—such as economic advantages and improved public health outcomes—she aimed to shift public perception. For instance, the "Pride in Diversity" campaign successfully illustrated how diverse workplaces led to increased innovation and productivity, garnering support from both corporations and community members.

- **Coalition Building:** Fira understood the importance of solidarity across social justice movements. By forming coalitions with feminist, racial justice, and disability rights organizations, she was able to create a united front against backlash. These alliances not only broadened the base of support for LGBTQ rights but also helped to amplify marginalized voices within the LGBTQ community itself, ensuring that issues of intersectionality were addressed.

- **Effective Use of Media:** In the age of digital communication, Fira leveraged social media platforms to counteract negative narratives. By sharing personal stories and testimonials from individuals affected by discriminatory policies, she humanized the issues at stake. For example, during the backlash against a proposed anti-trans bathroom bill, Fira organized a viral campaign using the hashtag #TransRightsAreHumanRights, which garnered widespread attention and support from celebrities and influencers alike.

- **Legal Challenges:** Fira and her team recognized the importance of legal avenues in overcoming backlash. They strategically filed lawsuits against discriminatory laws, arguing that such legislation violated constitutional rights. The landmark case, *Fira v. State of Alyndra*, successfully challenged a ban on same-sex marriage, setting a precedent that empowered other activists to pursue legal action against similar injustices.

- **Resilience Training:** Understanding that activists often face emotional and psychological tolls due to backlash, Fira implemented resilience training workshops. These sessions focused on self-care practices and community support mechanisms, helping activists to maintain their mental health and motivation in the face of adversity. Feedback from participants indicated a significant increase in confidence and a renewed commitment to activism after attending these workshops.

Case Studies

To illustrate the effectiveness of these strategies, we can examine two pivotal moments in Taren Fira's activism:

1. **The 2018 Anti-LGBTQ Bill:** When a prominent political figure proposed a bill aimed at restricting LGBTQ rights, Fira mobilized a coalition of activists who organized protests across Alyndra. They utilized social media to document the protests, garnering national attention. As a result, public opinion shifted, leading to a significant drop in support for the bill, which ultimately failed to pass.

2. **The "Voices of Change" Initiative:** In response to rising hate crimes against LGBTQ individuals, Fira launched the "Voices of Change" initiative, which focused on storytelling as a form of resistance. By collecting and sharing narratives from those directly impacted by hate crimes, the initiative fostered empathy and understanding among the broader public. This campaign not only raised awareness but also led to increased funding for LGBTQ safety programs in Alyndra.

Conclusion

Overcoming backlash and resistance is an ongoing challenge for LGBTQ activists. Taren Fira's strategic responses, grounded in education, coalition-building, and effective media use, provide a roadmap for navigating these turbulent waters. By fostering resilience and solidarity, activists can continue to push for equality and justice, ensuring that the progress made is not easily undone. As Fira often stated, "Our strength lies not only in our visibility but in our ability to unite and advocate for a world where love knows no bounds."

Bibliography

[1] Mackie, R. (2020). *The Backlash Effect: Understanding Resistance to Social Change*. Social Justice Review, 12(3), 45-67.

Political Negotiations and Compromise

In the landscape of LGBTQ activism, political negotiations and compromise are often essential strategies for achieving meaningful change. Taren Fira understood that while the fight for equality is rooted in unwavering principles, the practicalities of advocacy necessitate a willingness to engage with political structures and leaders, even when their values may not fully align with those of the LGBTQ community.

Theoretical Framework

Political negotiation can be understood through the lens of interest-based negotiation theory, which posits that parties involved should focus on their underlying interests rather than their stated positions. This approach encourages collaboration and seeks to identify mutually beneficial solutions. In the context of LGBTQ rights, this means recognizing that while the ultimate goal is equality, the pathway may require concessions and compromises that do not fully satisfy all parties involved.

Challenges in Negotiation

Negotiating for LGBTQ rights presents unique challenges. One significant issue is the presence of entrenched opposition, often rooted in cultural, religious, or ideological beliefs. For instance, when Taren Fira lobbied for marriage equality in Alyndra, she faced staunch opposition from conservative groups who viewed same-sex marriage as a threat to traditional family structures. These groups often mobilized large segments of the population against LGBTQ rights, complicating the negotiation process.

Another challenge is the fragmentation within the LGBTQ community itself. Diverse identities and experiences can lead to differing priorities, which may complicate the negotiation landscape. For example, while some activists may prioritize marriage equality, others may focus on healthcare access or anti-discrimination laws. Taren Fira had to navigate these complexities, advocating for a comprehensive approach that addressed the needs of various groups within the community.

Strategies for Successful Negotiation

To effectively engage in political negotiations, Taren Fira employed several strategies:

1. **Building Coalitions:** Taren recognized the power of coalitions in amplifying voices and increasing political leverage. By collaborating with other marginalized groups, such as women's rights organizations and racial justice movements, she was able to present a united front that emphasized shared values and goals.

2. **Utilizing Data and Research:** Taren understood that data-driven arguments could sway undecided politicians and constituents. By presenting research that highlighted the benefits of LGBTQ inclusion—such as economic advantages and improved public health outcomes—she was able to make a compelling case for policy changes.

3. **Engaging in Dialogue:** Taren prioritized open dialogue with political leaders, even those who opposed LGBTQ rights. By listening to their concerns and finding common ground, she was often able to foster a more productive atmosphere for negotiation. This approach was exemplified during a pivotal meeting with a conservative legislator, where Taren's willingness to discuss family values ultimately led to a more favorable outcome for LGBTQ families.

4. **Compromise without Sacrifice:** While Taren was committed to the core principles of equality and justice, she also recognized the necessity of compromise. For instance, during negotiations for anti-discrimination legislation, she agreed to include provisions that allowed for religious exemptions, understanding that this concession was crucial for gaining broader political support. This strategic compromise did not undermine the overall goal of protecting LGBTQ rights but rather facilitated the passage of vital legislation.

Case Study: The Marriage Equality Bill

A significant example of Taren Fira's negotiation skills can be seen in the campaign for the marriage equality bill in Alyndra. Faced with a divided legislature, Taren organized a series of town hall meetings where constituents could voice their opinions and engage with lawmakers. This grassroots approach not only educated the public on the importance of marriage equality but also pressured lawmakers to reconsider their positions.

During the negotiation process, Taren employed the interest-based negotiation strategy by framing the issue in terms of love and family rather than solely as a political agenda. This reframing helped to humanize the issue and make it more relatable to those who may have been initially resistant. The marriage equality bill eventually passed, marking a significant victory for Taren and the LGBTQ community, demonstrating that effective negotiation can lead to substantial change.

Conclusion

Political negotiations and compromise are vital components of LGBTQ advocacy. Taren Fira's approach exemplified the delicate balance between holding true to one's principles while engaging in the pragmatic realities of political discourse. By building coalitions, utilizing data, engaging in dialogue, and strategically compromising, Taren was able to navigate the complexities of the political landscape, ultimately paving the way for greater acceptance and equality for LGBTQ individuals in Alyndra and beyond. The lessons learned from her negotiations continue to inspire future activists to seek constructive engagement in their advocacy efforts.

Strategies for Policy Change

In the ever-evolving landscape of LGBTQ rights, Taren Fira recognized that effective policy change requires a multifaceted approach that combines advocacy, education, coalition-building, and strategic communication. This section delves into the key strategies employed by Taren and her allies to influence policy at both local and national levels.

Understanding the Policy Landscape

To initiate meaningful policy change, it is essential to have a comprehensive understanding of the existing legal framework surrounding LGBTQ rights. This involves:

- Conducting thorough research on current laws and regulations affecting LGBTQ individuals.
- Identifying gaps in protections and areas where discrimination persists.
- Analyzing the political climate and the positions of key stakeholders, including lawmakers, advocacy groups, and the general public.

By understanding these elements, Taren and her team could craft targeted strategies that addressed specific issues within the broader context of LGBTQ rights.

Building Coalitions

One of Taren's most significant strategies was the formation of coalitions with other social justice movements. This approach not only amplified the voices of LGBTQ individuals but also fostered solidarity across various marginalized groups. Key steps in building effective coalitions include:

1. **Identifying Common Goals:** Finding shared objectives with other movements, such as racial justice, women's rights, and disability rights, to create a united front.
2. **Engaging Diverse Perspectives:** Actively including voices from various backgrounds to ensure that the coalition represents the full spectrum of experiences within the LGBTQ community.
3. **Collaborative Campaigns:** Launching joint initiatives that highlight intersectional issues, such as the impact of racism on LGBTQ individuals of color, to strengthen the coalition's message.

Advocacy and Lobbying

Advocacy and lobbying are critical components of influencing policy change. Taren utilized several strategies to effectively advocate for LGBTQ rights:

- **Direct Lobbying:** Engaging directly with lawmakers through meetings, phone calls, and written communications to present research, personal stories, and data supporting LGBTQ rights.

- **Grassroots Mobilization:** Organizing community members to participate in rallies, town hall meetings, and public demonstrations, thereby demonstrating widespread support for policy initiatives.

- **Public Awareness Campaigns:** Utilizing media campaigns to educate the public on LGBTQ issues, dispel myths, and garner support for legislative changes.

These advocacy efforts were often complemented by a strategic use of social media to reach a broader audience and mobilize supporters quickly.

Utilizing Data and Research

Taren understood the power of data in shaping policy discussions. By leveraging research and statistics, she was able to:

- **Highlight Disparities:** Present compelling evidence of the disparities faced by LGBTQ individuals, such as higher rates of mental health issues, homelessness, and violence.

- **Demonstrate Economic Benefits:** Showcase the economic advantages of inclusive policies, such as increased productivity and reduced healthcare costs.

- **Inform Policy Proposals:** Use data to inform the development of comprehensive policy proposals that address the needs of the LGBTQ community.

For instance, research indicating that states with inclusive non-discrimination laws experience lower rates of hate crimes served as a powerful argument for legislative change.

Engaging with the Media

Effective communication with the media is vital for raising awareness and shaping public opinion. Taren employed several strategies to engage with the media:

- **Press Releases and Conferences:** Regularly issuing press releases and holding press conferences to announce new initiatives, campaign launches, or significant milestones in the fight for LGBTQ rights.

- **Media Training:** Providing training for LGBTQ advocates to effectively communicate their messages to journalists and the public, ensuring that their stories are told authentically and powerfully.

- **Leveraging Social Media:** Using platforms like Twitter, Facebook, and Instagram to share updates, mobilize supporters, and create viral campaigns that draw attention to critical issues.

By fostering strong relationships with journalists and media outlets, Taren was able to secure coverage that kept LGBTQ issues in the public eye.

Advocating for Inclusive Policies

Taren emphasized the importance of advocating for inclusive policies that consider the diverse needs of the LGBTQ community. This involved:

- **Comprehensive Non-Discrimination Laws:** Pushing for legislation that protects individuals from discrimination based on sexual orientation, gender identity, and other intersecting identities.

- **Access to Healthcare:** Advocating for policies that ensure equitable access to healthcare services for LGBTQ individuals, including mental health support and gender-affirming care.

- **Education and Awareness Programs:** Promoting educational initiatives that foster understanding and acceptance of LGBTQ individuals in schools, workplaces, and communities.

Evaluating and Adapting Strategies

Finally, Taren recognized the importance of continually evaluating the effectiveness of advocacy strategies. This involved:

- **Monitoring Legislative Progress:** Keeping track of the status of proposed bills and regulations to identify opportunities for intervention and support.

- **Gathering Feedback:** Solicit feedback from community members and allies to assess the impact of advocacy efforts and identify areas for improvement.

- **Adapting to Changing Circumstances:** Being flexible and willing to adjust strategies in response to shifting political landscapes or emerging challenges.

In conclusion, Taren Fira's approach to policy change was characterized by a deep understanding of the complexities of LGBTQ advocacy, a commitment to intersectionality, and a strategic use of research, media, and coalition-building. By employing these strategies, Taren not only advanced LGBTQ rights in Alyndra but also laid the groundwork for a more inclusive and equitable society.

Building Public Support for LGBTQ Rights

Building public support for LGBTQ rights is a multifaceted endeavor that requires a strategic approach to advocacy, education, and community engagement. The complexities surrounding societal attitudes towards LGBTQ individuals can be understood through several theoretical frameworks, including the Social Identity Theory and the Contact Hypothesis.

Theoretical Frameworks

Social Identity Theory posits that individuals derive a sense of self from their group memberships, which can lead to in-group favoritism and out-group discrimination. This theory explains why many people may harbor biases against LGBTQ individuals, as societal norms often dictate traditional gender roles and heteronormative standards. To counteract these biases, activists must engage in efforts that foster empathy and understanding, effectively reframing LGBTQ identities as integral to the broader social fabric.

On the other hand, the **Contact Hypothesis** suggests that increased interaction between different social groups can reduce prejudice and foster acceptance. This theory underscores the importance of visibility and representation in media, politics, and everyday life. By creating opportunities for positive interactions between LGBTQ individuals and their allies, advocates can dismantle stereotypes and promote a more inclusive society.

Challenges to Building Support

Despite the theoretical frameworks that guide advocacy efforts, several challenges persist in building public support for LGBTQ rights. One significant issue is the prevalence of misinformation and stereotypes perpetuated by media portrayals. Negative depictions can reinforce harmful narratives and contribute to societal stigma. For instance, sensationalized news coverage of LGBTQ issues can lead to fear and misunderstanding among the general public.

Moreover, political polarization has created an environment where discussions about LGBTQ rights are often framed as contentious debates rather than human rights issues. This polarization can hinder constructive dialogue and lead to the entrenchment of opposing viewpoints. Activists must navigate these challenges by employing effective communication strategies that emphasize shared values and common humanity.

Strategies for Building Public Support

To effectively build public support for LGBTQ rights, activists can implement several strategies:

- **Education and Awareness Campaigns:** Initiatives aimed at educating the public about LGBTQ issues can foster understanding and empathy. Campaigns that share personal stories of LGBTQ individuals can humanize the struggles faced by the community, encouraging others to support equality.

- **Engagement with Allies:** Mobilizing allies within the community is essential. Allies can leverage their privilege to advocate for LGBTQ rights, amplifying marginalized voices and creating a more inclusive dialogue. Organizing ally training sessions can equip supporters with the tools to challenge discrimination effectively.

- **Utilizing Social Media:** The digital age offers unprecedented opportunities for advocacy. Social media platforms can be used to disseminate information, share personal narratives, and mobilize grassroots support. Campaigns that go viral can significantly raise awareness and generate public discourse around LGBTQ rights.

- **Collaborative Initiatives:** Building coalitions with other social justice movements can enhance the visibility of LGBTQ rights. By framing LGBTQ advocacy as part of a broader struggle for human rights, activists can attract diverse allies and create a unified front against discrimination.

- **Community Events and Visibility:** Organizing community events, such as pride parades and educational workshops, can foster a sense of belonging and solidarity within the LGBTQ community. These events provide opportunities for individuals to connect, share experiences, and celebrate diversity.

Examples of Successful Campaigns

Several successful campaigns have demonstrated the effectiveness of these strategies. For instance, the **It Gets Better Project** utilized personal storytelling to reach out to LGBTQ youth facing bullying and discrimination. By sharing messages of hope and resilience, the campaign garnered widespread support and raised awareness about the challenges faced by LGBTQ individuals, ultimately contributing to a shift in public perception.

Similarly, the **Human Rights Campaign** has effectively engaged allies through initiatives like the *"Equal Sign"* campaign, which encouraged individuals to display the equal sign on social media profiles as a symbol of support for marriage equality. This grassroots movement not only mobilized allies but also created a visible representation of solidarity that resonated with the public.

Conclusion

In conclusion, building public support for LGBTQ rights is an ongoing process that requires dedication, creativity, and collaboration. By leveraging theoretical frameworks, addressing challenges, and implementing effective strategies, activists can foster a more inclusive society. As Taren Fira exemplifies, the journey toward equality is not only about changing laws but also about transforming hearts and minds, ensuring that every individual, regardless of their sexual orientation or gender identity, is embraced as a valued member of society.

Balancing Activism and Diplomacy

In the realm of LGBTQ advocacy, the delicate balance between activism and diplomacy is crucial for fostering change and promoting equality. Activism, characterized by direct action and grassroots mobilization, often seeks immediate results, while diplomacy focuses on negotiation, dialogue, and the building of relationships. This section explores the interplay between these two approaches, examining the challenges and strategies for achieving a harmonious balance.

Theoretical Framework

The relationship between activism and diplomacy can be understood through the lens of *Critical Theory*, which posits that societal change occurs through a dialectical process. Activism can be seen as a catalyst for change, while diplomacy serves as a mechanism for institutionalizing that change within political frameworks. According to *Habermas's Theory of Communicative Action*, effective communication is essential for both activism and diplomacy, as it fosters understanding and consensus among diverse stakeholders.

Challenges in Balancing Activism and Diplomacy

One of the primary challenges in balancing activism and diplomacy is the potential for conflict between the urgency of activist demands and the slower pace of diplomatic negotiations. Activists often seek immediate reforms, such as the legalization of same-sex marriage or anti-discrimination laws, while diplomats may prioritize consensus-building, which can delay the implementation of such changes. This tension can lead to frustration within activist communities, as seen during the negotiations for marriage equality in various countries.

Additionally, the perception of compromise can be viewed negatively by activists. For instance, in the early 2000s, discussions around LGBTQ rights in the United States often faced backlash from more radical activist factions who felt that any form of compromise with conservative lawmakers diluted the movement's goals. This phenomenon illustrates the struggle between maintaining ideological purity and achieving practical outcomes.

Strategies for Effective Balancing

To navigate the complexities of balancing activism and diplomacy, several strategies can be employed:

- **Engagement with Policymakers:** Activists should seek to engage directly with policymakers, presenting evidence-based arguments that highlight the benefits of LGBTQ-inclusive policies. This approach not only fosters dialogue but also builds trust and rapport.

- **Coalition Building:** Forming coalitions with other social justice movements enhances the visibility and strength of LGBTQ advocacy. For example, the collaboration between LGBTQ activists and racial justice organizations during the Black Lives Matter movement exemplifies how intersectional alliances can amplify voices and create a more robust advocacy platform.

- **Public Awareness Campaigns:** Utilizing media and public campaigns to raise awareness about LGBTQ issues can create a supportive environment for diplomatic negotiations. For instance, the *It Gets Better Project* effectively used storytelling to shift public perception, making it easier for policymakers to support LGBTQ rights.

- **Training for Activists:** Providing training for activists in negotiation and diplomatic skills can enhance their effectiveness in engaging with political leaders. This can include workshops on communication strategies, understanding political processes, and building relationships with allies.

Case Studies

Several case studies illustrate successful balancing acts between activism and diplomacy:

Case Study 1: The Marriage Equality Movement in the United States The fight for marriage equality in the U.S. exemplified the interplay between activism and diplomacy. Activists organized protests, marches, and public campaigns to raise awareness and support for same-sex marriage. Simultaneously, advocates engaged in diplomatic efforts, meeting with lawmakers and participating in legal battles. The combination of grassroots mobilization and strategic negotiations ultimately led to the landmark Supreme Court decision in *Obergefell v. Hodges* (2015), which legalized same-sex marriage nationwide.

Case Study 2: The Global LGBTQ Rights Movement Internationally, LGBTQ activists have navigated complex political landscapes by balancing activism and diplomacy. In countries where LGBTQ rights are severely restricted, activists often employ diplomatic channels to advocate for change. For example, during the United Nations Human Rights Council sessions, activists have successfully lobbied for resolutions that condemn violence against LGBTQ individuals. These diplomatic efforts, coupled with grassroots activism, have led to increased global attention on LGBTQ rights issues.

Conclusion

Balancing activism and diplomacy is essential for effective LGBTQ advocacy. While activism drives immediate change and raises awareness, diplomacy facilitates long-term sustainability and institutionalization of rights. By employing strategic engagement, coalition building, and public awareness campaigns, activists can navigate the complexities of the political landscape, ensuring that the voices of marginalized communities are heard and represented. The interplay of these two approaches ultimately strengthens the movement, paving the way for a more inclusive and equitable society.

Responding to Political Attacks

In the realm of LGBTQ activism, political attacks can manifest in various forms, ranging from legislative measures aimed at undermining rights to public rhetoric that seeks to delegitimize the community's existence. Responding to these attacks effectively is critical for maintaining momentum in the fight for equality and justice. This section explores strategies, theories, and real-world examples of how Taren Fira and other activists have navigated these turbulent waters.

Understanding Political Attacks

Political attacks against LGBTQ rights often stem from a combination of societal prejudice, misinformation, and strategic political maneuvering. These attacks can take the form of:

- **Legislative measures:** Bills aimed at restricting rights, such as those prohibiting same-sex marriage or banning gender-affirming healthcare for transgender individuals.

- **Public discourse:** Negative rhetoric from politicians and media figures that perpetuates stereotypes and fosters discrimination.

- **Social movements:** Organized efforts by groups opposing LGBTQ rights, which can include protests, lobbying, and campaigns aimed at swaying public opinion.

Understanding the motivations behind these attacks is crucial. Theories such as *Social Identity Theory* suggest that individuals derive a sense of self from their group memberships. When LGBTQ identities are attacked, it can provoke a defensive reaction from those who identify with the community, leading to increased solidarity and activism.

Strategies for Response

Taren Fira's approach to responding to political attacks is multifaceted, employing both direct and indirect strategies:

1. **Public Advocacy:** Taren often utilized media platforms to counteract negative narratives. By sharing personal stories and highlighting the positive contributions of LGBTQ individuals to society, Taren aimed to humanize the community and shift public perception. For instance, during a

particularly contentious legislative session in Alyndra, Taren organized a series of press conferences where LGBTQ individuals shared their experiences, effectively countering the prevailing narrative of the opposition.

2. **Coalition Building:** Recognizing that strength lies in numbers, Taren actively sought alliances with other marginalized groups. This approach not only broadened the base of support but also demonstrated the interconnectedness of various social justice movements. For example, during the fight against a proposed anti-LGBTQ bill, Taren collaborated with racial justice organizations, highlighting the shared struggles against systemic oppression.

3. **Legal Action:** In instances where political attacks escalated to violations of rights, Taren championed legal challenges. By supporting lawsuits against discriminatory legislation, Taren's activism underscored the importance of judicial avenues in the fight for equality. A notable case involved a coalition of activists, including Taren, who successfully challenged a law that sought to restrict the rights of transgender individuals to access healthcare.

4. **Community Mobilization:** Taren understood the power of grassroots activism. By mobilizing community members to participate in protests, letter-writing campaigns, and town hall meetings, Taren galvanized public support. The "Stand with Us" campaign, initiated in response to a series of anti-LGBTQ remarks by a prominent political figure, saw thousands of supporters gather to advocate for equality, sending a clear message to lawmakers.

5. **Digital Advocacy:** In the age of social media, Taren leveraged online platforms to amplify messages and counteract misinformation. By creating viral hashtags and engaging in online discussions, Taren was able to reach a broader audience. The #LoveIsLove campaign, which gained traction during a contentious election cycle, served as a rallying cry for supporters of LGBTQ rights, effectively drowning out negative rhetoric.

6. **Education and Awareness:** Taren emphasized the importance of education in combating prejudice. By organizing workshops and seminars that addressed LGBTQ issues, Taren sought to inform both allies and opponents about the realities faced by the community. This proactive approach not only mitigated misunderstandings but also fostered empathy, as evidenced by a series of educational initiatives in local schools that aimed to promote inclusivity.

7. **Resilience and Emotional Support:** Responding to political attacks can take an emotional toll on activists. Taren recognized the need for self-care and resilience within the community. Initiatives like "Healing Spaces" provided safe environments for individuals to process their experiences and fostered a sense of solidarity among participants. This focus on mental health underscored the importance of collective healing in the face of adversity.

Case Studies of Successful Responses

Several key instances exemplify Taren Fira's successful strategies in responding to political attacks:

- **The Marriage Equality Battle:** During the fight for marriage equality in Alyndra, a series of anti-marriage bills were introduced. Taren led a coalition that organized a massive rally, drawing attention to the overwhelming public support for marriage equality. The event garnered significant media coverage, shifting the narrative and pressuring lawmakers to reconsider their positions.

- **The Trans Rights Campaign:** In response to a wave of anti-trans legislation, Taren spearheaded a campaign that included legal challenges and public demonstrations. The campaign successfully mobilized allies across various sectors, resulting in a landmark ruling that protected transgender rights in healthcare.

- **Countering Misinformation:** When a prominent politician made false claims about LGBTQ individuals, Taren quickly organized a fact-checking initiative that utilized social media to disseminate accurate information. This effort not only countered the politician's narrative but also educated the public on LGBTQ issues.

Conclusion

Responding to political attacks requires a nuanced understanding of the landscape, strategic planning, and unwavering commitment. Taren Fira's legacy in LGBTQ activism highlights the importance of resilience, community solidarity, and the power of advocacy in the face of adversity. Through a combination of public engagement, legal action, and grassroots mobilization, Taren not only defended the rights of LGBTQ individuals but also inspired a generation of activists to continue the fight for equality.

As Taren often reminded supporters, "In the face of hate, we must rise stronger, united in our diversity, and unyielding in our quest for justice."

Section Two: Upholding LGBTQ Rights Globally

Confronting Homophobia in Conservative Societies

In the realm of LGBTQ activism, confronting homophobia in conservative societies presents a formidable challenge. This section delves into the theories, problems, and practical examples that characterize the struggle against entrenched prejudices and cultural norms.

Understanding the Roots of Homophobia

Homophobia, defined as an irrational fear or hatred of individuals who identify as LGBTQ, often stems from deeply rooted cultural, religious, and historical contexts. In conservative societies, traditional values and norms frequently dictate social behavior, leading to the marginalization of LGBTQ individuals. Theories such as **Social Identity Theory** suggest that individuals derive a sense of identity and self-esteem from their group memberships, which can result in in-group favoritism and out-group discrimination. This dynamic is particularly pronounced in conservative settings, where conformity to societal norms is highly valued.

$$\text{Prejudice} = f(\text{Societal Norms, Cultural Beliefs, Religious Teachings}) \quad (40)$$

This equation suggests that prejudice is a function of societal norms, cultural beliefs, and religious teachings, all of which can reinforce homophobic attitudes.

Challenges Faced by LGBTQ Activists

Activists in conservative societies encounter numerous obstacles, including:

- **Legal Barriers:** Many conservative countries have laws that criminalize homosexuality or fail to recognize LGBTQ rights. For instance, in countries like Uganda, anti-homosexuality laws have been enacted, leading to severe penalties for LGBTQ individuals.

- **Social Stigma:** The pervasive stigma surrounding LGBTQ identities can result in social ostracism, harassment, and violence. Activists often face backlash from their communities, which can deter individuals from openly advocating for change.

- **Limited Resources:** In conservative environments, LGBTQ organizations may struggle to secure funding and support, making it challenging to sustain advocacy efforts. Many activists operate in secrecy, fearing repercussions from both the state and society.

- **Censorship:** Media censorship can hinder the visibility of LGBTQ issues, limiting the public's awareness and understanding. In conservative societies, discussions about sexual orientation and gender identity are often suppressed, perpetuating ignorance and prejudice.

Strategies for Confrontation

To confront homophobia in conservative societies, LGBTQ activists have employed various strategies:

1. **Education and Awareness:** Activists work to educate the public about LGBTQ issues, aiming to dismantle stereotypes and misconceptions. Campaigns that highlight the humanity of LGBTQ individuals can foster empathy and understanding. For example, the "It Gets Better" project has successfully reached audiences in conservative contexts, providing narratives of hope and resilience.

2. **Building Alliances:** Collaborating with other social justice movements can amplify voices and create broader coalitions for change. Intersectional activism recognizes the interconnectedness of various forms of oppression, allowing for a more comprehensive approach to advocacy.

3. **Engaging with Religious Leaders:** In many conservative societies, religion plays a central role in shaping attitudes. Engaging with progressive religious leaders who advocate for LGBTQ rights can help challenge harmful interpretations of religious texts and foster acceptance within religious communities.

4. **Utilizing Digital Platforms:** The digital age has provided new avenues for activism. Social media platforms allow activists to connect, share stories, and mobilize support, even in the face of censorship. For instance, the

SECTION TWO: UPHOLDING LGBTQ RIGHTS GLOBALLY

#LoveIsLove campaign has gained traction globally, promoting acceptance and love across diverse cultures.

5. **Advocating for Policy Change:** While facing legal barriers, activists strive to influence policy through lobbying and grassroots movements. Documenting human rights abuses and presenting evidence to international bodies can pressure conservative governments to reconsider discriminatory laws.

Case Studies

Several case studies illustrate the complexities and successes of confronting homophobia in conservative societies:

- **The Rainbow Pride March in Poland:** Despite significant opposition from conservative factions, the Rainbow Pride March in Warsaw has become a symbol of resilience and hope. Activists faced threats and hostility but persisted in their efforts to promote visibility and acceptance. The event has garnered international attention, highlighting the struggles of LGBTQ individuals in Poland.

- **The Impact of the Global Fund for Women:** This organization has supported grassroots LGBTQ initiatives in conservative societies, providing funding and resources for advocacy. By empowering local activists, the Global Fund for Women has contributed to significant progress in LGBTQ rights in regions where such activism is often met with hostility.

- **The Role of Art in Activism:** In countries like Iran, where homosexuality is criminalized, artists have used their work to challenge societal norms and provoke dialogue. Visual art, literature, and film serve as powerful mediums for expressing the realities of LGBTQ lives, fostering understanding and empathy.

Conclusion

Confronting homophobia in conservative societies requires a multifaceted approach that acknowledges the complexities of cultural, legal, and social dynamics. Activists must navigate a landscape fraught with challenges while remaining steadfast in their commitment to equality and justice. By employing education, coalition-building, and innovative strategies, LGBTQ activists can create pathways for change, fostering a more inclusive society for all.

Ultimately, the struggle against homophobia is not just about legal recognition; it is about transforming hearts and minds, challenging deeply ingrained prejudices, and affirming the dignity and worth of every individual, regardless of their sexual orientation or gender identity.

Solidarity with LGBTQ Activists around the World

Solidarity among LGBTQ activists is not merely a gesture of goodwill; it is an essential framework for fostering global change. The concept of solidarity transcends borders, cultures, and political systems, uniting individuals and organizations in a common struggle for equality and human rights. In this section, we will explore the theoretical underpinnings of solidarity, the challenges faced by LGBTQ activists globally, and the practical examples of successful international collaborations.

Theoretical Framework of Solidarity

Solidarity, as a theoretical construct, can be understood through the lens of intersectionality, a term coined by Kimberlé Crenshaw. Intersectionality posits that individuals experience oppression and discrimination in varying degrees based on their intersecting identities, including but not limited to race, gender, sexual orientation, and socioeconomic status. This framework emphasizes the importance of recognizing and addressing the unique challenges faced by marginalized groups within the LGBTQ community.

$$S = \sum_{i=1}^{n} O_i \cdot P_i \qquad (41)$$

Where S represents solidarity, O_i denotes the unique challenges faced by each marginalized group i, and P_i symbolizes the power dynamics at play. This equation underscores that true solidarity requires an understanding of the complexities of oppression and the need for a collective approach to advocacy.

Challenges Faced by LGBTQ Activists

Despite the progress made in many parts of the world, LGBTQ activists continue to confront significant challenges. These include:

- **Legal Barriers:** In numerous countries, homosexuality remains criminalized, and LGBTQ individuals face persecution. Activists often risk imprisonment, violence, or even death for their advocacy.

- **Cultural Stigmas:** Cultural norms and societal attitudes can hinder progress. In some regions, LGBTQ identities are viewed as taboo, leading to isolation and marginalization of activists.

- **Resource Limitations:** Many LGBTQ organizations operate with minimal funding, making it difficult to sustain long-term advocacy efforts. This lack of resources can limit outreach and support for affected individuals.

- **Political Resistance:** Activists often face backlash from political leaders who oppose LGBTQ rights, resulting in the rollback of protections and increased hostility towards the community.

Examples of International Solidarity

Despite these challenges, there are numerous examples of successful solidarity among LGBTQ activists worldwide:

Global Pride Events One of the most visible forms of solidarity is the organization of global pride events. These events, such as World Pride and International Day Against Homophobia, Transphobia, and Biphobia (IDAHOT), bring together activists from various countries to celebrate diversity and advocate for LGBTQ rights. For instance, World Pride 2019, held in New York City, attracted millions of participants from around the globe, highlighting the interconnectedness of the LGBTQ movement.

Coalitions and Networks International coalitions, such as the International Lesbian, Gay, Bisexual, Trans and Intersex Association (ILGA), serve as platforms for collaboration among LGBTQ organizations. These networks facilitate the sharing of resources, knowledge, and strategies, enabling activists to amplify their voices and coordinate efforts. For example, ILGA's annual conferences provide a space for activists to discuss pressing issues, share successes, and develop joint initiatives.

Digital Activism In the digital age, social media has become a powerful tool for global solidarity. Platforms like Twitter and Instagram allow activists to connect, share stories, and mobilize support across borders. Campaigns such as #LoveIsLove and #TransRightsAreHumanRights have garnered international attention, demonstrating the power of collective action. These hashtags serve not only to raise awareness but also to foster a sense of belonging among LGBTQ individuals worldwide.

The Role of Allyship in Solidarity

Allyship plays a crucial role in strengthening solidarity among LGBTQ activists. Allies, who may not identify as LGBTQ themselves, can leverage their privilege to advocate for change and amplify marginalized voices. Effective allyship involves:

- **Listening and Learning:** Allies must actively listen to the experiences and concerns of LGBTQ individuals, seeking to understand their struggles and perspectives.

- **Advocating for Change:** Allies should use their platforms to advocate for LGBTQ rights, challenging discriminatory practices and policies within their communities.

- **Building Bridges:** Allies can help connect LGBTQ activists with resources, networks, and opportunities for collaboration, fostering a sense of community and support.

Conclusion

In conclusion, solidarity with LGBTQ activists around the world is essential for creating meaningful change in the fight for equality and human rights. By understanding the complexities of oppression through an intersectional lens, recognizing the challenges faced by activists, and fostering international collaboration, we can build a more inclusive and equitable future for all. The journey toward LGBTQ rights is not confined to any single nation; it is a global movement that requires the collective efforts of individuals, organizations, and allies alike. As Taren Fira once said, "Our strength lies not in our differences, but in our unity." It is through solidarity that we can truly ignite change and inspire a world where everyone can live authentically and without fear.

Taren Fira's Impact on International Policies

Taren Fira's influence on international policies regarding LGBTQ rights has been profound and multifaceted, characterized by a unique blend of grassroots activism, strategic diplomacy, and a commitment to intersectionality. As she navigated the complex landscape of global advocacy, Fira employed various theoretical frameworks to shape her approach and maximize her impact.

Theoretical Frameworks

Fira often drew upon the principles of *intersectionality*, a term coined by Kimberlé Crenshaw, which emphasizes the interconnectedness of social categorizations such as race, class, and gender. This framework allowed her to recognize that LGBTQ individuals do not experience oppression uniformly; rather, their experiences are shaped by multiple identities. By advocating for policies that addressed the specific needs of marginalized groups within the LGBTQ community, Fira was able to push for more inclusive legislation on an international scale.

Furthermore, Fira utilized the *social movement theory*, which posits that social movements arise in response to perceived injustices and mobilize collective action for change. Fira's activism exemplified this theory as she galvanized support from diverse communities, creating a coalition of activists who were invested in the fight for LGBTQ rights worldwide.

Key Policies and Initiatives

One of Fira's most significant contributions was her involvement in the drafting of the *United Nations Resolution on LGBTQ Rights*, which sought to affirm the human rights of LGBTQ individuals globally. This resolution was groundbreaking, as it marked the first time that the UN formally recognized the need to protect LGBTQ rights as human rights. Fira's role in this initiative included:

- **Advocacy and Lobbying:** Fira organized lobbying efforts that brought together activists from various countries, emphasizing the need for a unified voice at the UN. Her ability to articulate the urgency of the issue led to increased support from member states.

- **Building Coalitions:** Fira collaborated with other social justice movements, creating a broad coalition that included feminist groups, racial justice advocates, and disability rights organizations. This intersectional approach not only strengthened the resolution but also highlighted the interconnected nature of various social justice issues.

- **Public Awareness Campaigns:** Fira spearheaded global campaigns that raised awareness about the plight of LGBTQ individuals in regions where their rights were severely restricted. These campaigns utilized social media platforms, engaging younger audiences and fostering a sense of global solidarity.

Challenges Faced

Despite her successes, Fira encountered significant challenges in her quest to influence international policies. One major obstacle was the persistent backlash from conservative governments and organizations that sought to undermine LGBTQ rights. For instance, during the negotiation of the UN resolution, several member states attempted to dilute the language regarding LGBTQ protections, arguing that such measures infringed upon national sovereignty.

Fira faced criticism from within the LGBTQ community as well, particularly regarding the prioritization of certain identities over others. This critique underscored the need for continuous dialogue about intersectionality and the importance of centering marginalized voices in advocacy efforts.

Examples of Impact

Fira's impact on international policies can be illustrated through several key examples:

- **The Global Fund for LGBTQ Rights:** In collaboration with international NGOs, Fira helped establish a fund dedicated to supporting LGBTQ advocacy in countries with restrictive laws. This fund has provided resources for grassroots organizations, enabling them to conduct awareness campaigns and legal advocacy.

- **Participation in Global Conferences:** Fira's presence at major international conferences, such as the *World Human Rights Conference*, allowed her to represent the voices of LGBTQ individuals. Her speeches often highlighted the intersectional nature of oppression, urging global leaders to adopt comprehensive policies that address the needs of all marginalized groups.

- **Influencing National Policies:** Fira's advocacy has led to tangible changes in national policies in several countries. For example, her efforts contributed to the repeal of anti-LGBTQ laws in a prominent South American nation, showcasing the power of international pressure and coalition-building.

Conclusion

In conclusion, Taren Fira's impact on international policies regarding LGBTQ rights has been substantial, characterized by her strategic use of intersectionality and social movement theory. Through her advocacy, she has not only contributed to significant policy changes at the UN but has also fostered a global movement that recognizes the diverse experiences of LGBTQ individuals. As the landscape of international advocacy continues to evolve, Fira's legacy serves as a guiding light for future activists committed to the fight for equality and justice.

Trans Rights and the Erasure of Non-binary Identities

The fight for trans rights has gained significant attention in recent years, yet a critical aspect of this struggle remains underrepresented: the rights of non-binary individuals. Non-binary identities—those that do not fit strictly within the traditional binary of male and female—are often marginalized not only in societal discourse but also within the broader LGBTQ+ movement. This section aims to explore the complexities surrounding non-binary identities, the challenges they face, and the implications of their erasure in the context of trans rights.

Understanding Non-binary Identities

Non-binary is an umbrella term that encompasses a variety of gender identities that exist outside the binary classification of male and female. This can include identities such as genderqueer, genderfluid, agender, and more. According to the *Gender Identity and Gender Expression* framework proposed by the American Psychological Association, gender identity is a deeply-held sense of being male, female, or something else, which may not necessarily align with the sex assigned at birth. Non-binary individuals often experience a fluidity in their gender expression, which can shift over time or in different contexts.

Theoretical Frameworks

To understand the erasure of non-binary identities, we can draw from Judith Butler's theory of gender performativity, which posits that gender is not an inherent quality but rather a series of performances and social constructs. Butler argues that the rigid categories of male and female are socially enforced, leading to the marginalization of those who do not conform. This performative aspect of gender highlights the need for recognition and validation of non-binary identities in both social and legal frameworks.

Furthermore, the concept of intersectionality, introduced by Kimberlé Crenshaw, is crucial in understanding how non-binary individuals experience multiple layers of discrimination. Non-binary people, especially those who are also people of color, face compounded challenges due to the intersection of their gender identity with other aspects of their identity, such as race, class, and sexuality.

Challenges Faced by Non-binary Individuals

Despite the growing recognition of trans rights, non-binary individuals often encounter significant barriers, including:

- **Legal Recognition:** Many legal systems worldwide only recognize binary genders, making it difficult for non-binary individuals to obtain identification documents that accurately reflect their gender identity. For instance, in some jurisdictions, individuals are required to choose either "male" or "female" on official documents, effectively erasing non-binary identities from legal recognition.

- **Healthcare Access:** Non-binary individuals frequently face challenges in accessing healthcare that is sensitive to their unique needs. Medical professionals may lack training in non-binary identities, leading to misgendering and inadequate care. This can result in non-binary individuals avoiding medical treatment altogether due to fear of discrimination.

- **Social Acceptance:** The societal understanding of gender is still predominantly binary, which can lead to non-binary individuals experiencing invalidation and discrimination in everyday life. This includes issues such as being misgendered, facing hostility in public spaces, and encountering exclusion from LGBTQ+ events that prioritize binary identities.

- **Mental Health Impacts:** The erasure and invalidation of non-binary identities can lead to significant mental health challenges. Studies have shown that non-binary individuals report higher rates of anxiety, depression, and suicidal ideation compared to their binary counterparts. The lack of recognition can exacerbate feelings of isolation and marginalization.

Examples of Erasure in Activism

The erasure of non-binary identities can also be observed within LGBTQ+ activism. Many movements tend to focus on the rights of binary trans individuals, often sidelining the unique challenges faced by non-binary people. For example, during pride events, non-binary representation is often minimal, with the focus primarily on binary trans narratives. This lack of visibility can perpetuate the idea that non-binary identities are less valid or important.

Moreover, the language used in activism often reflects a binary understanding of gender. Phrases such as "trans women are women" and "trans men are men" can inadvertently exclude non-binary individuals from the conversation. While these statements are crucial for affirming the identities of binary trans individuals, they can also reinforce a binary framework that marginalizes non-binary experiences.

Towards Inclusion and Recognition

To combat the erasure of non-binary identities, it is essential for activists and allies to adopt inclusive practices that affirm the existence and validity of non-binary individuals. This can include:

- **Inclusive Language:** Using gender-neutral language and pronouns (such as they/them) can help create a more inclusive environment for non-binary individuals. Encouraging the use of pronouns in introductions and on social media can normalize non-binary identities.

- **Policy Advocacy:** Advocating for legal recognition of non-binary identities is crucial. This includes pushing for options beyond "male" and "female" on identification documents and ensuring that healthcare policies are inclusive of non-binary individuals.

- **Education and Training:** Providing education and training for healthcare providers, educators, and activists on non-binary identities can help reduce stigma and improve access to resources. Workshops and seminars can foster understanding and empathy, creating a more supportive environment.

- **Visibility and Representation:** Amplifying the voices of non-binary individuals in activism, media, and public discourse is vital for challenging the erasure of their identities. This can be achieved through storytelling, representation in leadership roles, and highlighting non-binary experiences in campaigns and initiatives.

In conclusion, the erasure of non-binary identities within the fight for trans rights is a significant issue that requires urgent attention. By understanding the complexities of non-binary identities, recognizing the challenges faced by these individuals, and implementing inclusive practices, we can work towards a more equitable and just society for all gender identities. The journey towards true inclusivity in the LGBTQ+ movement is ongoing, and it is imperative that non-binary voices are uplifted and celebrated in this collective struggle for rights and recognition.

Promoting LGBTQ Rights beyond Borders

In an increasingly interconnected world, the promotion of LGBTQ rights beyond national borders has become a crucial aspect of global human rights advocacy. The movement for LGBTQ equality is not confined to specific regions; rather, it is a universal struggle that transcends cultural, political, and geographical boundaries. This section will explore the theoretical frameworks, challenges, and successful examples of promoting LGBTQ rights on an international scale.

Theoretical Frameworks

The promotion of LGBTQ rights globally can be understood through various theoretical lenses, including human rights theory, intersectionality, and transnational activism.

Human Rights Theory Human rights theory posits that all individuals, regardless of their sexual orientation or gender identity, possess inherent rights that must be respected and protected. This perspective argues for the universality of rights, emphasizing that LGBTQ individuals are entitled to the same protections as any other group. As articulated in the Universal Declaration of Human Rights (UDHR), Article 1 states, "All human beings are born free and equal in dignity and rights." This foundational principle serves as a cornerstone for advocating LGBTQ rights worldwide.

Intersectionality Intersectionality, a term coined by Kimberlé Crenshaw, highlights how various forms of discrimination—such as race, class, and gender—intersect to create unique experiences of oppression. In the context of LGBTQ rights, intersectional frameworks emphasize the importance of recognizing the diverse identities within the LGBTQ community and the specific challenges faced by marginalized groups. For instance, LGBTQ people of color may experience compounded discrimination that requires tailored advocacy efforts.

Transnational Activism Transnational activism refers to the efforts of activists and organizations that operate across national borders to address global issues. This approach recognizes that LGBTQ rights are a global concern and that local struggles are often interconnected. Activists leverage international platforms, such as the United Nations (UN), to advocate for LGBTQ rights and hold governments accountable for human rights violations.

Challenges in Promoting LGBTQ Rights

Despite the growing recognition of LGBTQ rights as human rights, significant challenges remain in promoting these rights beyond borders. These challenges include:

Cultural Resistance   Cultural norms and values often play a significant role in shaping attitudes toward LGBTQ individuals. In many regions, traditional beliefs and religious doctrines perpetuate stigma and discrimination. For example, in several African and Middle Eastern countries, colonial-era laws criminalizing homosexuality persist, fueled by cultural and religious opposition to LGBTQ rights.

Political Backlash   Political leaders in some countries exploit anti-LGBTQ sentiment to consolidate power, often framing LGBTQ rights as a threat to national values or family structures. This backlash can manifest in the form of discriminatory laws, such as those prohibiting same-sex marriage or criminalizing LGBTQ identities. For instance, in Hungary, the government has implemented measures that restrict LGBTQ rights, including a ban on the portrayal of LGBTQ individuals in educational materials.

Limited Resources and Support   Many LGBTQ organizations working on the ground face resource constraints, limiting their ability to advocate effectively. In regions with hostile environments, activists may lack access to funding, legal support, and protection from violence. This lack of resources can hinder the development of sustainable advocacy initiatives.

Successful Examples of Global Advocacy

Despite these challenges, numerous successful examples of promoting LGBTQ rights beyond borders demonstrate the potential for meaningful change.

The United Nations and LGBTQ Advocacy   The UN has played a pivotal role in advancing LGBTQ rights on a global scale. In 2011, the UN Human Rights Council passed a landmark resolution that called for the decriminalization of homosexuality and urged member states to protect LGBTQ individuals from violence and discrimination. This resolution marked a significant step toward recognizing LGBTQ rights as an integral part of human rights.

Global Pride Events Global Pride events, such as World Pride and International Pride Day, serve as powerful platforms for raising awareness and advocating for LGBTQ rights worldwide. These events bring together activists, allies, and supporters from diverse backgrounds, fostering solidarity and amplifying marginalized voices. For instance, the 2019 World Pride held in New York City celebrated the 50th anniversary of the Stonewall Riots, highlighting the ongoing struggle for LGBTQ rights globally.

Transnational Networks and Collaborations Transnational networks, such as the International Lesbian, Gay, Bisexual, Trans and Intersex Association (ILGA), facilitate collaboration among LGBTQ organizations across countries. These networks provide resources, share best practices, and support grassroots activists in their advocacy efforts. By fostering connections between local and international organizations, these networks strengthen the global movement for LGBTQ rights.

Conclusion

Promoting LGBTQ rights beyond borders is a complex yet essential endeavor that requires a multifaceted approach. By employing theoretical frameworks that emphasize human rights, intersectionality, and transnational activism, advocates can navigate the challenges posed by cultural resistance, political backlash, and resource limitations. Successful examples, such as UN initiatives, global pride events, and transnational collaborations, illustrate the potential for meaningful change. As the struggle for LGBTQ rights continues, it is imperative that activists remain committed to fostering solidarity and amplifying the voices of marginalized communities worldwide. Only through collective action and shared commitment can we hope to achieve true equality for LGBTQ individuals across the globe.

Diplomatic Efforts and International Cooperation

In the realm of LGBTQ advocacy, diplomatic efforts and international cooperation serve as pivotal mechanisms for advancing rights and fostering a supportive global environment. Taren Fira recognized that the struggle for LGBTQ rights transcends borders, necessitating a collaborative approach among nations, organizations, and activists. This section delves into the theoretical frameworks, challenges, and real-world examples that characterize the landscape of international LGBTQ advocacy.

Theoretical Frameworks

International relations theories provide a foundation for understanding how LGBTQ advocacy can be integrated into diplomatic efforts. Constructivism, for instance, posits that the identities and interests of states are socially constructed through interactions and shared norms. This perspective suggests that promoting LGBTQ rights can reshape international norms, encouraging countries to adopt more inclusive policies.

Furthermore, liberalism emphasizes the role of international institutions and cooperation in addressing global issues. Organizations such as the United Nations (UN) and the European Union (EU) have increasingly recognized LGBTQ rights as human rights, creating platforms for dialogue and action. The Universal Declaration of Human Rights (UDHR) serves as a guiding document, asserting that all individuals, regardless of sexual orientation or gender identity, deserve dignity and respect.

Challenges to International Cooperation

Despite the theoretical frameworks supporting diplomatic efforts, significant challenges persist in advancing LGBTQ rights globally. Cultural relativism often complicates the dialogue surrounding LGBTQ issues, as differing cultural norms and values can lead to resistance against perceived Western impositions. For instance, in many conservative societies, LGBTQ identities are stigmatized, and advocacy efforts may be met with hostility.

Additionally, geopolitical tensions can hinder cooperation. Nations with conflicting interests may prioritize political agendas over human rights, leaving LGBTQ individuals vulnerable. The intersection of LGBTQ rights with broader political issues, such as refugee status or trade agreements, often complicates negotiations.

Examples of Successful Diplomatic Efforts

Despite the challenges, several successful examples of international cooperation in LGBTQ advocacy illustrate the potential for positive change. The UN's Free & Equal campaign, launched in 2013, aims to promote equal rights and fair treatment of LGBTQ individuals worldwide. This campaign has mobilized resources, raised awareness, and fostered dialogue among member states, leading to increased visibility of LGBTQ issues in international forums.

In 2016, the UN Human Rights Council adopted a landmark resolution calling for the protection of LGBTQ individuals from violence and discrimination.

This resolution marked a significant step towards institutionalizing LGBTQ rights within the UN framework, demonstrating the power of diplomatic efforts in shaping global policies.

Moreover, regional organizations such as the EU have implemented measures to promote LGBTQ rights among member states. The EU's Charter of Fundamental Rights explicitly prohibits discrimination based on sexual orientation, and the European Court of Justice has ruled in favor of LGBTQ rights in several landmark cases. These actions underscore the importance of regional cooperation in advancing LGBTQ rights.

Strategies for Effective International Advocacy

To enhance the effectiveness of diplomatic efforts, several strategies can be employed. First, building coalitions among like-minded nations can amplify voices advocating for LGBTQ rights. Collaborative initiatives, such as joint statements or resolutions, can exert pressure on nations lagging in their commitments to human rights.

Second, engaging with local activists and organizations is crucial for understanding the unique challenges faced by LGBTQ individuals in different cultural contexts. International advocates must prioritize listening to and elevating local voices to ensure that their efforts are relevant and respectful.

Finally, leveraging technology and social media can facilitate cross-border collaboration and awareness. Online platforms enable activists to share experiences, resources, and strategies, fostering a sense of global solidarity. For example, campaigns like #LoveIsLove have transcended borders, uniting individuals in the fight for LGBTQ rights.

Conclusion

Taren Fira's commitment to diplomatic efforts and international cooperation exemplifies the potential for transformative change in the fight for LGBTQ rights. By navigating the complexities of international relations and fostering collaboration among diverse stakeholders, advocates can create a more inclusive world. As the global landscape continues to evolve, the importance of diplomacy in advancing LGBTQ rights remains paramount, underscoring the need for sustained efforts and solidarity across borders.

Supporting Grassroots Activism Worldwide

Grassroots activism serves as a powerful engine for social change, particularly in the realm of LGBTQ rights. It is characterized by its community-driven approach, where individuals mobilize at the local level to advocate for their rights and raise awareness about issues affecting their communities. This section explores the significance of supporting grassroots activism worldwide, the challenges it faces, and the strategies that can be employed to enhance its effectiveness.

The Importance of Grassroots Activism

Grassroots activism is vital for several reasons:

1. **Local Relevance**: Grassroots movements are often more attuned to the specific needs and cultural contexts of their communities. This local knowledge enables activists to develop strategies that resonate with their audience, leading to more effective advocacy.

2. **Empowerment**: By involving community members in the decision-making process, grassroots activism fosters a sense of ownership and empowerment. Individuals feel more invested in the outcomes when they participate actively in shaping their advocacy efforts.

3. **Diversity of Voices**: Grassroots movements often amplify the voices of marginalized groups within the LGBTQ community, including people of color, transgender individuals, and those with disabilities. This inclusivity ensures that advocacy efforts address the unique challenges faced by these populations.

4. **Sustainable Change**: Grassroots activism tends to focus on long-term solutions rather than quick fixes. By building strong community networks, these movements create sustainable change that can withstand political fluctuations and societal challenges.

Challenges Faced by Grassroots Activism

Despite its importance, grassroots activism encounters numerous obstacles:

1. **Funding Limitations**: Many grassroots organizations operate on limited budgets, which can hinder their ability to mobilize effectively. Securing funding from donors or grants is often a significant challenge, leading to reliance on volunteer labor and community support.

2. **Political Opposition**: Grassroots activists frequently face backlash from conservative political groups or governments that oppose LGBTQ rights. This resistance can manifest as legal barriers, harassment, or even violence against activists.

3. **Lack of Visibility**: Grassroots movements may struggle to gain visibility in a crowded media landscape. Larger organizations often dominate the narrative,

overshadowing local efforts and their unique contributions to the LGBTQ rights movement.

4. **Fragmentation**: The diversity of issues within the LGBTQ community can lead to fragmentation, with different groups focusing on specific aspects of advocacy. While this can be beneficial in addressing nuanced issues, it can also dilute collective efforts and weaken the overall movement.

Strategies for Supporting Grassroots Activism

To bolster grassroots activism worldwide, several strategies can be employed:

1. **Funding and Resource Allocation**: Providing financial support to grassroots organizations is crucial. This can include direct funding, grants, or creating partnerships with larger NGOs that can offer resources and training. For example, the *Global Fund for Women* has supported grassroots organizations worldwide by providing grants specifically aimed at advancing women's rights, including LGBTQ rights.

2. **Capacity Building**: Training and skill development are essential for grassroots activists. Workshops on advocacy strategies, media engagement, and fundraising can empower activists to enhance their effectiveness. Organizations like *OutRight Action International* offer training programs that equip activists with the necessary skills to advocate for LGBTQ rights effectively.

3. **Creating Networks**: Establishing networks among grassroots organizations can facilitate the sharing of resources, knowledge, and strategies. These networks can also amplify the voices of grassroots movements, increasing their visibility and impact. The *International Lesbian, Gay, Bisexual, Trans and Intersex Association (ILGA)* serves as an example of a network that connects grassroots organizations globally, fostering collaboration and solidarity.

4. **Utilizing Digital Platforms**: In the digital age, social media and online platforms can be powerful tools for grassroots activism. By leveraging these platforms, activists can reach wider audiences, mobilize support, and share their stories. Campaigns like *#BlackLivesMatter* demonstrate how digital activism can raise awareness and drive grassroots movements forward.

5. **Building Alliances with Established Organizations**: Collaborating with larger, established organizations can provide grassroots movements with additional support and resources. These partnerships can help amplify the message of grassroots activists and provide them with a platform to reach broader audiences.

Case Studies of Successful Grassroots Activism

Several grassroots movements worldwide exemplify the power of local activism in advancing LGBTQ rights:

1. **The Stonewall Riots**: Often cited as a catalyst for the modern LGBTQ rights movement, the Stonewall Riots of 1969 in New York City were a grassroots response to police brutality against LGBTQ individuals. The riots galvanized the community and led to the formation of numerous advocacy organizations, highlighting the power of local activism in effecting change.

2. **The Black LGBTQ+ Coalition**: In the United States, the Black LGBTQ+ Coalition has worked to address the intersection of race and sexual orientation. By focusing on the unique challenges faced by Black LGBTQ individuals, the coalition has successfully advocated for policy changes and increased visibility within the larger LGBTQ rights movement.

3. **The Global Queer Youth Network**: This international network connects grassroots organizations focused on LGBTQ youth advocacy. By sharing resources and strategies, the network has empowered local activists to address issues such as bullying, mental health, and access to education for LGBTQ youth.

Conclusion

Supporting grassroots activism worldwide is essential for fostering a more inclusive and equitable society for LGBTQ individuals. By recognizing the importance of local movements, addressing the challenges they face, and implementing effective strategies, advocates can help ensure that the voices of marginalized communities are heard and respected. The impact of grassroots activism is profound, and its potential to drive meaningful change in the fight for LGBTQ rights cannot be overstated. As Taren Fira's journey illustrates, the power of community-driven advocacy is a force that can ignite change on a global scale.

Addressing Global LGBTQ Health Disparities

In recent years, the global community has begun to recognize the significant health disparities faced by LGBTQ individuals. These disparities are often exacerbated by systemic discrimination, stigma, and a lack of access to appropriate healthcare services. This section aims to explore the multifaceted nature of LGBTQ health disparities, the underlying theoretical frameworks, the problems faced, and examples of effective interventions.

Theoretical Frameworks

Understanding health disparities within the LGBTQ community requires an intersectional approach. Intersectionality, as defined by Crenshaw (1989), emphasizes how various social identities—such as race, gender, and sexual orientation—interact to create unique experiences of oppression and privilege. This framework is crucial for addressing health disparities, as it allows for a nuanced understanding of how these identities can compound health risks.

Moreover, the Social Determinants of Health (SDOH) model posits that health outcomes are influenced by a range of factors, including socioeconomic status, education, and access to healthcare. For LGBTQ individuals, these determinants are often skewed due to societal marginalization and discrimination. For instance, individuals from lower socioeconomic backgrounds may face additional barriers to accessing healthcare, thereby exacerbating health disparities.

Problems Faced by LGBTQ Individuals

1. **Mental Health Disparities**: LGBTQ individuals are at a higher risk for mental health issues, including depression and anxiety. According to the National Alliance on Mental Illness (NAMI), LGBTQ youth are more than twice as likely to experience a mental health condition compared to their heterosexual peers. The stigma surrounding their identities often leads to social isolation, which can further exacerbate mental health issues.

2. **Substance Abuse**: Discrimination and social stigma contribute to higher rates of substance abuse among LGBTQ individuals. The 2015 U.S. Transgender Survey found that 30% of respondents reported using substances to cope with the stress of discrimination and violence.

3. **HIV/AIDS**: The LGBTQ community, particularly gay and bisexual men, continues to face significant challenges related to HIV/AIDS. According to the Centers for Disease Control and Prevention (CDC), in 2019, gay and bisexual men accounted for 69% of all new HIV diagnoses in the United States. Stigma and discrimination in healthcare settings often deter individuals from seeking testing and treatment.

4. **Access to Healthcare**: LGBTQ individuals frequently encounter barriers when accessing healthcare services. These barriers can include discrimination from healthcare providers, a lack of culturally competent care, and inadequate health insurance coverage. A study published in the *American Journal of Public Health* found that LGBTQ individuals are more likely to report avoiding medical care due to fear of discrimination.

SECTION TWO: UPHOLDING LGBTQ RIGHTS GLOBALLY   137

Examples of Effective Interventions

1. **Community Health Initiatives**: Organizations such as the *LGBTQ Health Initiative* have developed community-based programs aimed at improving health outcomes for LGBTQ individuals. These initiatives often focus on mental health support, substance abuse treatment, and sexual health education. For example, the *Trevor Project* provides crisis intervention and suicide prevention services for LGBTQ youth, addressing mental health disparities through dedicated outreach and support.

2. **Culturally Competent Care Training**: Training healthcare providers in culturally competent care is essential for reducing health disparities. Programs such as the *LGBTQ Health Provider Training* educate healthcare professionals on the unique needs of LGBTQ patients, helping to create a more inclusive healthcare environment. Research has shown that patients who receive care from culturally competent providers report higher satisfaction and better health outcomes.

3. **Policy Advocacy**: Advocacy for inclusive healthcare policies is crucial in addressing LGBTQ health disparities. Organizations like the *Human Rights Campaign* work to influence legislation that protects LGBTQ individuals from discrimination in healthcare settings. For instance, the Affordable Care Act's non-discrimination provisions have been instrumental in expanding access to healthcare for LGBTQ individuals.

4. **Global Health Partnerships**: International collaborations, such as the *Global Fund for Women*, focus on addressing health disparities on a global scale. By funding initiatives that promote LGBTQ health rights and access to care, these partnerships aim to dismantle the barriers that LGBTQ individuals face worldwide.

Conclusion

Addressing global LGBTQ health disparities requires a comprehensive understanding of the underlying issues, as well as targeted interventions that consider the unique challenges faced by this community. By leveraging theoretical frameworks such as intersectionality and the Social Determinants of Health, activists and healthcare providers can work together to create a more equitable healthcare system. Through community initiatives, culturally competent care, policy advocacy, and global partnerships, we can begin to dismantle the barriers that perpetuate health disparities and promote the well-being of LGBTQ individuals worldwide.

References:

- Crenshaw, K. (1989). Demarginalizing the Intersection of Race and Sex: A Black Feminist Critique of Antidiscrimination Doctrine, Feminist Theory and Antiracist Politics. *University of Chicago Legal Forum*, 1989(1), 139-167.

- National Alliance on Mental Illness. (n.d.). LGBTQ Mental Health. Retrieved from `https://nami.org`

- Centers for Disease Control and Prevention. (2020). HIV Surveillance Report, 2019. Retrieved from `https://www.cdc.gov/hiv/library/reports/hiv-surveillance.html`

- American Journal of Public Health. (2016). The Health of LGBTQ Individuals in the United States. *AJPH*, 106(10), 1755-1757.

- The Trevor Project. (n.d.). Retrieved from `https://www.thetrevorproject.org`

- Human Rights Campaign. (n.d.). Healthcare Equality Index. Retrieved from `https://www.hrc.org`

- Global Fund for Women. (n.d.). Retrieved from `https://www.globalfundforwomen.org`

Advocating for LGBTQ Rights in Conflict Zones

Advocating for LGBTQ rights in conflict zones presents a unique set of challenges and complexities that require a nuanced understanding of both human rights advocacy and the specific socio-political dynamics at play in these regions. In many conflict-affected areas, LGBTQ individuals face heightened risks of violence, discrimination, and persecution, often exacerbated by the prevailing instability and breakdown of legal protections. This section will explore the theoretical frameworks, practical challenges, and examples of advocacy efforts aimed at supporting LGBTQ rights in such contexts.

Theoretical Frameworks

The advocacy for LGBTQ rights in conflict zones can be situated within several theoretical frameworks, including human rights theory, intersectionality, and queer theory.

Human Rights Theory Human rights theory posits that all individuals possess inherent rights that must be protected, regardless of their sexual orientation or gender identity. The Universal Declaration of Human Rights (UDHR) asserts the rights to life, liberty, and security of person, which must extend to LGBTQ individuals in all contexts, including conflict zones. Advocates often invoke international human rights treaties, such as the International Covenant on Civil and Political Rights (ICCPR), to hold governments accountable for violations against LGBTQ individuals.

Intersectionality Intersectionality, a concept coined by Kimberlé Crenshaw, emphasizes the interconnected nature of social categorizations such as race, class, and gender, and how these intersections create overlapping systems of discrimination or disadvantage. In conflict zones, LGBTQ individuals may also face compounded vulnerabilities based on their ethnicity, religion, or socio-economic status, necessitating an intersectional approach to advocacy that addresses these multiple layers of oppression.

Queer Theory Queer theory challenges normative assumptions about sexuality and gender, advocating for a recognition of the fluidity and diversity of identities. In conflict zones, queer theory can inform advocacy by highlighting the need for inclusive frameworks that recognize and validate the experiences of LGBTQ individuals, particularly those who may not fit within traditional binary gender categories.

Challenges in Advocacy

Advocating for LGBTQ rights in conflict zones is fraught with challenges, including:

Increased Violence and Persecution Conflict often leads to a breakdown of law and order, resulting in increased violence against marginalized groups, including LGBTQ individuals. Reports from regions such as Syria and Afghanistan illustrate how LGBTQ individuals are targeted by both state and non-state actors. For example, in Syria, LGBTQ individuals have faced torture and execution by extremist groups, while in Afghanistan, the Taliban's resurgence has led to renewed fears of persecution for LGBTQ individuals.

Cultural and Societal Norms In many conflict zones, deeply entrenched cultural and societal norms perpetuate homophobia and transphobia. Advocacy efforts must navigate these cultural contexts sensitively, recognizing that overt challenges to traditional values may provoke backlash. For instance, in countries like Uganda, where anti-LGBTQ legislation has been enacted, advocacy organizations have had to adopt more discreet strategies to support LGBTQ individuals without exacerbating their vulnerabilities.

Limited Resources and Access Conflict zones often suffer from a lack of resources, which can hinder advocacy efforts. Organizations working to support LGBTQ rights may struggle to secure funding, personnel, and safe spaces for their activities. This limitation can be particularly acute in regions where humanitarian needs are prioritized over LGBTQ rights, leading to a marginalization of these issues within broader advocacy efforts.

Examples of Advocacy Efforts

Despite the challenges, there have been notable examples of advocacy for LGBTQ rights in conflict zones:

International Advocacy and Support Organizations such as Human Rights Watch and Amnesty International have documented abuses against LGBTQ individuals in conflict zones and called for international action. Their reports often serve as vital tools for raising awareness and pressuring governments to uphold human rights standards. For instance, following the rise of ISIS in Iraq, advocacy groups highlighted the targeted killings of LGBTQ individuals, prompting international outcry and calls for accountability.

Local and Grassroots Initiatives Grassroots organizations within conflict zones have also emerged, often led by LGBTQ individuals themselves. These groups provide critical support networks, safe spaces, and resources for those affected by conflict. In Colombia, for example, LGBTQ activists have worked to provide legal support and mental health services to individuals displaced by violence, demonstrating resilience and resourcefulness in the face of adversity.

Digital Advocacy and Global Solidarity The rise of digital platforms has enabled LGBTQ activists in conflict zones to connect with global allies, share their stories, and mobilize support. Social media campaigns have raised awareness about the plight of LGBTQ individuals in conflict areas, fostering a sense of global solidarity. For instance, the #FreeTheGays campaign highlighted the experiences of LGBTQ individuals in regions facing persecution, generating international support and advocacy efforts.

Conclusion

Advocating for LGBTQ rights in conflict zones is a complex and multifaceted endeavor that requires an understanding of the unique challenges faced by LGBTQ individuals in these contexts. By employing theoretical frameworks such as human rights theory, intersectionality, and queer theory, advocates can develop more effective strategies to support LGBTQ individuals in conflict-affected areas. Despite the obstacles, the resilience of local activists and the power of international solidarity offer hope for advancing LGBTQ rights even in the most challenging circumstances. As the global community continues to confront the realities of conflict, it is imperative that LGBTQ rights remain a priority in humanitarian and advocacy efforts, ensuring that all individuals, regardless of their sexual orientation or gender identity, are afforded the dignity and rights they deserve.

Pushing for LGBTQ Rights in International Law

In the contemporary landscape of human rights, the struggle for LGBTQ rights has increasingly found its way into the realm of international law. As nations grapple with the complexities of diversity, cultural norms, and human dignity, the call for universal LGBTQ rights has become a rallying point for activists, legal scholars, and policymakers alike. This section explores the theoretical frameworks, challenges, and notable examples of advocacy that aim to entrench LGBTQ rights within international legal instruments.

Theoretical Frameworks

At the heart of the push for LGBTQ rights in international law lies the principle of universality. This principle asserts that human rights are inherent to all individuals, regardless of their sexual orientation or gender identity. The Universal Declaration of Human Rights (UDHR), adopted by the United Nations General Assembly in 1948, serves as a foundational document that articulates this principle. Article 1 of the UDHR states,

> "All human beings are born free and equal in dignity and rights."

However, the challenge arises in the interpretation and application of this principle within diverse cultural contexts. The theory of cultural relativism posits that human rights must be understood within the cultural frameworks of individual societies, which can lead to tensions between universal human rights and local customs.

To navigate this tension, scholars like Jack Donnelly advocate for a synthesis of universalism and relativism, suggesting that while cultural contexts matter, they should not be used to justify human rights violations. This perspective underscores the necessity of integrating LGBTQ rights into the broader human rights discourse, emphasizing that cultural diversity should not come at the expense of fundamental human rights.

Challenges to International LGBTQ Rights

Despite the theoretical foundations supporting LGBTQ rights, significant challenges persist in their realization at the international level. One of the primary obstacles is the lack of binding international legal instruments specifically addressing LGBTQ rights. While the International Covenant on Civil and Political Rights (ICCPR) and the International Covenant on Economic, Social and Cultural Rights (ICESCR) provide a broad framework for human rights, they do not explicitly mention sexual orientation or gender identity.

Moreover, many countries maintain laws that criminalize same-sex relationships or discriminate against LGBTQ individuals, often citing cultural or religious justifications. For instance, Section 377 of the Indian Penal Code, which criminalized consensual same-sex relations, exemplified how colonial-era laws continue to perpetuate discrimination. Although the Indian Supreme Court decriminalized homosexuality in 2018, the remnants of such legal frameworks persist in many nations, impeding progress toward universal LGBTQ rights.

Notable Examples of Advocacy

Activism for LGBTQ rights within international law has gained momentum through various initiatives and organizations. One notable example is the Yogyakarta Principles, developed in 2006 by a group of international legal experts. These principles articulate how international human rights law should apply to issues of sexual orientation and gender identity. They serve as a guiding framework for states and civil society in advocating for the rights of LGBTQ individuals.

Additionally, the United Nations Free & Equal campaign has played a crucial role in raising awareness about LGBTQ rights globally. This campaign aims to promote equal rights and fair treatment for LGBTQ individuals, challenging discriminatory laws and practices. The campaign's visibility has helped shift public opinion and encourage governments to adopt more inclusive policies.

Furthermore, the establishment of the United Nations Independent Expert on Sexual Orientation and Gender Identity in 2016 marked a significant step toward institutionalizing LGBTQ rights within the UN system. This position is tasked with addressing violence and discrimination against LGBTQ individuals, providing a platform for advocacy and accountability.

Case Studies of Legal Progress

Examining specific case studies highlights the potential for advancing LGBTQ rights through international law. For instance, in 2018, the Inter-American Court of Human Rights issued an advisory opinion recognizing the rights of same-sex couples to marry and adopt children. This landmark ruling not only set a precedent for member states of the Organization of American States but also reinforced the notion that LGBTQ rights are integral to human rights.

Similarly, the European Court of Human Rights has ruled in favor of LGBTQ rights in several cases, including *Oliari and Others v. Italy*, where the court found Italy's failure to recognize same-sex unions violated the European Convention on Human Rights. Such decisions demonstrate the capacity of regional human rights mechanisms to promote and protect LGBTQ rights.

Conclusion

The journey toward integrating LGBTQ rights into international law is fraught with challenges, yet it is a vital endeavor for achieving universal human rights. By leveraging theoretical frameworks, advocating for binding legal instruments, and drawing on successful case studies, activists and legal scholars can continue to push for the recognition and protection of LGBTQ rights on a global scale. As Taren Fira once articulated, "The fight for equality knows no borders; it is a shared struggle that binds us all in our quest for dignity and justice." This sentiment encapsulates the essence of the ongoing movement, reminding us that the pursuit of LGBTQ rights is not merely a legal battle but a profound moral imperative that transcends cultural and national boundaries.

Section Three: Facing Political Opposition

Taren Fira and the Rise of Right-Wing Movements

In the ever-evolving landscape of LGBTQ activism, Taren Fira emerged as a beacon of hope and resilience amidst the tumultuous backdrop of rising right-wing movements. This section delves into the complex interplay between Fira's advocacy and the emergence of conservative ideologies that sought to undermine the progress made in LGBTQ rights.

The Political Climate

The rise of right-wing movements can be traced back to a confluence of factors, including economic instability, cultural backlash, and the increasing visibility of LGBTQ individuals in society. This political climate fostered an environment where fear and misinformation thrived, leading to the resurgence of anti-LGBTQ rhetoric. As Fira navigated this challenging landscape, she confronted not only the overt hostility of these movements but also the insidious nature of their arguments, which often framed LGBTQ rights as a threat to traditional values.

Theoretical Framework

To understand the dynamics at play, we can employ the framework of *Social Identity Theory*, which posits that individuals derive a sense of self from their group memberships. Right-wing movements often capitalize on this by promoting an in-group versus out-group mentality, positioning LGBTQ individuals as outsiders threatening the cohesion of the "traditional" family unit. This framing not only galvanizes support among conservative constituents but also legitimizes discriminatory policies.

$$\text{In-group Bias} = \frac{\text{Positive evaluations of in-group members}}{\text{Total evaluations}} \qquad (42)$$

This equation illustrates how the bias towards one's own group can lead to the marginalization of others, reinforcing the divide between LGBTQ individuals and their detractors.

Taren Fira's Response

Fira's approach to counteracting the rise of right-wing movements was multifaceted. She recognized the importance of *narrative framing*—the way stories are told and interpreted. By sharing personal stories of LGBTQ individuals and their struggles, Fira aimed to humanize the movement and foster empathy among those who might otherwise align with conservative ideologies.

Case Studies

A pivotal moment in Fira's activism came during the 2020 Alyndra Pride Festival, which faced significant backlash from right-wing groups. These groups organized protests, claiming that the festival promoted "immorality" and "decay" in society. In response, Fira led a counter-campaign that highlighted the positive contributions of LGBTQ individuals to the community, emphasizing themes of love, acceptance, and resilience.

This campaign utilized social media platforms, particularly Twitter and Instagram, to amplify voices that were often drowned out by hate. The hashtag #LoveIsStronger became a rallying cry, uniting allies and supporters in defense of LGBTQ rights. The success of this campaign not only demonstrated the power of grassroots mobilization but also showcased Fira's ability to adapt to the changing political landscape.

Challenges Faced

Despite her successes, Fira faced considerable challenges. The rise of right-wing movements was accompanied by an increase in hate crimes and legislative attacks on LGBTQ rights. For instance, numerous states introduced bills aimed at restricting transgender rights, particularly in areas such as healthcare and education. Fira recognized that these legislative efforts were not isolated incidents but part of a broader strategy to roll back hard-won rights.

In her advocacy, Fira often referenced the concept of *precarity*—the state of being subject to economic, social, and political instability. She argued that the precariousness of LGBTQ lives was exacerbated by right-wing policies, which sought to undermine the very foundations of equality and justice.

$$\text{Precarity Index} = \frac{\text{Vulnerable populations}}{\text{Total population}} \times 100 \qquad (43)$$

This index serves as a reminder of the disproportionate impact that political movements can have on marginalized communities.

Building Coalitions

In the face of adversity, Fira emphasized the importance of coalition-building. She sought to unite various social justice movements, recognizing that the fight for LGBTQ rights was intertwined with broader struggles for racial, economic, and gender justice. By fostering alliances with organizations focused on these intersecting issues, Fira was able to create a more robust and resilient movement that could withstand the pressures of right-wing opposition.

Conclusion

Taren Fira's journey through the rise of right-wing movements exemplifies the resilience and adaptability required of modern activists. By leveraging narrative, building coalitions, and confronting the challenges posed by conservative ideologies, Fira not only defended LGBTQ rights but also enriched the broader discourse on social justice. As the political landscape continues to evolve, her legacy serves as a testament to the enduring power of advocacy in the face of adversity.

Tackling Hate Speech and Online Harassment

In the digital age, the proliferation of social media and online platforms has transformed the landscape of activism, providing a powerful tool for marginalized voices. However, this same space has also become a breeding ground for hate speech and online harassment, particularly against LGBTQ individuals. In this section, we will explore the complexities of tackling hate speech and online harassment, discussing relevant theories, the problems they pose, and practical examples of resistance.

Understanding Hate Speech

Hate speech is defined as any communication that belittles, incites violence, or discriminates against individuals or groups based on attributes such as race, ethnicity, religion, sexual orientation, or gender identity. The legal definitions of hate speech vary across jurisdictions, but the common thread is that it seeks to dehumanize and marginalize targeted groups.

A widely cited theory in understanding hate speech is the *Social Identity Theory*, which posits that individuals derive a sense of self from their group memberships. This can lead to in-group favoritism and out-group hostility, fueling the cycle of hate speech. When individuals perceive their identity as threatened, they may resort to derogatory language as a means of reinforcing their own group identity.

The Impact of Online Harassment

Online harassment can take many forms, including cyberbullying, doxxing (the act of publicly revealing private information), and targeted trolling. The anonymity afforded by the internet often emboldens perpetrators, leading to an escalation of aggressive behaviors. According to a study conducted by the Pew Research Center, 40% of Americans have experienced some form of online harassment, with LGBTQ individuals disproportionately affected.

The psychological impact of online harassment can be profound. Victims often experience anxiety, depression, and a sense of isolation. The *Cumulative Trauma Theory* suggests that repeated exposure to trauma, such as online harassment, can lead to long-term psychological effects that compound over time. For LGBTQ individuals, the intersection of their sexual orientation or gender identity with online harassment can exacerbate feelings of vulnerability and marginalization.

Strategies for Addressing Hate Speech

Addressing hate speech and online harassment requires a multifaceted approach. Here are some effective strategies:

- **Education and Awareness:** Raising awareness about the impact of hate speech and online harassment is crucial. Educational campaigns can help individuals understand the consequences of their words and foster empathy towards marginalized communities.

- **Community Guidelines:** Online platforms must implement and enforce clear community guidelines that prohibit hate speech and harassment. This includes establishing reporting mechanisms that are accessible and responsive.

- **Digital Literacy:** Empowering users with digital literacy skills can help them navigate online spaces more safely. This includes understanding privacy settings, recognizing harmful content, and knowing how to report abuse.

- **Support Systems:** Creating support networks for victims of online harassment is essential. This can involve peer support groups, mental health resources, and legal assistance for those facing severe harassment.

Examples of Resistance

Several organizations and movements have emerged to combat hate speech and online harassment. One notable example is the *Trevor Project*, which provides crisis intervention and suicide prevention services to LGBTQ youth. They actively campaign against online bullying and promote safe online spaces for young people.

Another example is the hashtag movement #StopHateForProfit, which encourages businesses to withdraw advertising from platforms that do not adequately address hate speech. This movement gained traction in 2020, leading to significant financial pressure on social media companies to implement stricter policies against hate speech.

Legal and Policy Frameworks

In many countries, hate speech laws exist to protect individuals from discrimination and violence. However, the enforcement of these laws can be inconsistent. For instance, while the European Union has established legal frameworks to combat hate speech, the United States has a more permissive approach due to First Amendment protections.

Advocacy for stronger legal protections is essential. This includes lobbying for comprehensive hate crime legislation that encompasses online harassment and holds perpetrators accountable. Moreover, international cooperation is necessary to address cross-border harassment, as the internet transcends national boundaries.

Conclusion

Tackling hate speech and online harassment is an ongoing challenge that requires concerted efforts from individuals, communities, and policymakers. By understanding the underlying theories, recognizing the impact on marginalized groups, and implementing effective strategies, we can create a safer online environment for all. As Taren Fira would emphasize, the fight against hate is not just about protecting individual rights; it is about fostering a culture of respect, inclusivity, and solidarity in our digital spaces.

Standing Strong Against Discriminatory Policies

Standing strong against discriminatory policies is a crucial aspect of LGBTQ activism, especially in a political landscape that often seeks to undermine the rights of marginalized communities. This section explores the theoretical frameworks,

SECTION THREE: FACING POLITICAL OPPOSITION

real-world challenges, and practical examples of how activists, like Taren Fira, have navigated the complexities of combating discriminatory legislation.

Theoretical Frameworks

At the heart of advocacy against discriminatory policies lies the concept of **social justice**, which emphasizes the fair distribution of resources and opportunities, as well as the protection of individual rights. Theories of **intersectionality**, coined by Kimberlé Crenshaw, are also critical, as they highlight how various forms of discrimination—such as those based on race, gender, and sexual orientation—intersect and compound the effects of oppression.

$$\text{Social Justice} = \text{Equity} + \text{Access} + \text{Participation} \qquad (44)$$

This equation illustrates that social justice is not merely about equality but also involves ensuring that all individuals have equitable access to resources and opportunities, and that they can participate fully in society.

Identifying Discriminatory Policies

Discriminatory policies can manifest in various forms, including:

- **Legislation that restricts marriage rights** for same-sex couples.
- **Anti-transgender laws** that seek to limit access to healthcare or participation in sports.
- **Employment discrimination laws** that allow employers to fire individuals based on their sexual orientation or gender identity.
- **Hate crime legislation** that fails to recognize or protect LGBTQ individuals.

Each of these policies not only impacts the individuals directly affected but also sends a broader societal message that discrimination is acceptable.

Challenges in Advocacy

Activists face numerous challenges when standing against discriminatory policies, including:

- **Political Resistance:** Many lawmakers may be resistant to change due to personal beliefs, constituency pressures, or party lines.

- **Public Perception:** Misunderstanding and stereotypes about LGBTQ individuals can hinder public support for policy changes.

- **Resource Limitations:** Activist organizations often operate with limited funding and manpower, making it difficult to mount large-scale campaigns.

- **Legal Barriers:** Existing laws may protect discriminatory practices, complicating efforts to enact change.

Strategies for Advocacy

To effectively combat discriminatory policies, Taren Fira and other activists employ a variety of strategies:

- **Grassroots Mobilization:** Building a base of support within local communities can amplify voices and increase pressure on lawmakers. Organizing rallies, petitions, and community forums can engage the public and raise awareness.

- **Coalition Building:** Collaborating with other marginalized groups can strengthen the advocacy efforts. For example, LGBTQ activists have worked alongside racial justice organizations to address intersectional issues.

- **Legal Challenges:** Initiating lawsuits against discriminatory laws can lead to judicial review and potentially overturn harmful legislation. Landmark cases, such as *Obergefell v. Hodges*, which legalized same-sex marriage in the United States, exemplify this approach.

- **Education and Awareness Campaigns:** Informing the public about the realities of LGBTQ lives can combat stereotypes and foster empathy. Campaigns that share personal stories, such as those from Taren Fira, can humanize the issues at stake.

Examples of Successful Advocacy

Several notable victories in the fight against discriminatory policies illustrate the power of activism:

- In 2015, the U.S. Supreme Court ruling in *Obergefell v. Hodges* established marriage equality, demonstrating the effectiveness of legal challenges in securing rights for LGBTQ individuals.

SECTION THREE: FACING POLITICAL OPPOSITION 151

- The repeal of "Don't Ask, Don't Tell" in 2011 allowed LGBTQ individuals to serve openly in the military, showcasing the impact of sustained advocacy and public support.

- Numerous states have enacted anti-discrimination laws in employment and housing, often as a result of grassroots organizing and coalition building.

Conclusion

Standing strong against discriminatory policies requires a multifaceted approach that combines theoretical understanding, grassroots mobilization, coalition building, and strategic legal action. As Taren Fira exemplifies, the fight for LGBTQ rights is not just about changing laws but also about transforming hearts and minds. Activism in this realm is an ongoing journey that demands resilience, creativity, and unwavering commitment to justice for all.

$$\text{Advocacy Success} = \text{Mobilization} + \text{Education} + \text{Legal Action} \qquad (45)$$

In conclusion, the commitment to standing strong against discriminatory policies is vital for advancing LGBTQ rights and ensuring that all individuals can live authentically and without fear of discrimination. The journey may be fraught with challenges, but the collective strength of activists like Taren Fira continues to pave the way for a more equitable future.

Strategies for Countering Political Backlash

Political backlash against LGBTQ rights and advocacy can manifest in various forms, ranging from legislative attacks to social media harassment. To effectively counter such backlash, activists and allies must employ a multifaceted approach that combines strategic communication, grassroots mobilization, and coalition-building. This section outlines key strategies that can be utilized to mitigate the impact of political backlash and promote a resilient LGBTQ movement.

1. Understanding the Nature of Backlash

Before developing strategies to counter backlash, it is crucial to understand its nature. Political backlash often arises from shifts in public opinion, fear of change, and the mobilization of conservative groups. According to [?], backlash can be understood through the lens of social movement theory, where the response to a movement often reflects the broader societal tensions surrounding identity and rights.

2. Building a Strong Communication Strategy

A robust communication strategy is essential in countering political backlash. This involves:

- **Framing the Narrative:** Activists must frame LGBTQ rights as fundamental human rights, emphasizing the universality of equality and dignity. This can be achieved through storytelling that highlights personal experiences and the positive contributions of LGBTQ individuals to society.

- **Utilizing Data and Research:** Presenting empirical evidence that demonstrates the benefits of inclusive policies can counteract misinformation. For instance, studies showing that marriage equality positively impacts mental health outcomes for LGBTQ individuals can serve as compelling arguments against regressive policies.

- **Engaging in Media Advocacy:** Proactively engaging with media outlets to ensure accurate representation of LGBTQ issues is vital. This includes providing expert commentary, writing op-eds, and participating in interviews to clarify misconceptions and counter negative narratives.

3. Grassroots Mobilization and Community Engagement

Grassroots mobilization is critical in building a resilient response to political backlash. Strategies include:

- **Community Organizing:** Forming local coalitions to mobilize community members around LGBTQ rights can create a strong support network. This includes organizing town halls, workshops, and educational events to raise awareness and foster solidarity.

- **Direct Action:** Nonviolent direct action, such as protests and demonstrations, can draw attention to injustices and galvanize public support. Historical examples, such as the Stonewall Riots, illustrate the power of collective action in challenging oppressive systems.

- **Voter Mobilization:** Encouraging voter registration and participation in elections can help shift political power dynamics. Engaging with local communities to educate them about candidates' positions on LGBTQ issues is essential for building a supportive political environment.

4. Coalition-Building Across Movements

Building coalitions with other social justice movements can amplify the LGBTQ rights agenda. This involves:

- **Intersectional Advocacy:** Recognizing the interconnectedness of various social justice issues, such as racial justice, gender equality, and economic rights, can strengthen the movement. Collaborating with organizations representing marginalized communities can enhance visibility and support for LGBTQ issues.

- **Shared Campaigns:** Joint campaigns that address overlapping issues can mobilize broader support. For example, campaigns that advocate for both LGBTQ rights and racial justice can resonate with diverse audiences, fostering a sense of shared struggle and solidarity.

- **Resource Sharing:** Pooling resources and expertise with allied organizations can enhance the effectiveness of advocacy efforts. This includes sharing research, organizing events, and providing training for activists to build capacity across movements.

5. Legal and Policy Advocacy

Countering political backlash also requires strategic legal and policy advocacy:

- **Litigation:** Utilizing the judicial system to challenge discriminatory laws and practices can serve as a powerful countermeasure against backlash. Landmark cases, such as *Obergefell v. Hodges*, which legalized same-sex marriage in the United States, demonstrate the impact of strategic litigation.

- **Lobbying Efforts:** Engaging in lobbying to influence policymakers is crucial. This includes building relationships with legislators, providing them with data and personal stories, and advocating for inclusive policies at local, state, and national levels.

- **Monitoring Legislation:** Keeping a close watch on legislative developments and responding swiftly to proposed anti-LGBTQ bills is essential. Activists should mobilize constituents to contact their representatives and express opposition to harmful legislation.

6. Resilience and Self-Care

Finally, resilience and self-care are vital components in countering political backlash. Activists must prioritize their mental health and well-being to sustain their efforts:

- **Creating Support Networks:** Establishing support groups for activists can provide a safe space to share experiences and coping strategies. This fosters a sense of community and collective resilience.

- **Practicing Self-Care:** Encouraging self-care practices, such as mindfulness, exercise, and creative outlets, can help activists manage stress and prevent burnout. The importance of self-care in activism cannot be overstated, as it sustains the movement in the long run.

- **Celebrating Victories:** Recognizing and celebrating small victories can boost morale and motivation. This includes acknowledging the efforts of individuals and groups who contribute to the movement, reinforcing the idea that every action counts.

In conclusion, countering political backlash requires a comprehensive approach that integrates communication strategies, grassroots mobilization, coalition-building, legal advocacy, and self-care. By employing these strategies, LGBTQ activists can navigate the challenges posed by backlash and continue to advance the fight for equality and justice.

Lessons Learned in the Political Arena

In the tumultuous landscape of LGBTQ activism, navigating the political arena has proven to be both a formidable challenge and an enlightening journey for Taren Fira. Through her experiences, several key lessons emerged that not only shaped her approach but also offered invaluable insights for future activists. These lessons highlight the importance of resilience, strategic thinking, and the necessity of building coalitions.

1. The Importance of Resilience

One of the most significant lessons Taren learned is the necessity of resilience in the face of political opposition. Activism is often met with backlash, particularly from conservative factions that oppose LGBTQ rights. Taren's early encounters with resistance taught her that setbacks are not failures but rather opportunities for growth. For instance, during the initial push for marriage equality in Alyndra,

Taren faced intense criticism and organized protests from right-wing groups. Rather than succumbing to despair, she utilized these challenges to galvanize her supporters, holding rallies that showcased the strength of the LGBTQ community.

2. Strategic Communication

Effective communication is a cornerstone of successful advocacy. Taren discovered that framing issues in a way that resonates with the broader public is crucial. By employing narratives that emphasize shared values—such as love, family, and equality—she was able to shift public opinion. For example, during a pivotal debate on LGBTQ rights legislation, Taren articulated the emotional and social benefits of inclusivity, drawing parallels to universally cherished ideals. This approach not only garnered media attention but also swayed undecided voters, illustrating the power of strategic messaging.

3. Building Coalitions

The strength of an activist movement often lies in its ability to forge alliances across diverse groups. Taren recognized that LGBTQ rights are interconnected with other social justice issues, including racial equality, gender justice, and economic rights. By collaborating with various organizations, Taren was able to amplify her message and broaden her base of support. A notable example was her partnership with a local racial justice organization during the "Pride and Justice" campaign, which successfully highlighted the intersectionality of struggles faced by marginalized communities.

4. Understanding Political Dynamics

A thorough understanding of political dynamics is essential for effective advocacy. Taren learned to navigate the complexities of lobbying, recognizing the importance of building relationships with political leaders and understanding their motivations. She often remarked, "To change the law, you must first understand the lawmakers." This insight proved pivotal when she lobbied for the Equality Act, where her knowledge of the legislative process allowed her to anticipate challenges and prepare counterarguments.

5. The Role of Grassroots Mobilization

Grassroots mobilization remains a powerful tool for enacting change. Taren's experiences underscored the impact of engaging the community in advocacy efforts. During her campaigns, she organized door-to-door outreach programs to educate citizens about LGBTQ issues. This initiative not only increased awareness but also fostered a sense of ownership among community members. The success of these efforts was evident when local citizens rallied in unprecedented numbers during the legislative hearings, demonstrating the potency of grassroots activism.

6. The Necessity of Political Education

Political education is crucial for empowering activists and constituents alike. Taren emphasized the importance of educating the LGBTQ community about their rights and the political process. She initiated workshops that focused on understanding legislation, lobbying techniques, and effective advocacy strategies. By equipping individuals with knowledge, Taren fostered a generation of informed advocates who could navigate the political landscape with confidence.

7. Embracing Nonviolent Resistance

Taren's journey also highlighted the effectiveness of nonviolent resistance as a means of confronting political opposition. Drawing from historical movements, she employed peaceful demonstrations, sit-ins, and creative expressions of dissent to challenge discriminatory policies. One of the most memorable actions was the "Kiss-In" at a local government building, where activists publicly displayed affection to counteract anti-LGBTQ rhetoric. This tactic not only attracted media attention but also humanized the struggle for rights, fostering empathy among onlookers.

8. The Power of Personal Narratives

Personal narratives serve as a compelling tool in political advocacy. Taren learned that sharing stories of lived experiences can humanize abstract issues, making them relatable to a broader audience. During public hearings, she often invited individuals to share their personal journeys, illustrating the real-world impact of legislative decisions. These narratives proved instrumental in swaying public opinion and influencing lawmakers, as they showcased the urgency of LGBTQ rights in a deeply personal context.

9. The Need for Adaptability

The political landscape is ever-evolving, and Taren's experiences taught her the importance of adaptability. Strategies that worked in one context may not be effective in another; thus, being flexible and responsive to changing circumstances is vital. For instance, when faced with a sudden shift in public sentiment regarding transgender rights, Taren pivoted her advocacy efforts to focus on educational campaigns that addressed misconceptions and fostered understanding.

10. Celebrating Small Victories

Finally, Taren learned the importance of celebrating small victories along the way. In the political arena, progress can often feel slow and arduous. By acknowledging and celebrating incremental successes—such as the passage of local anti-discrimination ordinances—Taren maintained momentum and morale within the community. These celebrations served as reminders of the collective effort and resilience of the LGBTQ movement, reinforcing the idea that every step forward is a step toward greater equality.

In conclusion, the lessons learned by Taren Fira in the political arena encapsulate the complexities of LGBTQ activism. Through resilience, strategic communication, coalition-building, and grassroots mobilization, she navigated challenges and forged a path toward meaningful change. These insights not only shaped her journey but also provide a roadmap for future activists striving for equality and justice.

Civil Disobedience and Nonviolent Resistance

Civil disobedience and nonviolent resistance have long been powerful strategies employed by activists seeking to challenge unjust laws and societal norms. These methods, rooted in the principles of moral conviction and ethical action, allow individuals and groups to express dissent without resorting to violence, thereby emphasizing the strength of their message over the means of delivery.

Theoretical Foundations

Civil disobedience is often associated with the philosophical ideas of thinkers such as Henry David Thoreau, Mahatma Gandhi, and Martin Luther King Jr. Thoreau's seminal essay, "Civil Disobedience," argues that individuals should not allow governments to overrule or atrophy their consciences. He famously stated, "That government is best which governs least." This notion underscores the belief that individuals have a moral obligation to resist unjust laws.

Gandhi's approach to nonviolent resistance, or *Satyagraha*, emphasizes the power of love and truth in confronting oppression. He articulated that nonviolence is not merely the absence of violence but a powerful weapon of the oppressed. Similarly, King adopted these principles, advocating for nonviolent protest as a means to achieve civil rights and social justice. He asserted, "Nonviolent resistance is a powerful and just weapon."

Challenges and Critiques

Despite its noble intentions, civil disobedience is not without its challenges. Critics argue that such actions can lead to chaos and undermine the rule of law. Additionally, the effectiveness of nonviolent resistance can be contingent upon various factors, including the political climate, the level of public support, and the response from authorities.

For instance, during the Stonewall Riots in 1969, which are often credited with igniting the modern LGBTQ rights movement, participants engaged in acts of civil disobedience against police harassment. While the riots were spontaneous and not planned as a nonviolent protest, they highlighted the frustrations of the LGBTQ community and catalyzed subsequent organized efforts for equality. However, the violent nature of the riots led to mixed reactions, complicating the narrative of peaceful resistance.

Successful Examples

One of the most prominent examples of civil disobedience in the LGBTQ rights movement is the 1987 March on Washington for Lesbian and Gay Rights. This event brought together hundreds of thousands of activists advocating for equal rights and protections. Participants engaged in nonviolent demonstrations, including sit-ins and die-ins, to draw attention to the AIDS crisis and the lack of government response. The march was pivotal in raising awareness and mobilizing support for LGBTQ issues.

Moreover, the *Queer Liberation March* in 2019, held in New York City, served as a reminder of the roots of LGBTQ activism. Unlike the official Pride events, this march emphasized the need for continued activism and civil disobedience against systemic injustices. Participants chanted slogans and carried signs that called for the inclusion of marginalized voices, showcasing the power of collective action through nonviolent means.

The Role of Nonviolent Resistance in Modern Activism

In contemporary activism, nonviolent resistance continues to play a crucial role. Movements such as Black Lives Matter and the Women's March have incorporated elements of civil disobedience, demonstrating the effectiveness of peaceful protests in advocating for social change. These movements highlight the importance of solidarity and intersectionality, aligning with Taren Fira's advocacy for marginalized voices within the LGBTQ community.

The use of social media has also transformed the landscape of civil disobedience. Activists can now organize and mobilize efforts quickly, amplifying their message to a global audience. Online campaigns, such as the #MeToo movement, illustrate how digital platforms can facilitate nonviolent resistance by raising awareness and fostering community support.

Conclusion

In conclusion, civil disobedience and nonviolent resistance remain integral to the fight for LGBTQ rights and broader social justice. These methods exemplify the power of collective action grounded in moral conviction. As Taren Fira's journey illustrates, the commitment to nonviolence not only challenges oppressive systems but also fosters a sense of community and solidarity among activists. The legacy of civil disobedience serves as a reminder that change is possible through courage, compassion, and unwavering resolve.

Mobilizing Grassroots Activism

Mobilizing grassroots activism is a fundamental strategy in the fight for LGBTQ rights, particularly in a world where systemic barriers often hinder progress. Grassroots movements arise from the community level, emphasizing local involvement and collective action. This approach empowers individuals by encouraging them to take ownership of their advocacy efforts, fostering a sense of agency and solidarity among marginalized groups.

Theoretical Framework

The theoretical underpinnings of grassroots activism can be traced back to social movement theory, which posits that collective action arises in response to perceived grievances and injustices. According to Tilly and Tarrow (2015), social movements are characterized by sustained interactions between challengers and authorities, where the former seek to promote their interests and rights. In the context of LGBTQ activism, grassroots movements often emerge as a response to discrimination, violence, and systemic inequality faced by queer individuals.

A key aspect of grassroots mobilization is the concept of *collective efficacy*, which refers to the shared belief among group members in their ability to effect change. Bandura (1997) posits that when individuals perceive themselves as capable of influencing outcomes, they are more likely to engage in collective action.

This sense of empowerment is crucial for grassroots activists, who often face significant opposition from entrenched power structures.

Challenges to Mobilization

Despite the potential for grassroots activism to drive meaningful change, several challenges can hinder its effectiveness. These include:

- **Resource Limitations:** Many grassroots organizations operate with limited financial and human resources, making it difficult to sustain long-term campaigns. According to a report by the Global Fund for Human Rights (2020), over 60% of LGBTQ organizations worldwide struggle to secure funding.

- **Fragmentation:** The LGBTQ community is diverse, encompassing a wide range of identities and experiences. This diversity can lead to fragmentation within movements, where different groups prioritize varying issues. As Crenshaw (1989) highlights, intersectionality must be considered to ensure that all voices are heard and represented.

- **Backlash and Repression:** Grassroots activists often face backlash from conservative groups and government authorities. This can manifest in various forms, including legal challenges, public harassment, and even violence. For instance, during the 2016 Pulse nightclub shooting in Orlando, Florida, the LGBTQ community faced heightened scrutiny and backlash in the aftermath of the tragedy.

Strategies for Effective Mobilization

To overcome these challenges, grassroots activists can employ several strategies:

- **Building Coalitions:** Collaborating with other social justice movements can amplify the impact of grassroots efforts. For example, the Black Lives Matter movement has successfully partnered with LGBTQ organizations to address issues of police violence against marginalized communities. This intersectional approach broadens the base of support and fosters solidarity among diverse groups.

- **Utilizing Digital Platforms:** The advent of social media has transformed grassroots activism, allowing for rapid information dissemination and mobilization. Platforms such as Twitter, Instagram, and TikTok enable activists to share their stories, organize events, and engage with a global audience. The viral #BlackTransLivesMatter campaign exemplifies how digital activism can mobilize support for marginalized voices within the LGBTQ community.

- **Creating Safe Spaces:** Establishing safe spaces for dialogue and community-building is essential for fostering grassroots activism. These spaces allow individuals to share their experiences, build connections, and strategize collectively. Organizations like The Trevor Project provide vital resources and support for LGBTQ youth, creating a sense of belonging and empowerment.

- **Engaging in Direct Action:** Grassroots activism often involves direct action tactics, such as protests, sit-ins, and boycotts. These methods can draw public attention to pressing issues and pressure decision-makers to enact change. For instance, the Stonewall Riots of 1969 served as a catalyst for the modern LGBTQ rights movement, highlighting the power of direct action in challenging systemic oppression.

- **Education and Awareness:** Raising awareness about LGBTQ issues is crucial for mobilizing grassroots activism. Educational campaigns can inform the public about the challenges faced by queer individuals and promote empathy and understanding. Initiatives such as the Human Rights Campaign's "Coming Out Project" encourage individuals to share their stories, fostering a culture of acceptance and support.

Case Studies of Successful Grassroots Mobilization

Several notable examples illustrate the power of grassroots activism in advancing LGBTQ rights:

- **Marriage Equality Movement:** The grassroots campaign for marriage equality in the United States gained momentum through local efforts, community organizing, and strategic litigation. Organizations such as Freedom to Marry mobilized supporters across the country, culminating in the landmark Supreme Court decision in *Obergefell v. Hodges* (2015), which legalized same-sex marriage nationwide.

- **Trans Rights Advocacy:** The #TransIsBeautiful campaign, initiated by activist and actor Geena Rocero, exemplifies grassroots efforts to uplift trans voices and advocate for their rights. Through social media and community engagement, the campaign has raised awareness about the challenges faced by transgender individuals, fostering a sense of pride and visibility.

- **Global LGBTQ Solidarity:** In countries where LGBTQ rights are severely restricted, grassroots activists have mobilized to create change. For instance, in Uganda, the activists of the organization Sexual Minorities Uganda (SMUG) have faced significant challenges, yet they continue to advocate for the rights of LGBTQ individuals through community organizing and international solidarity efforts.

Conclusion

Mobilizing grassroots activism is essential for advancing LGBTQ rights and fostering a more inclusive society. By empowering individuals, building coalitions, and utilizing digital platforms, grassroots activists can overcome challenges and effect meaningful change. As Taren Fira exemplified in her journey, the power of collective action and community engagement can ignite a movement that resonates far beyond local boundaries, inspiring future generations to continue the fight for equality and justice.

Engaging with Political Adversaries

Engaging with political adversaries is a nuanced and often challenging aspect of LGBTQ activism. It requires a delicate balance of assertiveness, empathy, and strategic communication. This section explores the complexities of such engagements, the theoretical frameworks that inform them, and practical examples of successful interactions.

Theoretical Frameworks

To understand the dynamics of engaging with political adversaries, we can draw upon several theoretical frameworks. One prominent theory is the **Conflict Resolution Theory**, which posits that conflicts can be resolved through dialogue and negotiation rather than through adversarial tactics. This theory emphasizes the importance of understanding the interests and motivations of opposing parties.

Another relevant framework is **Interest-Based Negotiation**, which focuses on the underlying interests rather than positions. According to Fisher and Ury in their seminal work, *Getting to Yes*, successful negotiations occur when parties move from a position-based stance to one that addresses the interests of all involved. This approach is particularly useful in LGBTQ advocacy, where the goal is not merely to win a debate but to foster understanding and create lasting change.

Challenges in Engagement

Engaging with political adversaries presents several challenges. One significant issue is the **polarization** of political discourse, particularly regarding LGBTQ rights. Adversaries often hold deeply entrenched beliefs, which can lead to hostile interactions. This polarization can be exacerbated by social media, where misinformation and extreme viewpoints can spread rapidly.

Another challenge is the potential for **emotional fatigue**. Activists may feel overwhelmed by the constant need to defend their identities and rights, leading to burnout. This emotional toll can hinder effective engagement, as activists may approach conversations with frustration rather than openness.

Strategies for Effective Engagement

Despite these challenges, there are effective strategies for engaging with political adversaries. One key approach is to **practice active listening**. By genuinely listening to the concerns and viewpoints of adversaries, activists can identify common ground and areas of potential collaboration. This technique not only fosters respect but can also disarm hostility.

For example, during a heated debate on marriage equality, Taren Fira participated in a town hall meeting where opponents expressed fears about the implications of same-sex marriage on traditional family structures. Instead of countering with anger, Taren acknowledged these fears and shared personal stories that illustrated the positive impacts of marriage equality on families. This approach transformed a potentially confrontational discussion into a dialogue that highlighted shared values of love and commitment.

Utilizing Empathy and Shared Values

Empathy plays a crucial role in engaging with adversaries. Activists can employ **narrative empathy**, which involves sharing personal stories that resonate on an emotional level. This strategy can humanize the LGBTQ experience and challenge stereotypes.

For instance, Taren Fira often recounted her own journey of coming out and the struggles faced by her family to accept her identity. By framing the conversation around personal experiences rather than abstract concepts, she was able to connect with individuals who may have initially opposed her views. This method not only fosters understanding but also encourages adversaries to reconsider their positions.

Building Alliances

Another effective strategy is to seek out **allies within opposing camps.** Engaging with individuals who may not fully agree with LGBTQ rights but are open to discussion can create opportunities for dialogue. These allies can help bridge the gap between opposing viewpoints and facilitate more constructive conversations.

For instance, Taren collaborated with moderate political figures who had previously opposed LGBTQ legislation but were willing to engage in discussions about the implications of their stances. By focusing on shared goals, such as community safety and family welfare, Taren was able to foster a more collaborative atmosphere.

Examples of Successful Engagement

One notable example of successful engagement with political adversaries occurred during a legislative session concerning anti-discrimination laws. Taren organized a coalition of LGBTQ advocates and moderate conservatives to present a united front advocating for the protection of all individuals, regardless of sexual orientation or gender identity.

Through this coalition, Taren and her allies were able to demonstrate that supporting LGBTQ rights did not threaten traditional values but rather aligned with broader principles of fairness and justice. This approach not only garnered bipartisan support but also shifted the narrative from one of conflict to one of collaboration.

Conclusion

Engaging with political adversaries is a critical component of effective LGBTQ activism. By employing strategies rooted in conflict resolution, active listening, empathy, and coalition-building, activists can navigate the complexities of political discourse. Taren Fira's experiences illustrate that while challenges abound, the potential for meaningful dialogue and change remains a powerful tool in the fight for equality.

Ultimately, the goal is not merely to win arguments but to foster understanding and create a more inclusive society for all. As Taren often reminded her supporters, "In the end, we are all human, and it is our shared humanity that will guide us toward a brighter future."

Protecting LGBTQ Rights in Changing Political Landscapes

In the ever-evolving political climate of Alyndra, protecting LGBTQ rights has become a pressing challenge. As political landscapes shift, often influenced by populist movements and conservative agendas, the fight for equality and justice requires innovative strategies and steadfast resolve. This section explores the complexities of safeguarding LGBTQ rights in such a volatile environment, emphasizing the necessity for adaptability, resilience, and strategic engagement.

Theoretical Framework

Understanding the dynamics of political change is crucial for effective advocacy. Theories of social movement dynamics, particularly those articulated by Charles Tilly and Sidney Tarrow, suggest that successful movements must adapt their strategies in response to changing political opportunities and constraints. They propose a framework where the success of social movements hinges on the interplay between mobilization, political opportunities, and framing processes.

$$S = f(M, P, F) \tag{46}$$

Where:

- S = Success of the social movement
- M = Mobilization of resources and supporters
- P = Political opportunities available
- F = Framing of issues to resonate with broader audiences

This equation highlights the necessity of a multi-faceted approach to advocacy, particularly in times of political uncertainty.

Identifying Challenges

One of the primary challenges in protecting LGBTQ rights amidst changing political landscapes is the rise of anti-LGBTQ rhetoric and legislation. In recent years, several regions in Alyndra have witnessed a surge in bills aimed at undermining LGBTQ rights, including those targeting marriage equality, healthcare access, and anti-discrimination protections. For instance, the introduction of the "Alyndra Family Protection Act" sought to redefine marriage in a way that excluded same-sex couples, sparking widespread protests and mobilization among activists.

Moreover, the increasing normalization of hate speech, particularly online, has created an environment where LGBTQ individuals face heightened discrimination and violence. This necessitates a robust response from the LGBTQ community and its allies, emphasizing the need for counter-narratives and public education campaigns to challenge harmful stereotypes.

Strategies for Advocacy

To effectively protect LGBTQ rights in this shifting landscape, several strategies can be employed:

- **Building Coalitions:** Forming alliances with other marginalized groups can amplify voices and create a united front against discrimination. For example, collaborations with racial justice movements have proven effective in addressing intersectional issues within the LGBTQ community, fostering a broader understanding of inclusivity.

- **Engaging in Political Lobbying:** Direct engagement with political leaders is vital. This includes lobbying for supportive legislation while actively opposing harmful bills. The success of the "United for Equality" campaign, which rallied thousands to advocate for LGBTQ rights in legislative sessions, serves as a testament to the power of organized political action.

- **Utilizing Media and Social Media:** Harnessing the power of media can shape public perception and mobilize support. Campaigns that highlight personal stories of LGBTQ individuals can humanize issues and foster empathy. The viral success of the "#LoveIsLove" campaign exemplifies how social media can galvanize public support and challenge discriminatory narratives.

- **Legal Challenges:** Engaging in strategic litigation to challenge discriminatory laws is another critical avenue for advocacy. The landmark case of "Fira v. Alyndra State" demonstrated how legal action could protect the rights of LGBTQ individuals against unjust legislation, setting a precedent for future cases.

Resilience and Adaptation

The ability to adapt to changing circumstances is paramount. As political tides shift, LGBTQ activists must remain vigilant and responsive. This requires continuous education about the political landscape, regular assessment of strategies, and a commitment to resilience. The concept of "strategic resilience," as articulated by activists such as Taren Fira, emphasizes the importance of maintaining momentum and morale within the community, even in the face of adversity.

Conclusion

Protecting LGBTQ rights in changing political landscapes is a multifaceted challenge that requires a combination of theoretical understanding, strategic action, and unwavering commitment. By leveraging coalition-building, political lobbying, media engagement, and legal strategies, activists can navigate the complexities of the political arena. As Taren Fira once said, "In the face of opposition, we must stand together, adapt, and continue to fight for the rights that are inherently ours." This spirit of resilience and unity will be crucial in ensuring that the progress made in LGBTQ rights is not only protected but expanded in the future.

Reclaiming the Narrative

The act of reclaiming the narrative is a powerful tool in LGBTQ activism, particularly in the face of political opposition and societal backlash. This process involves taking control of the stories, identities, and representations that have historically been marginalized or distorted. By asserting their own narratives, LGBTQ activists not only challenge prevailing stereotypes but also foster a deeper understanding of the complexities of queer identities.

Theoretical Framework

Reclaiming the narrative is grounded in several theoretical frameworks, including queer theory, post-colonial theory, and critical race theory. Queer theory, as articulated by scholars such as Judith Butler and Eve Kosofsky Sedgwick, emphasizes the fluidity of identity and the importance of personal narratives in shaping societal understanding. This perspective argues that identities are not fixed but are instead constructed through language, culture, and experience.

Post-colonial theory adds another layer to this conversation by addressing how colonial legacies impact marginalized communities, particularly LGBTQ individuals of color. The intersection of race and sexuality complicates the narratives surrounding identity, requiring activists to confront both homophobia and racism. Critical race theory, championed by scholars like Kimberlé Crenshaw, advocates for an intersectional approach, recognizing that the experiences of LGBTQ individuals cannot be divorced from their racial and cultural contexts.

Problems in Narrative Representation

The challenges of reclaiming the narrative are manifold. One significant problem is the prevalence of heteronormative frameworks that dominate mainstream media and political discourse. These frameworks often reduce LGBTQ identities to simplistic stereotypes, stripping away the richness and diversity of queer experiences. For instance, the portrayal of gay men as flamboyant and lesbians as masculine can perpetuate harmful clichés that do not reflect the true spectrum of identities within the community.

Moreover, the voices of marginalized groups within the LGBTQ community, such as transgender individuals and queer people of color, are frequently sidelined. This erasure not only perpetuates a monolithic view of queerness but also undermines the potential for solidarity and coalition-building across different identities. The lack of representation in media and politics means that the narratives that do emerge are often crafted by those who do not share the lived experiences of the communities they portray.

Strategies for Reclaiming the Narrative

To effectively reclaim the narrative, LGBTQ activists have employed various strategies:

- **Storytelling and Personal Narratives:** Activists have harnessed the power of storytelling to share their experiences and challenge stereotypes. Platforms such as social media, blogs, and public speaking engagements allow individuals to present their own narratives, fostering empathy and understanding among broader audiences.

- **Art and Creative Expression:** Art has long been a vehicle for social change. LGBTQ artists utilize various mediums—such as visual art, music, and theater—to express their identities and experiences. For example, the work of artists like Keith Haring and Audre Lorde not only celebrates queer identity but also critiques societal norms.

- **Community Engagement:** Building community through workshops, support groups, and activism fosters a sense of belonging and empowerment. These spaces allow individuals to share their stories in a safe environment, reinforcing the idea that every narrative is valid and important.

- **Advocacy for Inclusive Representation:** Activists advocate for more inclusive representation in media and politics, pushing for narratives that reflect the diversity of the LGBTQ community. This includes lobbying for policies that promote visibility and inclusion in educational curricula, media production, and governmental representation.

Examples of Successful Narrative Reclamation

One notable example of reclaiming the narrative is the #BlackAndQueer campaign, which highlights the intersectionality of race and sexuality within the LGBTQ community. This campaign amplifies the voices of queer people of color, challenging the dominant narratives that often exclude them. By sharing personal stories and experiences, participants in the campaign work to reshape public perceptions and advocate for greater inclusivity.

Another example is the rise of queer literature and media, which has seen a surge in works that authentically represent LGBTQ experiences. Authors like Ocean Vuong and Carmen Maria Machado have garnered critical acclaim for their narratives that delve into the complexities of queer identities, challenging the heteronormative storytelling that has long prevailed.

Conclusion

Reclaiming the narrative is an essential aspect of LGBTQ activism, serving as a means to challenge stereotypes, foster understanding, and advocate for inclusivity. By asserting control over their own stories, LGBTQ individuals can dismantle harmful representations and create a more nuanced understanding of queer identities. As Taren Fira and other activists have demonstrated, the power of personal narrative can inspire change and promote solidarity within and beyond the LGBTQ community.

Chapter Three: The Power of Personal Narratives

Section One: Changing Hearts and Minds

Storytelling as a Tool for Social Change

Storytelling has long been recognized as a powerful instrument for social change. In the context of LGBTQ activism, it serves not merely as a means of communication but as a catalyst for empathy, understanding, and ultimately, transformation. This section explores the theoretical underpinnings of storytelling, the challenges faced in its application, and real-world examples that illustrate its profound impact on social movements.

Theoretical Framework

At its core, storytelling taps into the human experience, allowing individuals to connect on an emotional level. According to narrative theory, stories can shape perceptions and influence behaviors. As noted by Bruner (1991), narratives are fundamental to human cognition; they help us make sense of our experiences and the world around us. This is particularly pertinent in marginalized communities, where traditional forms of representation may fail to encapsulate their lived realities.

The concept of "narrative empathy," as articulated by Keen (2007), further elucidates the role of storytelling in fostering understanding across diverse groups. By sharing personal experiences, individuals can evoke empathy in others, bridging gaps of misunderstanding and prejudice. This emotional connection is crucial in LGBTQ activism, where the stakes often involve identity, belonging, and acceptance.

Challenges in Storytelling

Despite its potential, storytelling as a tool for social change is fraught with challenges. One significant issue is the risk of oversimplification. Personal narratives can sometimes be reduced to stereotypes, perpetuating rather than dismantling harmful perceptions. For instance, the portrayal of LGBTQ individuals in mainstream media often leans towards sensationalism, which can overshadow the complexity of their experiences.

Moreover, there is the challenge of authenticity. In a society that frequently marginalizes queer voices, individuals may feel pressured to conform to certain narratives that align with societal expectations. This can lead to a phenomenon known as "performative allyship," where allies may amplify certain stories that fit their agenda while ignoring others that do not conform to their ideals.

Real-World Examples

Despite these challenges, numerous examples demonstrate the efficacy of storytelling in driving social change. One notable instance is the "It Gets Better" campaign, which began as a response to the alarming rates of bullying and suicide among LGBTQ youth. The campaign encouraged individuals to share their personal stories of struggle and triumph, creating a vast repository of narratives that offered hope and solidarity. The impact of this initiative was profound, leading to increased awareness and support for LGBTQ youth.

Another example is the use of storytelling in the documentary "Paris is Burning," which chronicles the lives of drag queens and LGBTQ individuals in New York City during the 1980s. This film not only provided visibility to marginalized voices but also sparked discussions about race, class, and gender within the LGBTQ community. By presenting authentic narratives, it challenged viewers to confront their biases and broaden their understanding of queer culture.

Conclusion

In conclusion, storytelling is an invaluable tool for social change within the LGBTQ movement. It allows individuals to share their experiences, foster empathy, and challenge societal norms. While challenges such as oversimplification and authenticity persist, the power of personal narratives to inspire, educate, and mobilize cannot be understated. As Taren Fira exemplifies in her advocacy, harnessing the power of storytelling can lead to meaningful change and a more inclusive society.

$$E = mc^2 \qquad (47)$$

Where E represents the energy of change, m signifies the mass of collective narratives, and c is the speed at which stories can spread through communities, igniting movements and fostering understanding. The equation illustrates that the more narratives we share, the greater the potential for societal transformation.

The Impact of Personal Narratives in LGBTQ Activism

In the realm of LGBTQ activism, personal narratives serve as powerful tools for fostering understanding, empathy, and change. These narratives, often rich in emotion and authenticity, allow individuals to share their lived experiences and challenge societal norms. By illuminating the complexities of queer identities, personal stories can dismantle stereotypes and create connections that transcend differences.

Theoretical Framework

The use of personal narratives in activism can be framed through the lens of narrative theory, which posits that stories shape our understanding of the world. According to Bruner (1991), narratives are fundamental to human cognition; they help individuals make sense of their experiences and communicate their realities to others. In the context of LGBTQ activism, these narratives can serve as a means of countering dominant discourses that marginalize queer identities.

Furthermore, the concept of "testimonial activism" (Hirsch, 1997) emphasizes the role of personal accounts in social movements. By sharing their stories, activists can assert their existence and demand recognition, thereby challenging the silencing of marginalized voices. This process not only validates individual experiences but also fosters solidarity within the LGBTQ community and beyond.

Addressing Problems through Personal Narratives

One of the significant problems faced by the LGBTQ community is the pervasive stigma and discrimination that often stem from ignorance and misinformation. Personal narratives can effectively address these issues by humanizing the experiences of queer individuals. For instance, when a person shares their story of coming out, they provide insight into the emotional turmoil and courage required to embrace their identity. This vulnerability can evoke empathy in listeners, prompting them to reconsider their preconceived notions about LGBTQ individuals.

Moreover, personal narratives can highlight the intersectionality of LGBTQ identities, illustrating how factors such as race, gender, and socioeconomic status intersect to shape unique experiences of oppression. For example, the story of a queer person of color navigating both racial and sexual discrimination can shed light on the compounded challenges faced by individuals at these intersections. This nuanced understanding is crucial for fostering inclusive advocacy efforts that address the diverse needs of the LGBTQ community.

Examples of Impactful Personal Narratives

Several prominent figures in LGBTQ activism have utilized personal narratives to effect change. One notable example is the late Marsha P. Johnson, a Black transgender activist whose experiences during the Stonewall uprising in 1969 are often recounted as pivotal moments in the fight for LGBTQ rights. Johnson's story not only highlights the contributions of transgender individuals to the movement but also underscores the importance of intersectionality in activism.

Another example is the viral impact of social media campaigns like "#MeToo" and "#LoveIsLove," which have encouraged individuals to share their personal experiences of discrimination and love. These movements have demonstrated the power of personal narratives in mobilizing communities and sparking broader societal conversations about LGBTQ rights.

Empathy and Understanding through Shared Experiences

The sharing of personal narratives fosters empathy by allowing individuals to see the world through the eyes of others. Research indicates that exposure to personal stories can lead to increased empathy and a greater willingness to support social change (Bennett, 2016). When individuals hear stories of love, loss, and resilience from LGBTQ individuals, they are more likely to recognize the humanity in those experiences and advocate for equality.

For instance, the documentary "Disclosure" presents the personal narratives of transgender individuals in media, revealing how harmful representations have shaped public perceptions. By sharing their stories, the filmmakers challenge viewers to confront their biases and reconsider the narratives they consume.

Amplifying Marginalized Voices

In the pursuit of social justice, it is essential to amplify the voices of those who have been historically marginalized. Personal narratives provide a platform for individuals to share their experiences and contribute to the broader narrative of LGBTQ activism. This amplification is particularly crucial for underrepresented groups, such as transgender individuals, people of color, and those with disabilities.

Activists can leverage various mediums—such as blogs, podcasts, and social media—to share personal stories and create a sense of community. By elevating these narratives, activists can foster a culture of inclusivity and solidarity that recognizes the diverse experiences within the LGBTQ community.

Conclusion

In conclusion, personal narratives play a vital role in LGBTQ activism by humanizing experiences, fostering empathy, and amplifying marginalized voices. As activists continue to share their stories, they not only challenge societal norms but also inspire others to join the fight for equality. The power of personal narratives lies in their ability to connect individuals across differences, creating a collective movement that advocates for justice and understanding.

Bibliography

[1] Bruner, J. (1991). *The Narrative Construction of Reality*. Critical Inquiry, 18(1), 1-21.

[2] Hirsch, M. (1997). *Family Frames: Photography, Narrative, and Postmemory*. Harvard University Press.

[3] Bennett, M. (2016). *The Role of Storytelling in Social Change*. Social Change Review, 14(2), 45-67.

Empathy and Understanding through Shared Experiences

Empathy is often described as the ability to understand and share the feelings of another. In the context of LGBTQ activism, fostering empathy is crucial for building bridges across diverse communities and promoting inclusivity. This section explores how shared experiences can cultivate empathy and understanding, ultimately leading to more effective advocacy for LGBTQ rights.

Theoretical Framework

The concept of empathy can be grounded in various psychological theories. One such theory is the **Social Identity Theory**, which posits that individuals derive a sense of self from their group memberships. According to Henri Tajfel and John Turner, people categorize themselves and others into social groups, which can lead to in-group favoritism and out-group discrimination. Understanding this framework helps activists recognize how shared identities—be they related to sexual orientation, gender identity, or other social categories—can foster empathy among individuals.

Furthermore, the **Empathy-Altruism Hypothesis** proposed by C. Daniel Batson suggests that empathy leads to altruistic behavior. When individuals feel empathy towards those in marginalized communities, they are more likely to take action to support them. This hypothesis is particularly relevant in LGBTQ activism, where shared narratives can evoke empathy and spur advocacy efforts.

Shared Experiences as a Tool for Empathy

Shared experiences often serve as a catalyst for empathy. When individuals hear personal stories of struggle and triumph, they are more likely to connect emotionally with the storyteller. For example, during LGBTQ pride events, individuals from various backgrounds share their journeys of coming out, facing discrimination, and finding acceptance. These narratives create a tapestry of shared experiences that can resonate with listeners, fostering a sense of understanding and solidarity.

Consider the case of a young queer person attending their first pride event. They may initially feel isolated and apprehensive, but as they listen to stories of resilience from older activists, their sense of belonging deepens. This connection not only validates their own experiences but also inspires them to engage in advocacy, reinforcing the cycle of empathy and action.

Case Studies and Examples

One powerful example of empathy through shared experiences is the **It Gets Better Project**, which began in 2010 as a response to the alarming rates of suicide among LGBTQ youth. The project features video testimonials from individuals sharing their experiences of bullying, acceptance, and hope. These narratives have reached millions, providing comfort and understanding to those who may feel alone in their struggles. The project's success underscores the importance of visibility and shared experiences in fostering empathy.

Another illustrative case is the annual **Transgender Day of Remembrance**, which honors the lives lost to anti-trans violence. During this event, communities come together to share stories of those who have been lost, creating a space for collective mourning and reflection. This shared grief fosters empathy among attendees, encouraging them to advocate for policy changes and social justice for transgender individuals.

Challenges to Fostering Empathy

While shared experiences can cultivate empathy, challenges remain. One significant barrier is the phenomenon of **empathy fatigue**, where individuals become desensitized to the suffering of others due to constant exposure to distressing narratives. This fatigue can lead to a lack of engagement and advocacy, undermining the efforts of LGBTQ activists.

Additionally, the **intersectionality** of identities complicates the landscape of empathy. Activists must navigate the diverse experiences within the LGBTQ community, recognizing that individuals from different backgrounds may have varying levels of privilege and access to resources. For example, the experiences of a white, cisgender gay man may differ significantly from those of a Black transgender woman. Acknowledging these differences is essential for fostering genuine empathy and understanding.

Strategies for Enhancing Empathy through Shared Experiences

To effectively enhance empathy through shared experiences, activists can employ several strategies:

- **Storytelling Workshops:** Organizing workshops where individuals can share their narratives in a safe and supportive environment encourages vulnerability and fosters connections among participants.

- **Collaborative Art Projects:** Engaging in artistic endeavors that reflect personal stories can create a powerful medium for empathy. Art allows individuals to express their experiences in creative ways, inviting others to engage with their narratives on a deeper level.

- **Community Dialogues:** Facilitating open dialogues within diverse groups can help bridge gaps in understanding. Encouraging participants to share their experiences and listen actively can promote empathy and strengthen community ties.

Conclusion

In conclusion, empathy and understanding through shared experiences play a vital role in LGBTQ activism. By harnessing the power of personal narratives, activists can create a more inclusive and supportive environment for all individuals. While challenges exist, the potential for empathy to drive social change remains a powerful tool in the ongoing fight for LGBTQ rights. As Taren Fira exemplified in her journey, fostering empathy is not just about understanding others; it is about building a collective movement that honors and uplifts every voice within the LGBTQ community.

Overcoming Stereotypes and Misconceptions

In the realm of LGBTQ activism, the journey towards acceptance and equality is often hindered by pervasive stereotypes and misconceptions. These preconceived notions not only distort the reality of queer identities but also create barriers that impede progress. This section explores the various stereotypes faced by LGBTQ individuals, the implications of these misconceptions, and the strategies employed to dismantle them.

Understanding Stereotypes

Stereotypes are oversimplified and generalized beliefs about a group of people. They often arise from a lack of understanding or exposure to diverse identities. In the context of LGBTQ individuals, common stereotypes include the belief that all gay men are effeminate, that lesbians are merely confused heterosexuals, and that transgender individuals are simply seeking attention. These stereotypes contribute to a narrow understanding of the rich diversity within the LGBTQ community.

The Impact of Stereotypes

The consequences of such stereotypes can be profound. They can lead to discrimination, social ostracism, and internalized homophobia among LGBTQ individuals. For example, a study conducted by Herek (2009) indicated that individuals who internalize negative stereotypes about their sexual orientation are more likely to experience mental health issues, including depression and anxiety. This internalization can stem from societal messages that devalue queer identities, leading individuals to question their self-worth.

Challenging Misconceptions

To effectively challenge stereotypes, it is essential to engage in education and awareness-raising efforts. Activists like Taren Fira have utilized storytelling as a potent tool for combating misconceptions. By sharing personal narratives, LGBTQ individuals can humanize their experiences, dispelling myths and fostering empathy among allies and the general public.

For instance, during the first LGBTQ Pride event organized by Taren Fira, participants were encouraged to share their stories in a safe and supportive environment. This initiative not only celebrated diverse identities but also provided a platform for individuals to confront and dismantle harmful stereotypes. The act of storytelling allows for the expression of complexity and nuance, illustrating that LGBTQ identities cannot be reduced to simplistic labels.

The Role of Media and Representation

Media representation plays a critical role in shaping societal perceptions of LGBTQ individuals. Historically, mainstream media has perpetuated harmful stereotypes, often portraying queer characters as caricatures or reinforcing negative tropes. However, recent shifts towards more authentic representation have begun to challenge these narratives.

The success of television shows like *Pose* and *Schitt's Creek* illustrates the power of positive representation. These shows feature multifaceted LGBTQ characters who navigate their identities with depth and complexity, allowing audiences to see them as relatable individuals rather than stereotypes. Such representation is crucial in fostering understanding and acceptance, as it provides a counter-narrative to the stereotypes that have long dominated media portrayals.

Intersectionality and Stereotypes

It is also essential to recognize that stereotypes do not operate in isolation. Intersectionality, a term coined by Kimberlé Crenshaw, refers to the interconnected nature of social categorizations such as race, class, and gender, which can create overlapping systems of discrimination or disadvantage. LGBTQ individuals who belong to multiple marginalized groups often face compounded stereotypes that further complicate their experiences.

For example, queer people of color may encounter stereotypes that not only relate to their sexual orientation but also to their racial identity. This intersectional lens is vital in understanding the diverse experiences within the LGBTQ community and addressing the unique challenges faced by individuals at the intersections of various identities.

Strategies for Overcoming Stereotypes

To effectively overcome stereotypes, a multifaceted approach is necessary. Some key strategies include:

- **Education and Awareness:** Hosting workshops and discussions that educate individuals about LGBTQ identities and the harmful effects of stereotypes can foster understanding and empathy.

- **Storytelling:** Encouraging individuals to share their personal narratives can humanize experiences and challenge preconceived notions.

- **Media Advocacy:** Supporting and promoting positive representations of LGBTQ individuals in media can help reshape societal perceptions.

- **Intersectional Advocacy:** Recognizing and addressing the unique challenges faced by individuals at the intersections of various identities can lead to more inclusive activism.

- **Community Building:** Creating safe spaces for LGBTQ individuals to connect and share their experiences can empower them to confront stereotypes collectively.

Conclusion

Overcoming stereotypes and misconceptions is a crucial aspect of LGBTQ activism. By challenging harmful narratives and fostering understanding, activists like Taren Fira are paving the way for a more inclusive and equitable society. Through education, storytelling, and community engagement, the LGBTQ community can dismantle the barriers created by stereotypes, ultimately leading to a world where all identities are celebrated and valued.

Amplifying Marginalized Voices

In the realm of LGBTQ activism, amplifying marginalized voices is not merely an act of support but a fundamental necessity for achieving true inclusivity and equity. Marginalized groups within the LGBTQ community—such as queer people of color, transgender individuals, and those with disabilities—often face compounded discrimination that can silence their experiences and needs. To address this, activists and allies must consciously work to elevate these voices, ensuring they are heard and represented in all facets of advocacy.

Theoretical Framework

The concept of amplifying marginalized voices is deeply rooted in intersectionality, a term coined by legal scholar Kimberlé Crenshaw. Intersectionality posits that individuals experience overlapping social identities, which can lead to unique forms of discrimination and privilege. This framework allows activists to understand that the struggles faced by LGBTQ individuals cannot be separated from other aspects of their identity, such as race, gender, and socioeconomic status.

Mathematically, we can represent the intersectional experience as follows:

$$E = \sum_{i=1}^{n}(P_i \cdot D_i) \tag{48}$$

Where: - E represents the overall experience of an individual, - P_i is the privilege associated with identity i, - D_i is the discrimination faced due to identity i, - n is the number of intersecting identities.

This equation illustrates that the experiences of marginalized individuals are the result of a complex interplay between privilege and discrimination across multiple identities.

Challenges in Amplifying Voices

Despite the importance of amplifying marginalized voices, several challenges persist:

- **Tokenism:** Organizations may superficially include marginalized voices without genuinely integrating their perspectives into decision-making processes. This can lead to a sense of alienation and mistrust within the community.

- **Access Barriers:** Many marginalized individuals face systemic barriers that hinder their ability to participate in activism, such as lack of access to education, healthcare, or safe spaces.

- **Misrepresentation:** When marginalized voices are amplified, there is a risk of misrepresentation or misinterpretation of their experiences, particularly when those outside the community attempt to speak on their behalf.

Strategies for Amplification

To effectively amplify marginalized voices, activists can employ several strategies:

1. **Create Platforms:** Establishing platforms—be it through social media, community forums, or art—where marginalized individuals can share their stories and experiences is essential. For example, the online campaign #BlackAndTransInAmerica has successfully highlighted the unique struggles faced by Black transgender individuals.

2. **Collaborative Storytelling:** Engaging in collaborative storytelling projects can empower marginalized individuals to share their narratives in their own

words. Initiatives like StoryCorps have demonstrated the power of personal stories in fostering understanding and empathy.

3. **Education and Training:** Providing training for allies on how to listen to and elevate marginalized voices can foster a more inclusive environment. Workshops that focus on active listening and understanding intersectionality are effective in this regard.

4. **Resource Allocation:** Ensuring that resources—financial, educational, and emotional—are directed toward marginalized communities can help amplify their voices. For instance, funding LGBTQ organizations led by people of color can significantly impact advocacy efforts.

Real-World Examples

Several organizations and movements have successfully amplified marginalized voices within the LGBTQ community:

- **The Audre Lorde Project:** This community organization focuses on mobilizing the LGBTQ community of color and emphasizes the importance of intersectional activism. Their programs are designed to uplift the voices of those often overlooked in mainstream advocacy.

- **Transgender Law Center:** By prioritizing the legal rights of transgender individuals, particularly those of color, this organization has been pivotal in amplifying marginalized voices within legal frameworks and advocating for policy changes.

- **Black Lives Matter:** While not exclusively an LGBTQ organization, BLM has highlighted the intersectionality of race and gender identity, advocating for the rights of Black LGBTQ individuals and ensuring their voices are central to the movement.

Conclusion

Amplifying marginalized voices is not just an ethical obligation but a strategic necessity in the fight for LGBTQ equality. By understanding the complexities of intersectionality and actively working to elevate those who are often silenced, activists can create a more inclusive and effective movement. This commitment to inclusivity not only enriches the advocacy landscape but also fosters a deeper sense of community and solidarity among all LGBTQ individuals.

By centering marginalized voices, the movement can ensure that all narratives are heard, valued, and integrated into the broader struggle for justice and equality. In the words of Audre Lorde, "There is no such thing as a single-issue struggle because we do not live single-issue lives." Therefore, the call to action remains clear: listen, uplift, and amplify.

Crafting Personal Stories for Advocacy

The art of crafting personal stories for advocacy is a powerful tool that can bridge the gap between lived experiences and the broader social issues at hand. Personal narratives serve not only to humanize abstract statistics but also to foster empathy and understanding among diverse audiences. This section delves into the theory, challenges, and exemplary practices involved in using personal storytelling as an advocacy strategy.

Theoretical Foundations

The use of personal narratives in advocacy is grounded in narrative theory, which posits that stories are fundamental to human experience and understanding. According to Bruner (1991), narrative serves as a means of making sense of the world, allowing individuals to process their experiences and communicate them effectively. This is particularly relevant in LGBTQ advocacy, where personal stories can illuminate the complexities of identity, discrimination, and resilience.

One key theoretical concept is the notion of **empathy**. As defined by Cohen and Strachan (2002), empathy involves the ability to understand and share the feelings of another. When advocates share their personal stories, they invite others to step into their shoes, fostering a sense of connection that can motivate action. This empathetic engagement is crucial for breaking down stereotypes and combating prejudice.

Challenges in Crafting Personal Stories

While personal storytelling is a potent advocacy tool, it is not without its challenges. One significant issue is the **vulnerability** that comes with sharing personal experiences. Advocates may fear backlash, misrepresentation, or emotional distress. It is essential to navigate this landscape carefully, ensuring that the storytelling process is both empowering and safe.

Another challenge is the potential for **oversimplification**. Personal narratives can sometimes reduce complex identities and experiences to simplistic tropes, which may inadvertently reinforce stereotypes rather than dismantle them.

Advocates must strive to present multifaceted stories that capture the richness of their experiences while avoiding the pitfalls of reductionism.

Strategies for Effective Storytelling

To craft compelling personal stories for advocacy, several strategies can be employed:

1. **Authenticity:** Authenticity is paramount in storytelling. Advocates should strive to present their true selves, sharing both triumphs and struggles. This honesty resonates with audiences and builds trust.

2. **Contextualization:** Providing context is crucial for understanding. Advocates should situate their personal experiences within broader societal issues, illustrating how individual stories reflect systemic challenges.

3. **Emotional Resonance:** Effective stories evoke emotions. Advocates can use vivid imagery, sensory details, and emotional language to draw audiences in and foster empathy.

4. **Call to Action:** Every personal narrative should culminate in a clear call to action. Advocates must articulate what they want their audience to do with the information shared, whether it be to support legislation, participate in activism, or engage in dialogue.

Examples of Successful Personal Storytelling

Numerous activists have successfully utilized personal storytelling to advance LGBTQ rights. One notable example is the work of **Harvey Milk**, who shared his journey as a gay man to galvanize support for LGBTQ rights in the 1970s. His candid discussions about his life experiences helped to humanize the struggle for equality, making it relatable to a wider audience.

Another powerful example is the campaign **"It Gets Better"**, which features personal videos from LGBTQ individuals sharing their stories of overcoming adversity. These narratives have had a profound impact, providing hope and solidarity to young LGBTQ people facing discrimination and bullying.

Conclusion

Crafting personal stories for advocacy is a vital practice that can transform perceptions and inspire action. By grounding narratives in authenticity, providing context, evoking emotions, and articulating clear calls to action, advocates can effectively use their experiences to drive social change. As Taren Fira exemplifies, the power of personal storytelling lies in its ability to connect individuals, foster empathy, and mobilize communities toward a common goal of justice and equality.

Bibliography

[1] Bruner, J. (1991). *The Narrative Construction of Reality*. Critical Inquiry, 18(1), 1-21.

[2] Cohen, J., & Strachan, A. (2002). *Empathy and the Role of Narrative in Social Change*. In R. B. Smith (Ed.), *Narrative and Social Change: The Role of Storytelling in Advocacy* (pp. 45-67). New York: Advocacy Press.

The Role of Art and Media in Personal Storytelling

Art and media serve as powerful vehicles for personal storytelling, particularly within the LGBTQ community, where narratives often challenge societal norms and foster understanding. The intersection of art, media, and personal narrative can be understood through various theoretical frameworks, including narrative theory, queer theory, and the concept of representation.

Narrative Theory

Narrative theory posits that stories shape our understanding of the world and ourselves. According to [?], narratives are fundamental to human cognition, allowing individuals to construct meaning from their experiences. This process is especially significant for marginalized communities, where personal stories can illuminate shared struggles and resilience. For example, Taren Fira's own journey, as chronicled in this biography, illustrates how personal storytelling can transform individual experiences into collective movements for change.

Queer Theory

Queer theory further complicates traditional narratives by questioning the binaries of gender and sexuality. As articulated by [?], identity is performative; thus, storytelling becomes a means of both expressing and constructing identity. Artistic expressions—whether through visual art, literature, or performance—allow LGBTQ individuals to explore and articulate their identities in ways that defy societal expectations. For instance, performance art pieces that incorporate personal narratives can challenge the audience's perceptions of gender and sexuality, creating space for empathy and understanding.

Representation and Visibility

Representation in media is crucial for the visibility of LGBTQ narratives. The concept of representation addresses how individuals and communities are portrayed in various media forms, influencing public perception and acceptance. [?] argues that representation is not merely about reflecting reality but actively shaping it. When LGBTQ individuals share their stories through art and media, they contribute to a broader narrative that counters stereotypes and fosters inclusivity.

For example, the documentary film *Paris is Burning* (1990) provides a poignant exploration of the drag ball culture in New York City, highlighting the lives of LGBTQ individuals who navigate societal marginalization. Through personal storytelling, the film captures the complexities of identity, community, and the pursuit of dreams, offering viewers a glimpse into a vibrant subculture often overlooked by mainstream media.

Challenges in Representation

Despite the potential of art and media to amplify personal narratives, challenges remain. The commercialization of LGBTQ stories can lead to a dilution of their authenticity. As noted by [?], when queer narratives are co-opted by mainstream media, they risk losing their original context and meaning. This phenomenon can result in the perpetuation of stereotypes rather than their dismantling.

Furthermore, the accessibility of platforms for storytelling can create disparities within the LGBTQ community itself. Not all voices are equally represented; marginalized subgroups, such as transgender individuals and queer people of color, often face additional barriers in gaining visibility. The importance of intersectionality, as discussed by [Crenshaw(1989)], highlights the need for diverse narratives that reflect the multifaceted experiences within the LGBTQ community.

Examples of Art and Media in Personal Storytelling

Artistic mediums such as literature, visual arts, and digital media have been instrumental in sharing personal stories. For instance, the graphic memoir *Fun*

Home by Alison Bechdel explores themes of identity, family, and sexuality through the lens of the author's relationship with her father. The graphic novel format allows for a unique interplay of text and imagery, enhancing the emotional resonance of Bechdel's narrative.

Similarly, social media platforms have emerged as vital spaces for personal storytelling. Hashtags like #MeToo and #BlackLivesMatter have demonstrated the power of collective storytelling in raising awareness and mobilizing communities. Within the LGBTQ context, campaigns like #LoveIsLove have utilized social media to share personal stories of love and acceptance, fostering a sense of solidarity and support among individuals facing discrimination.

Conclusion

In conclusion, the role of art and media in personal storytelling is multifaceted and transformative. Through the lenses of narrative theory and queer theory, we see how personal narratives can challenge societal norms, foster empathy, and create visibility for marginalized voices. However, it is essential to remain vigilant about the challenges of representation and the need for diverse narratives that reflect the complexities of the LGBTQ experience. As Taren Fira's journey illustrates, personal storytelling through art and media not only empowers individuals but also serves as a catalyst for broader social change.

Using Personal Narratives to Educate and Inspire

Personal narratives serve as powerful tools in the realm of LGBTQ activism, providing not only a voice to individual experiences but also fostering empathy and understanding among diverse audiences. This section explores the theoretical underpinnings of narrative as a form of advocacy, the challenges faced in sharing personal stories, and the transformative impact these narratives can have on both the storyteller and the listener.

Theoretical Framework

At the heart of using personal narratives in activism lies the theory of narrative identity, which posits that individuals construct their identities through the stories they tell about themselves. According to [?], narratives shape our understanding of the world and our place within it. This theory suggests that personal stories can illuminate the complexities of LGBTQ identities, challenging stereotypes and broadening perspectives.

Moreover, the concept of *empathy* plays a critical role in this process. Research by [?] indicates that personal narratives can evoke empathetic responses in listeners, allowing them to connect emotionally with experiences that may differ significantly from their own. This emotional connection can lead to increased awareness and support for LGBTQ rights.

Challenges in Sharing Personal Narratives

While personal narratives can be powerful, sharing them is not without challenges. Activists may face fears of vulnerability, potential backlash, or misinterpretation of their stories. The risk of exposing oneself to discrimination or harassment can deter individuals from speaking out. Furthermore, there is the concern of *tokenization*, where an individual's story may be used to represent an entire community, which can lead to oversimplification and erasure of diverse experiences.

For instance, consider the story of *Alex*, a non-binary activist who shared their journey of coming out in a conservative community. While their narrative garnered support from some, it also attracted negative attention from those who felt threatened by the challenge to traditional gender norms. Alex's experience highlights the need for a supportive environment when sharing personal stories, as well as the importance of framing narratives in a way that emphasizes collective experiences rather than individual struggles alone.

Examples of Impactful Personal Narratives

One of the most notable examples of personal narratives in LGBTQ activism is the *It Gets Better Project*, which began as a response to the alarming rates of bullying and suicide among LGBTQ youth. The project encourages individuals to share their stories of resilience and hope, illustrating that life can improve despite adversity. This initiative has inspired countless videos and testimonials, creating a vast repository of narratives that educate and uplift.

Another significant example is the memoir *Fun Home* by Alison Bechdel, which explores her experiences growing up with a gay father. The graphic novel not only resonates with those who share similar backgrounds but also educates readers about the complexities of LGBTQ identities and familial relationships. Bechdel's narrative has been adapted into a successful musical, further amplifying its reach and impact.

Strategies for Effective Storytelling

To harness the power of personal narratives effectively, activists can employ several strategies:

- **Authenticity:** Sharing stories that reflect genuine experiences fosters trust and connection. Authenticity resonates with audiences, making them more likely to engage with the message.

- **Inclusivity:** When crafting narratives, it is essential to acknowledge the diversity within the LGBTQ community. Highlighting intersectional experiences can broaden the narrative's appeal and relevance.

- **Clarity and Focus:** Effective storytelling often requires clarity of purpose. Activists should identify the key messages they wish to convey and structure their narratives to support those themes.

- **Call to Action:** Personal narratives can inspire action. By concluding stories with a call to action, activists can motivate audiences to engage in advocacy or support LGBTQ initiatives.

Conclusion

Using personal narratives in LGBTQ activism is a potent method for education and inspiration. By sharing their stories, activists can foster empathy, challenge stereotypes, and build connections within and beyond the community. Despite the challenges associated with vulnerability and representation, the impact of these narratives can be profound, leading to increased awareness, support, and ultimately, social change. As Taren Fira exemplifies through their journey, the power of personal storytelling can ignite movements and inspire future generations of activists to continue the fight for equality and justice.

The Ethics of Sharing Personal Stories

In the realm of LGBTQ activism, personal narratives serve as powerful tools for fostering empathy, understanding, and social change. However, the act of sharing personal stories is not without its ethical considerations. These ethical dimensions must be carefully navigated to ensure that storytelling contributes positively to the movement while respecting the dignity and privacy of individuals involved.

Understanding the Impact of Personal Narratives

Personal stories can humanize abstract issues, making them relatable and impactful. As noted by narrative theorist [?], storytelling is a fundamental way through which individuals make sense of their experiences and convey meaning. This is particularly relevant in LGBTQ activism, where the lived experiences of queer individuals can challenge stereotypes and misconceptions. However, the ethical implications of sharing these stories must be considered, especially in contexts where individuals may be vulnerable or marginalized.

The Dilemma of Consent

One of the primary ethical concerns in sharing personal stories is the issue of consent. Activists must ensure that individuals who share their stories do so willingly and with full understanding of how their narratives will be used. This is particularly critical when stories involve sensitive topics such as trauma, discrimination, or violence. According to [?], obtaining informed consent is not just a legal obligation but a moral imperative that fosters trust and respect within the community.

Potential for Harm

While sharing personal stories can empower individuals, it can also expose them to potential harm. This includes the risk of re-traumatization, public backlash, or further marginalization. [?] emphasizes the importance of considering the psychological impact on individuals who recount painful experiences. Activists should be mindful of how the sharing of personal narratives might affect the storyteller's mental health and well-being, and provide support mechanisms where necessary.

The Role of Intersectionality

The ethics of storytelling are further complicated by intersectionality—the interconnected nature of social categorizations such as race, gender, and class. [Crenshaw(1989)] highlights that individuals with multiple marginalized identities may face unique challenges and vulnerabilities. When sharing stories, it is essential to recognize these intersections and ensure that narratives do not perpetuate stereotypes or erase the complexities of individual experiences.

Authenticity vs. Representation

Another ethical consideration is the balance between authenticity and representation. Activists must navigate the fine line between sharing genuine experiences and the potential for those narratives to be co-opted or misrepresented. [?] discusses the concept of "front stage" and "back stage" behaviors, suggesting that individuals curate their narratives based on audience expectations. Activists should strive to present authentic stories while being cautious of how these narratives may be interpreted or appropriated by others.

Examples of Ethical Storytelling

To illustrate ethical storytelling, consider the case of the "It Gets Better" campaign, which encouraged LGBTQ individuals to share their experiences of overcoming adversity. While the campaign successfully raised awareness and provided hope, it also faced criticism for potentially oversimplifying complex issues and failing to address systemic inequalities. This highlights the need for activists to frame personal narratives within broader social contexts, ensuring that they do not inadvertently minimize the struggles faced by others.

Creating Safe Spaces for Sharing

To ethically navigate the sharing of personal stories, activists should prioritize creating safe spaces where individuals feel comfortable expressing their experiences. This involves establishing guidelines for storytelling that emphasize consent, confidentiality, and the option to withdraw narratives at any time. By fostering an environment of respect and support, activists can empower individuals to share their stories in ways that honor their experiences and promote healing.

Conclusion

In conclusion, the ethics of sharing personal stories in LGBTQ activism are multifaceted and require careful consideration. By prioritizing consent, acknowledging the potential for harm, and recognizing the complexities of intersectionality, activists can navigate these ethical dilemmas effectively. Ultimately, the goal of sharing personal narratives should be to uplift marginalized voices, foster understanding, and contribute to meaningful social change. As [?] reminds us, storytelling is not just an act of sharing; it is a powerful means of resistance and transformation.

Creating Safe Spaces for Sharing Stories

In the journey of activism, the creation of safe spaces for sharing stories is paramount. These spaces serve as sanctuaries where individuals can express their identities, experiences, and emotions without fear of judgment or reprisal. The significance of safe spaces lies not only in the comfort they provide but also in their ability to foster community, understanding, and healing.

Theoretical Framework

The concept of safe spaces is rooted in several theoretical frameworks, including feminist theory, queer theory, and social constructivism. Feminist theory emphasizes the importance of creating environments where marginalized voices can be heard, challenging the patriarchal structures that often silence them. Similarly, queer theory advocates for the recognition and validation of diverse sexual and gender identities, promoting inclusivity and acceptance. Social constructivism posits that knowledge and meaning are constructed through social interactions, highlighting the importance of dialogue in shaping individual and collective identities.

The establishment of safe spaces can be understood through the lens of *psychological safety*, a term coined by Amy Edmondson. Psychological safety refers to an environment where individuals feel safe to take risks, share ideas, and express vulnerabilities without fear of negative consequences. In LGBTQ activism, psychological safety is crucial for encouraging open dialogue about personal experiences, which can lead to greater empathy and understanding among community members.

Challenges in Creating Safe Spaces

Despite the importance of safe spaces, several challenges can impede their establishment. One significant barrier is the internalized stigma that many individuals within the LGBTQ community face. This stigma can manifest as self-doubt or fear of rejection, preventing individuals from sharing their stories. Furthermore, external societal pressures, including discrimination and violence against LGBTQ individuals, can create an atmosphere of fear that hinders open communication.

Another challenge is the diversity within the LGBTQ community itself. Different identities, backgrounds, and experiences can lead to varying perspectives on what constitutes a safe space. For example, a space that feels safe for a cisgender gay man may not feel the same for a transgender person of color. This intersectionality necessitates a nuanced approach to creating safe spaces that are truly inclusive and reflective of the community's diversity.

Examples of Safe Spaces

Numerous organizations and initiatives have successfully created safe spaces for sharing stories within the LGBTQ community. One notable example is the *StoryCorps* project, which encourages individuals to record and share their personal narratives. By providing a platform for storytelling, StoryCorps has enabled many LGBTQ individuals to articulate their experiences, fostering understanding and connection among diverse audiences.

Another example is the establishment of LGBTQ community centers, which often host support groups, workshops, and events focused on storytelling. These centers provide a physical space where individuals can gather, share their stories, and connect with others who have similar experiences. For instance, the *LGBTQ Center* in New York City offers various programs aimed at empowering individuals through storytelling, including open mic nights and writing workshops.

Best Practices for Creating Safe Spaces

To effectively create safe spaces for sharing stories, several best practices should be considered:

- **Establish Ground Rules:** Setting clear guidelines for respectful communication can help create an environment where individuals feel comfortable sharing their stories. Ground rules may include active listening, refraining from interrupting, and maintaining confidentiality.

- **Facilitate Inclusivity:** It is essential to actively seek out and include diverse voices within the space. This can be achieved by inviting individuals from various backgrounds and identities to share their experiences and perspectives.

- **Provide Support:** Offering resources such as counseling services or peer support groups can help individuals navigate the emotional aspects of sharing their stories. This support can be crucial for those who may experience trauma or distress when recounting their experiences.

- **Encourage Vulnerability:** Creating an atmosphere where vulnerability is embraced can lead to deeper connections among participants. Facilitators can model vulnerability by sharing their own stories and experiences, encouraging others to do the same.

- **Utilize Technology:** Online platforms can also serve as safe spaces for sharing stories, especially for individuals who may not have access to physical spaces. Social media campaigns, blogs, and virtual storytelling events can provide alternative avenues for expression and connection.

Conclusion

Creating safe spaces for sharing stories is a vital component of LGBTQ activism. These spaces not only empower individuals to voice their experiences but also foster community, understanding, and healing. By overcoming challenges and implementing best practices, activists can cultivate environments that celebrate diversity and inclusivity. As Taren Fira exemplified in her advocacy, the power of storytelling can ignite change, inspire others, and ultimately contribute to a more equitable society.

Section Two: Taren Fira's Personal Journey

Moments of Vulnerability and Strength

In the journey of activism, moments of vulnerability often intertwine with profound strength, creating a unique tapestry of experiences that define the activist's identity. For Taren Fira, these moments were not just personal experiences; they were critical turning points that shaped her understanding of herself and her mission within the LGBTQ community.

Vulnerability, as defined by Brené Brown, is the birthplace of innovation, creativity, and change. It is in these raw, unguarded moments that individuals can connect deeply with themselves and others. Taren's early experiences of vulnerability stemmed from her struggle to accept her queer identity in a world that often marginalized and discriminated against those who dared to be different.

One pivotal moment occurred during her first public speech at a local LGBTQ event. Standing before a crowd of supportive yet expectant faces, Taren felt a rush of fear and uncertainty. The weight of her truth pressed heavily on her chest. She recalled the words of her mentor, who once told her, "Your story is your power." With a deep breath, she began to share her journey of coming out, detailing the fear of rejection from her family and friends. As she spoke, she felt the warmth of empathy radiating from the audience, transforming her vulnerability into a source of strength.

This experience highlights a crucial aspect of activism: the power of storytelling. Research by social psychologists indicates that personal narratives can foster empathy and understanding, bridging gaps between diverse experiences. Taren's willingness to share her vulnerabilities resonated with many in the audience, creating a sense of solidarity that transcended individual struggles.

However, vulnerability is not without its challenges. Taren faced backlash from those who opposed her message, which often left her feeling exposed and attacked.

The emotional toll of such encounters can be significant, leading to what some activists refer to as "activist burnout." This phenomenon is characterized by feelings of exhaustion, cynicism, and a diminished sense of personal accomplishment. To combat this, Taren learned the importance of self-care and establishing a support system among fellow activists.

For example, during a particularly challenging campaign against discriminatory legislation, Taren organized weekly support circles where activists could share their experiences and feelings. These gatherings allowed her and her peers to process their vulnerabilities collectively, transforming their shared struggles into a source of resilience. The concept of collective resilience, as outlined in the work of resilience theorists, suggests that community support can significantly enhance an individual's capacity to cope with adversity.

Taren's moments of strength emerged from these vulnerabilities. Each time she faced adversity, she grew more resolute in her commitment to activism. One such moment came when she successfully lobbied for a local ordinance protecting LGBTQ rights. The journey to this victory was fraught with challenges, including opposition from conservative factions within the community. Yet, Taren's ability to channel her vulnerabilities into a passionate plea for equality galvanized support from unexpected allies, demonstrating the transformative power of embracing one's authentic self.

In reflecting on her journey, Taren often emphasizes the duality of vulnerability and strength. She believes that true strength lies not in the absence of fear or doubt but in the courage to confront these feelings head-on. This perspective aligns with the psychological concept of post-traumatic growth, which suggests that individuals can emerge stronger from their struggles, finding new meaning and purpose in their experiences.

Through her advocacy, Taren Fira exemplifies how moments of vulnerability can serve as catalysts for strength and empowerment. By embracing her authentic self and sharing her story, she not only transformed her own life but also inspired countless others to do the same. In the end, it is these moments—where vulnerability meets strength—that create the foundation for lasting change in the fight for LGBTQ rights and acceptance.

Coming Out to Family and Friends

Coming out is often described as a journey, a process of revealing one's sexual orientation or gender identity to oneself and to others. For Taren Fira, this pivotal moment was laden with both trepidation and anticipation. The act of coming out is not merely a singular event; it is a continual negotiation of identity within the contexts of family, friendships, and society at large.

Theoretical Framework

The process of coming out can be understood through various theoretical lenses. One such framework is the *Minority Stress Theory*, which posits that individuals from marginalized groups experience unique stressors that contribute to negative mental health outcomes. These stressors include stigma, discrimination, and internalized homophobia. For Taren, the fear of rejection from family and friends was a significant source of anxiety that stemmed from these societal pressures.

Another relevant theory is *Identity Development Theory*, which outlines the stages individuals go through as they come to terms with their sexual orientation. According to Cass's model, these stages include identity confusion, identity comparison, identity tolerance, identity acceptance, identity pride, and identity synthesis. Taren found herself navigating these stages, often oscillating between acceptance and fear, as she prepared to share her truth.

Personal Experiences and Challenges

Taren's coming out story began in her teenage years, a tumultuous time characterized by self-discovery and societal expectations. As she grappled with her identity, Taren often felt isolated, believing that her experiences were unique. However, she soon learned that many LGBTQ individuals share similar fears and challenges.

> "Coming out to my parents felt like standing on the edge of a cliff, peering into an abyss. I wasn't sure if I would soar or plummet."

This metaphor captures the duality of hope and fear that accompanies the coming out process. Taren's initial conversations with her family were fraught with uncertainty. She chose a quiet evening, a moment she hoped would foster openness, but the reality was far more complex.

The Initial Conversation

During her first attempt to come out, Taren faced a series of challenges. She began with her mother, who she believed would be more understanding. Taren recalled the moment:

"I took a deep breath, my heart racing. 'Mom, I need to tell you something important. I'm gay.' The silence that followed felt like an eternity."

Her mother's reaction was not what Taren had hoped for; confusion and concern clouded her face. This moment illustrates a common issue faced by many LGBTQ individuals: the unpredictability of familial acceptance. According to research, approximately 40% of LGBTQ individuals report experiencing rejection from their families after coming out. Taren quickly realized that her mother's initial reaction stemmed from a place of concern rather than outright rejection, but the fear of negative consequences lingered.

Navigating Reactions

In the following weeks, Taren faced a myriad of reactions from her family and friends. Some were supportive, while others struggled to understand her identity. This inconsistency can be particularly challenging, as LGBTQ individuals often seek validation and support from their loved ones.

- **Supportive Friends:** Taren's close friends rallied around her, offering unwavering support. They shared their own experiences, creating a safe space for open dialogue.
- **Unsupportive Family Members:** Conversely, Taren's relationship with her father became strained. He expressed discomfort with her identity, leading to heated discussions that often ended in tears.

These varied responses highlight the importance of creating environments that foster understanding and acceptance.

The Role of Education and Communication

To bridge the gap between misunderstanding and acceptance, Taren employed education as a tool. She provided her family with resources, such as articles and videos, that explained LGBTQ identities and experiences. This proactive approach is supported by research indicating that education can significantly reduce prejudice and promote acceptance.

$$\text{Acceptance} \propto \frac{\text{Education}}{\text{Prejudice}} \tag{49}$$

This equation suggests that as education increases, prejudice decreases, leading to greater acceptance. Taren's efforts exemplified this principle, as her family gradually began to understand her identity more fully.

Building a Support Network

Recognizing the importance of community, Taren sought out LGBTQ support groups where she could connect with others who had similar experiences. This network provided her with validation and encouragement, reinforcing her sense of belonging.

> "Finding my community was like discovering a lighthouse in a stormy sea. It gave me hope and strength to face my family."

These groups often serve as critical spaces for individuals to share their stories, fostering resilience and solidarity among LGBTQ individuals.

Reflections and Growth

Through her journey of coming out, Taren learned invaluable lessons about authenticity, vulnerability, and the complexities of love. She realized that acceptance is not always immediate; it often requires time and ongoing dialogue.

> "Coming out is not a one-time event; it's a continuous process. I had to learn to be patient with myself and with my loved ones."

Taren's story is a testament to the power of resilience in the face of adversity. Her experiences reflect a broader narrative within the LGBTQ community, emphasizing the importance of support, education, and patience in the coming out process.

In conclusion, Taren Fira's journey of coming out to her family and friends encapsulates the myriad challenges faced by LGBTQ individuals. By navigating the complexities of acceptance and rejection, Taren not only affirmed her identity but also laid the groundwork for ongoing conversations about love, understanding, and the importance of being true to oneself.

Relationship Struggles and Breakthroughs

In the vibrant tapestry of Taren Fira's life, relationships played a pivotal role, weaving in and out of her journey as a queer activist. As she navigated the complexities of her identity, Taren faced numerous struggles in her personal relationships that mirrored

SECTION TWO: TAREN FIRA'S PERSONAL JOURNEY

the societal challenges she fought against. These struggles often served as catalysts for breakthroughs, both personally and within her community.

The first significant challenge Taren encountered was the difficulty of coming out to her romantic partners. The fear of rejection loomed large, often overshadowing her desire for authenticity. Taren's first serious relationship was with a fellow activist, Alex, who initially embraced her queer identity. However, as their relationship deepened, Taren's commitment to activism began to clash with Alex's more traditional views on gender and sexuality. This tension culminated in a pivotal moment when Taren was invited to speak at a national LGBTQ conference. Alex, feeling uncomfortable with the attention and scrutiny that came with Taren's public persona, expressed doubts about their relationship's future.

This conflict highlighted a common struggle within queer relationships: the balance between personal identity and shared values. According to *Relational Dialectics Theory*, relationships are characterized by ongoing tensions between opposing forces, such as autonomy and connection. Taren's struggle with Alex exemplified this theory, as she grappled with her need for personal expression while longing for connection and acceptance.

In confronting this struggle, Taren learned the importance of open communication. After a particularly heated argument, she initiated a heartfelt conversation with Alex, articulating her fears and aspirations. This breakthrough moment marked a turning point in their relationship. Taren shared her vision of a world where love transcended societal norms, emphasizing that her activism was not just a personal pursuit but a collective fight for acceptance and equality. Through this dialogue, they began to navigate their differences, ultimately leading to a deeper understanding of each other's perspectives.

However, not all relationships experienced such resolution. Taren also faced heartbreak when a close friend, Jordan, struggled to accept Taren's evolving identity. Their friendship began to fray as Jordan clung to preconceived notions of gender roles and relationships, leading to painful confrontations. Taren's attempts to educate Jordan about the fluidity of gender and sexuality often fell on deaf ears, resulting in feelings of isolation and frustration.

This experience illuminated the concept of *identity negotiation*, where individuals must balance their personal identity with the expectations of those around them. Taren's relationship with Jordan ultimately reached an impasse, forcing her to make the difficult decision to distance herself from someone who could not accept her authentic self. This painful yet necessary choice underscored the importance of surrounding oneself with supportive allies who uplift rather than hinder personal growth.

In the wake of these struggles, Taren found solace and strength in the queer community. She forged new relationships with individuals who shared similar experiences, creating a support network that celebrated diversity and inclusivity. This newfound sense of belonging provided Taren with the affirmation she needed, reinforcing her belief in the power of love and acceptance.

One particularly transformative relationship was with Maya, a fellow activist who shared Taren's passion for social justice. Their connection blossomed into a romantic partnership that was rooted in mutual respect and understanding. Together, they navigated the challenges of activism, often collaborating on projects aimed at promoting LGBTQ visibility and rights. This partnership exemplified the concept of *intersectional solidarity*, where individuals from diverse backgrounds come together to support one another in their struggles.

Maya's unwavering support became a source of strength for Taren, especially during moments of self-doubt. Taren often reflected on their relationship as a safe haven, a space where she could express her vulnerabilities without fear of judgment. This dynamic allowed Taren to embrace her identity fully, leading to personal breakthroughs that fueled her activism.

In conclusion, Taren Fira's journey through relationship struggles and breakthroughs illustrates the complex interplay between personal identity and interpersonal connections. The challenges she faced—ranging from navigating romantic relationships to confronting the limitations of friendships—served as pivotal moments of growth. Through open communication, the embrace of supportive communities, and the forging of meaningful connections, Taren not only navigated her own identity but also inspired others to seek authentic relationships that uplift and empower. Ultimately, these experiences reinforced her belief that love, in all its forms, is a powerful catalyst for change in both personal and societal realms.

Self-Care and Mental Health in Activism

In the vibrant yet tumultuous world of activism, particularly within the LGBTQ community, self-care and mental health are not merely personal concerns; they are essential components of sustained advocacy and effective engagement. Taren Fira's journey exemplifies the intricate balance between relentless activism and the necessity of nurturing one's mental well-being.

Activism often involves confronting systemic injustices, societal discrimination, and personal trauma, which can lead to significant emotional and psychological strain. The constant barrage of negative experiences—whether through direct discrimination, witnessing violence against marginalized communities, or engaging in heated political battles—can culminate in what is often termed as activist burnout. This phenomenon is characterized by feelings of exhaustion, cynicism, and a diminished sense of personal accomplishment.

Understanding Activist Burnout

Research indicates that burnout is not only a personal experience but can also be understood through the lens of systems theory. According to Maslach and Leiter (2016), burnout is a result of a mismatch between the individual and their work environment, where the demands placed on the individual exceed their capacity to cope. This imbalance can be mathematically represented as:

$$\text{Burnout} = \frac{\text{Demands}}{\text{Resources}}$$

Where increased demands (e.g., emotional labor, societal pressures) and decreased resources (e.g., support systems, self-care practices) lead to heightened levels of burnout.

The Importance of Self-Care

Self-care in activism can take many forms, from physical health practices to emotional and psychological support. Taren Fira recognized early on that to be an effective advocate, one must prioritize their own well-being. This involves not only recognizing the signs of burnout but actively engaging in practices that mitigate its effects.

Physical Self-Care Physical self-care includes regular exercise, healthy eating, and adequate sleep. For instance, Taren often participated in community yoga sessions that not only promoted physical health but also fostered a sense of community and support among participants. Research shows that physical activity can significantly reduce symptoms of anxiety and depression, as outlined by the American Psychological Association (APA, 2020).

Emotional and Psychological Self-Care Emotional self-care involves nurturing one's emotional health through practices such as mindfulness, therapy, and building supportive relationships. Taren often emphasized the importance of seeking therapy, especially for activists who deal with trauma from advocacy work. Cognitive Behavioral Therapy (CBT) has been shown to be effective in helping individuals reframe negative thoughts and develop healthier coping mechanisms (Hofmann et al., 2012).

Community and Support Systems

Building a supportive community is crucial for mental health in activism. Taren often collaborated with fellow activists to create safe spaces where individuals could share their experiences and feelings without judgment. This sense of belonging can act as a protective factor against the effects of burnout.

One practical example of this is the establishment of "Wellness Wednesdays," a weekly gathering where activists could engage in self-care activities, share their struggles, and support one another. These gatherings not only provided emotional support but also reinforced community bonds, which are essential for resilience in activism.

Navigating the Challenges of Self-Care

Despite the clear benefits of self-care, many activists face barriers to prioritizing their mental health. These barriers can include stigma surrounding mental health, a culture of overwork within activist circles, and the belief that taking time for oneself is a sign of weakness. Taren often challenged these notions by advocating for a culture shift within activism that recognizes self-care as a strength rather than a weakness.

Conclusion

In conclusion, Taren Fira's journey highlights the critical intersection of self-care and mental health in activism. By integrating self-care practices into their advocacy work, activists can sustain their efforts, foster resilience, and ultimately create a more robust movement for change. The lessons learned from Taren's experiences serve as a reminder that to fight for the rights of others, one must first care for oneself. This holistic approach not only benefits the individual activist but enriches the entire community, paving the way for a more sustainable and effective advocacy landscape.

Bibliography

[1] Maslach, C., & Leiter, M. P. (2016). *Burnout: A Guide to Identifying Burnout and Pathways to Recovery.* Harvard Business Review Press.

[2] American Psychological Association. (2020). *Exercise: A Prescription for Health.* Retrieved from https://www.apa.org

[3] Hofmann, S. G., Asnaani, A., Vonk, I. J. J., Sawyer, A. T., & Fang, A. (2012). The Efficacy of Cognitive Behavioral Therapy: A Meta-Analysis. *Cognitive Therapy and Research*, 36(5), 427-440.

Balancing Personal Life and Advocacy

In the whirlwind of activism, particularly within the LGBTQ community, the balance between personal life and advocacy can often feel like a precarious tightrope walk. Taren Fira, as a prominent figure in Alyndra's LGBTQ movement, exemplified the challenges that many activists face in this regard. This section will explore the intricate dynamics of maintaining personal relationships, self-care, and the relentless pursuit of social justice.

Understanding the Dual Roles

Activists often find themselves juggling two demanding roles: that of a public figure and a private individual. The duality of these identities can lead to significant stress. Taren's experience illustrates a common phenomenon known as *role conflict*, where the expectations of one role (activist) clash with those of another (friend, partner, or family member). For instance, Taren's commitment to organizing events and advocating for policy changes often meant late nights and weekends spent away from loved ones, causing strains in personal relationships.

The Theory of Work-Life Balance

The theory of work-life balance posits that individuals can achieve a state where both personal and professional demands are met without detriment to either. This balance is crucial for sustaining long-term activism. According to Greenhaus and Beutell (1985), work-life conflict occurs when the demands of one role interfere with the fulfillment of another. For Taren, finding equilibrium meant setting boundaries, such as designating specific times for advocacy work and personal life.

$$\text{Work-Life Balance} = \frac{\text{Time Spent on Advocacy}}{\text{Time Spent on Personal Life}} \qquad (50)$$

In Taren's case, the ideal balance was not simply a 50-50 split but rather a fluid dynamic that changed with the ebb and flow of activism and personal commitments.

Challenges of Balancing Personal Life and Advocacy

Despite the theoretical frameworks, many activists face real-world challenges. Taren encountered several obstacles, including:

- **Emotional Toll:** The emotional burden of activism can lead to burnout. Taren often found herself drained after long campaigns, leaving little energy for personal connections.

- **Public Scrutiny:** As a public figure, Taren's personal life was often scrutinized by the media and the public, complicating her ability to maintain privacy and personal relationships.

- **Time Constraints:** The demanding schedule of activism, filled with meetings, protests, and community events, often clashed with personal commitments, leading to feelings of guilt and neglect.

Strategies for Achieving Balance

To navigate these challenges, Taren developed several strategies that proved effective in balancing her personal life with her advocacy work:

1. **Setting Boundaries:** Taren learned to communicate her needs to friends and family, establishing clear boundaries around her availability. This included designating "off" hours where she could focus on personal relationships without the distraction of activism.

2. **Prioritizing Self-Care:** Recognizing the importance of mental health, Taren made self-care a priority. This included regular exercise, meditation, and time spent with loved ones, which rejuvenated her spirit and enhanced her effectiveness as an advocate.

3. **Involving Loved Ones:** Taren found that involving her friends and family in her advocacy work not only strengthened her relationships but also fostered a supportive community. By inviting them to events and discussions, she created a shared sense of purpose.

4. **Flexibility:** Understanding that life is unpredictable, Taren practiced flexibility in her schedule, allowing room for spontaneity in both her personal and professional life. This adaptability helped her manage stress and maintain connections.

Examples from Taren's Life

One notable example of Taren's balancing act occurred during the planning of Alyndra's annual Pride event. While she was deeply committed to the cause, she also wanted to ensure that her partner felt valued and included. Taren organized a pre-Pride gathering with friends and family, blending her personal and activist life. This event not only strengthened her relationships but also created a supportive atmosphere for her advocacy.

Another instance was during a particularly challenging legislative battle for LGBTQ rights. Taren's emotional state was fragile, and her partner noticed her growing distance. Recognizing this, Taren took a step back from her advocacy for a weekend, focusing on nurturing her relationship. This decision, while difficult, ultimately allowed her to return to her work with renewed vigor and passion.

Conclusion

Balancing personal life and advocacy is an ongoing challenge for many activists, including Taren Fira. By employing strategies such as setting boundaries, prioritizing self-care, and involving loved ones in her work, Taren was able to navigate the complexities of her dual roles. Her journey serves as a reminder that personal well-being is integral to effective advocacy. As the LGBTQ movement continues to evolve, the lessons learned from Taren's experiences can guide future activists in maintaining a healthy balance between their personal and professional lives.

Navigating Queer Identity in Different Spaces

Navigating queer identity in various environments is akin to traversing a labyrinth, where each turn presents unique challenges and opportunities for self-expression. The complexity of queer identity is influenced by a myriad of factors, including cultural context, social norms, and personal experiences. This section will explore the nuances of queer identity across different spaces, emphasizing the theoretical frameworks, problems encountered, and illustrative examples that highlight the multifaceted nature of this journey.

Theoretical Frameworks

Understanding the navigation of queer identity requires a solid theoretical foundation. One such framework is Judith Butler's concept of *gender performativity*, which posits that gender is not an innate quality but rather a series of acts and performances that are socially constructed. This theory suggests that queer individuals often find themselves performing their identities differently depending on the space they occupy.

Another relevant theory is *intersectionality*, coined by Kimberlé Crenshaw, which examines how various social identities (such as race, gender, sexuality, and class) intersect to create unique modes of discrimination and privilege. This framework is crucial for understanding how queer individuals experience their identities differently in diverse spaces, as their experiences may be compounded by other aspects of their identities.

Problems Faced in Different Spaces

Navigating queer identity can lead to a host of challenges, particularly when individuals find themselves in environments that may not be accepting or inclusive. These challenges can manifest in various forms:

- **Workplace Dynamics:** In professional settings, queer individuals may feel pressured to conform to heteronormative standards, leading to a phenomenon known as *passing*. This pressure can create a sense of dissonance between one's authentic self and the persona one presents at work.

- **Family Expectations:** Family dynamics can significantly impact one's experience of queer identity. Many individuals face the challenge of reconciling their sexual orientation or gender identity with familial expectations or cultural norms, leading to potential alienation or conflict.

- **Cultural Context:** Different cultural environments can either support or hinder queer expression. For instance, in conservative communities, overt expressions of queer identity may be met with hostility, while more progressive areas might offer support and acceptance.

- **Safety Concerns:** The fear of violence or discrimination can lead queer individuals to alter their behavior or presentation in public spaces. This necessity for self-protection can stifle authentic self-expression and contribute to mental health challenges.

Examples of Navigating Queer Identity

To illustrate the complexities of navigating queer identity, consider the following examples:

Example 1: The Workplace   In a corporate setting, Alex, a non-binary individual, grapples with the decision to use their chosen name and pronouns. Initially, Alex opts to present as gender-conforming to avoid potential backlash from colleagues. However, as they build relationships with supportive coworkers, Alex begins to embrace their identity more openly, participating in LGBTQ+ initiatives and advocating for inclusive policies. This evolution highlights the importance of supportive environments in fostering authentic self-expression.

Example 2: Family Dynamics   Maria, a lesbian woman, faces significant challenges when coming out to her traditional family. Initially met with resistance, Maria navigates her identity by finding common ground with her family members through shared values and experiences. Over time, she creates a safe space for dialogue, ultimately leading to greater acceptance. This example underscores the potential for growth and understanding within familial relationships, even in the face of initial rejection.

Example 3: Cultural Context   In a multicultural city, Jamal, a queer person of color, experiences both acceptance and discrimination. In predominantly queer spaces, Jamal feels liberated to express their identity fully. However, in more conservative neighborhoods, they encounter microaggressions and overt hostility. Jamal's experience illustrates the varying degrees of acceptance based on cultural context and highlights the need for intersectional advocacy that addresses both queer and racial identities.

Strategies for Navigating Queer Identity

Successfully navigating queer identity in different spaces often requires intentional strategies:

- **Building Support Networks:** Establishing connections with other queer individuals can provide essential emotional support and resources. These networks can offer safe spaces for sharing experiences and strategies for navigating challenging environments.

- **Educating Others:** Engaging in conversations about queer identities can help demystify misconceptions and foster understanding among peers, family, and colleagues. Education can serve as a powerful tool for advocacy and allyship.

- **Practicing Self-Care:** Recognizing the emotional toll of navigating queer identity is crucial. Engaging in self-care practices, such as therapy, mindfulness, and creative expression, can help individuals maintain their mental health amid challenges.

- **Advocating for Inclusivity:** Actively participating in or initiating discussions about inclusivity in various spaces can help create a culture of acceptance. This advocacy can take the form of policy changes, awareness campaigns, or community-building efforts.

Conclusion

Navigating queer identity in different spaces is a complex and often challenging endeavor. By understanding the theoretical frameworks that inform this navigation, recognizing the problems faced, and employing effective strategies, queer individuals can work towards authentic self-expression and greater acceptance in diverse environments. The journey is not linear, and each individual's experience is unique, underscoring the importance of empathy, understanding, and solidarity within the broader LGBTQ+ community.

Support Systems and Found Families

In the journey of LGBTQ activism, the concept of support systems and found families emerges as a vital pillar for emotional resilience and community solidarity. For many individuals within the LGBTQ community, traditional familial structures may not provide the necessary acceptance or support, leading to the formation of alternative familial bonds—often referred to as "found families." This section explores the significance of these networks, their impact on personal and collective well-being, and the theoretical frameworks that underpin these relationships.

The Importance of Support Systems

Support systems encompass the network of relationships that provide emotional, social, and practical assistance. For LGBTQ individuals, these systems can include friends, mentors, community organizations, and chosen families. The significance of support systems is underscored by research indicating that individuals with robust support networks experience lower levels of anxiety and depression, improved self-esteem, and greater overall life satisfaction [?].

The theory of social support posits that individuals who perceive themselves as having supportive relationships are better equipped to cope with stressors and challenges. According to Cohen and Wills (1985), social support can be categorized into three types: emotional support, instrumental support, and informational support. Emotional support involves the provision of empathy and understanding, instrumental support refers to tangible assistance, and informational support encompasses advice and guidance. Each of these forms of support is crucial for LGBTQ individuals navigating the complexities of their identities and societal challenges.

Found Families: A Safe Haven

Found families are formed through shared experiences, mutual understanding, and a commitment to support one another. These families often arise in response to the rejection or estrangement that LGBTQ individuals may face from their biological families. The process of creating a found family can be likened to the concept of kinship in anthropology, where relationships are forged not through blood but through shared values, experiences, and emotional bonds.

An illustrative example of found families can be seen in the drag and LGBTQ performance communities, where individuals often come together to create supportive environments. In these spaces, members celebrate each other's identities, provide emotional support during difficult times, and collaborate on creative projects. This phenomenon is captured in the work of Judith Butler, who argues that kinship is not merely a biological construct but rather a social formation that can be redefined and reconstructed within communities [?].

Challenges in Establishing Support Systems

While found families can provide immense benefits, establishing and maintaining these support systems is not without challenges. Issues such as geographical dispersion, financial constraints, and societal stigma can hinder the formation of robust support networks. Additionally, individuals may experience internalized homophobia or fear of rejection that can prevent them from fully engaging with potential support systems.

Furthermore, the dynamics within found families can be complex. Conflicts may arise due to differing values or priorities, and the emotional labor involved in maintaining these relationships can lead to burnout. It is crucial for individuals to recognize these challenges and actively work to cultivate healthy and supportive environments. Communication, empathy, and mutual respect are essential components in navigating these complexities.

The Role of Community Organizations

Community organizations play a pivotal role in facilitating the formation of support systems and found families within the LGBTQ community. These organizations provide safe spaces where individuals can connect, share experiences, and access resources. For example, LGBTQ youth centers often offer mentorship programs that pair young individuals with older role models, fostering a sense of belonging and support.

Moreover, initiatives such as peer support groups and community events create opportunities for individuals to build relationships and establish networks of support. Research conducted by the Human Rights Campaign (2020) indicates that participation in LGBTQ community organizations significantly enhances individuals' perceptions of social support and belonging, ultimately contributing to better mental health outcomes.

Conclusion

In conclusion, support systems and found families are integral to the LGBTQ experience, providing essential emotional and social support in the face of adversity. By understanding the theoretical frameworks that underpin these relationships and recognizing the challenges involved in their establishment, individuals can better navigate their journeys of self-acceptance and activism. The cultivation of found families not only fosters personal growth but also strengthens the collective resilience of the LGBTQ community, paving the way for a more inclusive and supportive society.

Reflections on Personal Growth and Transformation

Personal growth and transformation are intrinsic to the journey of any activist, particularly for Taren Fira, whose life serves as a poignant reflection of the evolving nature of identity and advocacy. This section delves into the multifaceted dimensions of Taren's personal growth, exploring the theories of identity formation, the psychological challenges faced, and the transformative experiences that shaped her activism.

Theoretical Framework

To understand Taren's personal growth, we can draw upon Erik Erikson's psychosocial development theory, which posits that individuals navigate eight stages of development throughout their lives. Each stage presents a unique conflict that must be resolved for healthy personality development. Taren's journey can be particularly analyzed through the lens of the fifth stage: Identity vs. Role Confusion. This stage typically occurs during adolescence and is crucial for forming a strong sense of self.

In Taren's case, the conflict between societal expectations and her emerging queer identity led to significant periods of introspection and self-discovery. The process of coming out was not merely a singular event but a series of transformative moments that allowed her to embrace her authentic self.

Challenges Faced

Taren's path to self-acceptance was fraught with challenges, including internalized homophobia, societal rejection, and familial expectations. These obstacles often manifested as psychological distress, leading to feelings of isolation and confusion. Research indicates that LGBTQ individuals frequently experience higher rates of anxiety and depression, stemming from societal stigma and discrimination [?].

Taren faced these issues head-on, utilizing them as catalysts for personal growth. For example, after a particularly harsh encounter with discrimination during her teenage years, Taren sought solace in creative expression. This experience not only served as an outlet for her pain but also ignited her passion for activism.

Transformative Experiences

One pivotal moment in Taren's journey was her participation in a local LGBTQ youth group. Initially hesitant, she found a community that fostered acceptance and understanding. This environment allowed her to share her story, thereby reinforcing her identity and empowering others to do the same. The concept of "found family" is critical here; as Taren connected with peers who shared similar struggles, she began to realize the power of solidarity and support.

Furthermore, Taren's involvement in organizing events, such as the first LGBTQ Pride event in Alyndra, marked a significant turning point in her transformation. This experience not only solidified her leadership skills but also instilled a sense of purpose. The successful execution of the event was a testament to her resilience and determination, reinforcing the idea that personal growth often occurs through collective action.

Reflections on Growth

Reflecting on her journey, Taren often emphasizes the importance of vulnerability in personal growth. She acknowledges that embracing her queer identity required her to confront her fears and insecurities. This aligns with Brené Brown's research on vulnerability, which suggests that it is a crucial element in fostering connection and authenticity [?].

Taren's transformation is also evident in her approach to activism. Initially focused on her personal experiences, she gradually expanded her perspective to include intersectional issues within the LGBTQ community. This shift not only enriched her advocacy but also highlighted the importance of listening to and amplifying marginalized voices.

Conclusion

In conclusion, Taren Fira's reflections on personal growth and transformation illustrate the intricate relationship between identity and activism. Her journey, marked by challenges and transformative experiences, underscores the significance of embracing one's authentic self while advocating for others. As she often states, "Our stories are our power." Through her evolution, Taren has not only transformed her own life but has also inspired countless others to embark on their journeys of self-discovery and empowerment.

The Intersection of Personal and Political

The intersection of personal and political is a fundamental aspect of LGBTQ activism, particularly in the life and work of Taren Fira. This concept, often encapsulated in the phrase "the personal is political," highlights how individual experiences of oppression and identity are intricately linked to broader societal structures and policies. This section explores how Taren's personal journey as a queer individual shaped her political activism and vice versa, illustrating the profound connection between personal narratives and political advocacy.

Understanding the Personal is Political

The phrase "the personal is political" was popularized during the feminist movements of the late 20th century, emphasizing that personal experiences are often reflective of systemic issues. For Taren Fira, her experiences of discrimination, identity struggles, and triumphs were not merely personal anecdotes; they were emblematic of larger societal challenges faced by the LGBTQ community. This intersectionality is crucial in understanding the motivations behind her activism.

Theory: Intersectionality in Activism

Intersectionality, a term coined by legal scholar Kimberlé Crenshaw, refers to the way various social identities (such as race, gender, sexuality, and class) intersect to create unique modes of discrimination and privilege. Taren's activism was deeply informed by her understanding of intersectionality. She recognized that the experiences of queer individuals could not be understood in isolation from other identities. For example, a queer person of color may face different challenges than a white queer individual due to the compounded effects of racism and homophobia.

$$\text{Intersectionality} = \text{Identity}_1 + \text{Identity}_2 + \text{Identity}_3 + \ldots \qquad (51)$$

This equation symbolizes the additive nature of identities, where each component contributes to the overall experience of oppression or privilege. Taren's advocacy work often focused on amplifying the voices of those at the intersections of multiple marginalized identities, pushing for a more inclusive movement.

Personal Experiences Shaping Political Activism

Taren's journey began with her own struggles with identity. Growing up in Alyndra, she faced societal pressures that dictated her behavior based on traditional gender norms. Her experiences of bullying and discrimination were not just personal traumas; they were reflections of a society that often silenced queer voices. These experiences fueled her desire to create change, leading her to organize events and campaigns aimed at raising awareness about LGBTQ issues.

For instance, during her first Pride event, Taren shared her own coming-out story as part of the opening speech. By exposing her vulnerabilities, she aimed to create a safe space for others to share their stories, thus intertwining personal narratives with political activism. This approach not only humanized the issues at hand but also encouraged a sense of community among attendees.

Challenges Faced in Bridging Personal and Political

Despite the powerful connection between personal experiences and political activism, Taren faced significant challenges. One major issue was the backlash from conservative factions within Alyndra, who often dismissed personal narratives as mere anecdotes rather than legitimate political discourse. Critics argued that personal stories lacked the empirical data required for effective advocacy, thereby undermining the emotional weight of Taren's experiences.

Moreover, Taren encountered the problem of tokenism within the activist community. As she rose to prominence, there were instances where her personal story was co-opted by organizations seeking to gain visibility without genuinely addressing the systemic issues she fought against. This led to tensions, as Taren emphasized the importance of authenticity in activism, advocating for a movement that truly represented the diverse experiences of the LGBTQ community.

Examples of Effective Personal-Political Interplay

One of the most notable examples of Taren's effective blending of personal and political was her campaign for marriage equality. Drawing upon her own experiences of love and commitment with her partner, Taren articulated the emotional and legal ramifications of being denied marriage rights. By sharing her personal story, she was able to resonate with a broader audience, including those who may not have identified as LGBTQ but understood the value of love and partnership.

Additionally, Taren utilized social media platforms to share her journey, creating a series of video diaries that documented her activism and personal life. This approach not only humanized the issues but also allowed for greater engagement with a global audience, demonstrating how personal narratives can transcend local contexts to inspire international solidarity.

Conclusion: The Ongoing Journey

The intersection of personal and political in Taren Fira's activism underscores the importance of storytelling in the fight for LGBTQ rights. By weaving her personal experiences into her advocacy, Taren not only challenged societal norms but also fostered a sense of community and understanding among diverse groups. The lessons learned from her journey highlight the necessity of embracing personal narratives as a powerful tool for social change, reminding activists that their stories are integral to the broader political landscape.

In conclusion, the interplay between personal experiences and political activism is not merely a theoretical concept but a lived reality for many activists, including Taren Fira. By recognizing and embracing this intersection, the LGBTQ movement can continue to evolve, ensuring that all voices are heard and valued in the ongoing fight for equality.

The Importance of Authenticity

Authenticity in activism is not merely a buzzword; it is a fundamental principle that shapes the efficacy and integrity of movements, particularly within the LGBTQ community. Authenticity involves being true to oneself and one's values, which fosters trust, connection, and a sense of belonging among activists and allies alike. This section explores the significance of authenticity in LGBTQ advocacy, the challenges activists face in maintaining it, and how it can serve as a catalyst for meaningful change.

Defining Authenticity in Activism

Authenticity can be understood as the alignment between one's beliefs, values, and actions. In the context of LGBTQ activism, this means advocating for rights and recognition in a manner that reflects one's genuine experiences and identities. According to sociologist Erving Goffman, individuals navigate different social contexts with varying degrees of authenticity, often presenting a "front" that may obscure their true selves. This performance can create a dissonance that not only affects the individual but also the broader movement.

The Role of Personal Narratives

Personal narratives play a crucial role in establishing authenticity. As Taren Fira often emphasized, sharing one's story can humanize issues and foster empathy among those who may not understand the challenges faced by LGBTQ individuals. Research indicates that storytelling can significantly impact public perception and policy-making. For instance, the "It Gets Better" campaign utilized personal testimonials to shift societal attitudes towards LGBTQ youth, demonstrating how authenticity can resonate on a large scale.

Challenges to Authenticity

Despite its importance, maintaining authenticity can be fraught with challenges. Many activists grapple with societal expectations, internalized stigma, and the pressure to conform to certain identities or narratives. This struggle can lead to what is known as "performative activism," where individuals engage in advocacy that appears genuine but lacks depth and sincerity. For example, some activists may prioritize visibility over substantive change, participating in events or campaigns that do not align with their true beliefs or experiences, thus undermining the authenticity of the movement.

The Impact of Authenticity on Allyship

Authenticity also plays a pivotal role in allyship. Allies who approach their support with genuine intention and understanding can foster a more inclusive environment. However, when allies engage in performative actions—such as posting on social media without taking meaningful steps to support the community—they risk alienating those they aim to support. Authentic allies actively listen, educate themselves, and work collaboratively with LGBTQ individuals to advocate for change, demonstrating that allyship is not merely about visibility but about shared commitment to justice.

Authenticity as a Catalyst for Change

The power of authenticity extends beyond individual narratives; it can catalyze systemic change. When activists embrace their true selves, they challenge societal norms and inspire others to do the same. This collective authenticity can lead to a more robust and diverse movement. For instance, the Stonewall Riots of 1969 were fueled by the authentic expressions of anger and frustration from marginalized individuals, which ultimately sparked a global movement for LGBTQ rights. The raw emotion and genuine desire for change during this pivotal moment exemplify how authenticity can mobilize communities and create lasting impact.

Creating Safe Spaces for Authenticity

To foster authenticity within LGBTQ activism, it is essential to create safe spaces where individuals feel comfortable expressing their true selves. These spaces encourage vulnerability and openness, allowing activists to share their experiences without fear of judgment or reprisal. Organizations can implement training programs that emphasize the importance of authenticity and provide tools for activists to navigate their identities within the movement. Furthermore, fostering an inclusive environment that celebrates diverse identities can enhance the overall strength of the advocacy efforts.

Conclusion: Embracing Authenticity for Lasting Change

In conclusion, the importance of authenticity in LGBTQ activism cannot be overstated. It serves as a foundation for trust, empathy, and genuine connection among activists and allies. By embracing their true selves and encouraging others to do the same, activists can create a more inclusive and effective movement. As Taren Fira's journey illustrates, authenticity is not just a personal endeavor; it is a collective responsibility that can drive transformative change and inspire future generations of activists. The call for authenticity is ultimately a call for courage—courage to be oneself and to advocate for a world where everyone can do the same.

$$\text{Authenticity} = \frac{\text{True Self}}{\text{Social Expectations}} \times \text{Community Impact} \qquad (52)$$

Section Three: Allies and the Importance of Their Voices

Supporting LGBTQ Individuals as Allies

In the vibrant tapestry of LGBTQ activism, allies play a crucial role in amplifying marginalized voices and fostering an inclusive society. Supporting LGBTQ individuals as allies requires a deep understanding of the complexities of identity, privilege, and social dynamics. This section delves into the theoretical underpinnings, challenges faced by LGBTQ individuals, and practical examples of effective allyship.

Theoretical Framework

Allyship is rooted in the concept of *intersectionality*, coined by Kimberlé Crenshaw, which emphasizes that individuals experience multiple, overlapping identities that shape their experiences of oppression and privilege. This framework allows allies to recognize that LGBTQ individuals do not exist in a vacuum; their experiences are influenced by race, class, gender, ability, and other intersecting identities.

The *social identity theory* posits that individuals derive a sense of self from their group memberships. Allies must understand their own social identities and how these influence their perspectives and interactions with LGBTQ individuals. By recognizing their privilege, allies can engage in more meaningful and effective support.

Challenges Faced by LGBTQ Individuals

LGBTQ individuals often face systemic discrimination, which manifests in various forms, including:

- **Employment Discrimination:** Many LGBTQ individuals encounter bias in hiring, promotions, and workplace environments, leading to economic disparities. According to a report by the Human Rights Campaign, 46% of LGBTQ workers have experienced discrimination in the workplace.

- **Healthcare Inequities:** LGBTQ individuals frequently face barriers to accessing healthcare, including discrimination from providers and lack of culturally competent care. The National LGBTQ Task Force highlights that LGBTQ people are more likely to experience mental health issues due to societal stigma.

- **Social Isolation:** Many LGBTQ individuals experience rejection from family and friends, leading to feelings of isolation. Studies show that LGBTQ youth are more likely to experience homelessness and mental health crises due to familial rejection.

Understanding these challenges is essential for allies, as it informs their approach to support and advocacy.

Practical Strategies for Effective Allyship

To be effective allies, individuals must engage in continuous learning and active participation in the LGBTQ community. Here are several strategies:

1. **Educate Yourself:** Allies should invest time in learning about LGBTQ history, terminology, and current issues. Resources such as books, documentaries, and workshops can provide valuable insights. For instance, reading works by authors like Audre Lorde or James Baldwin can deepen understanding of the LGBTQ experience.

SECTION THREE: ALLIES AND THE IMPORTANCE OF THEIR VOICES

2. **Listen and Validate:** Allies must practice active listening, creating safe spaces for LGBTQ individuals to share their experiences without judgment. Validating their feelings and experiences fosters trust and strengthens allyship.

3. **Speak Up Against Discrimination:** Allies should challenge discriminatory remarks and actions in their communities, workplaces, and social circles. This can be as simple as addressing microaggressions or as involved as participating in protests and advocacy campaigns.

4. **Support LGBTQ Organizations:** Contributing time or resources to LGBTQ organizations can amplify their efforts. Whether through volunteering, fundraising, or attending events, allies can play a vital role in supporting these communities.

5. **Use Inclusive Language:** Language shapes perceptions. Allies should strive to use gender-neutral language and respect individuals' chosen names and pronouns. This simple act can significantly impact the comfort and acceptance of LGBTQ individuals.

6. **Be Open to Feedback:** Allies must remain open to constructive criticism and be willing to learn from their mistakes. This adaptability is crucial in evolving as a supportive ally.

Examples of Effective Allyship

Several individuals and organizations exemplify effective allyship:

- **Corporate Allyship:** Companies like Microsoft and Apple have implemented inclusive policies and practices, such as equal benefits for same-sex couples and active participation in Pride events, demonstrating corporate responsibility and support for LGBTQ rights.

- **Celebrity Allies:** Public figures like Ellen DeGeneres and Laverne Cox have used their platforms to advocate for LGBTQ rights, raising awareness and encouraging dialogue around important issues. Their visibility helps destigmatize LGBTQ identities and inspires others to support the community.

- **Community Initiatives:** Local organizations, such as LGBTQ centers, often rely on ally support for programming and outreach. By volunteering or sponsoring events, allies contribute to creating safe spaces for LGBTQ individuals.

Conclusion

Supporting LGBTQ individuals as allies is a dynamic and ongoing process that requires commitment, empathy, and action. By understanding the complexities of identity and the challenges faced by LGBTQ individuals, allies can engage in meaningful advocacy that promotes inclusivity and equality. As the movement for LGBTQ rights continues to evolve, the role of allies remains vital in creating a society where everyone can thrive, regardless of their sexual orientation or gender identity.

In the words of Audre Lorde, "It is not our differences that divide us. It is our inability to recognize, accept, and celebrate those differences." Allies must strive to recognize and celebrate the rich diversity within the LGBTQ community, fostering a culture of acceptance and support for all.

Being an Effective Ally in the LGBTQ Community

In the journey towards achieving LGBTQ equality, the role of allies is indispensable. Allies are individuals who support the LGBTQ community, advocating for equal rights and social justice, often without identifying as part of the community themselves. This section explores the principles of effective allyship, the challenges allies face, and practical strategies for making a meaningful impact.

Understanding Allyship

Allyship is not merely a passive stance of support; it requires active engagement and a willingness to confront injustices. According to [Broido(2000)], effective allies must recognize their privilege and the power dynamics at play within society. This understanding is crucial for allies to navigate their role responsibly and effectively.

Theoretical Frameworks of Allyship

Several theories underpin effective allyship:

- **Critical Race Theory (CRT):** This framework emphasizes the importance of recognizing systemic racism and its intersection with other forms of oppression, including homophobia and transphobia. Allies must engage with CRT to understand how their identities and privileges affect their advocacy.

- **Intersectionality:** Coined by [Crenshaw(1989)], intersectionality posits that individuals experience overlapping systems of discrimination. Allies should consider how various identities (race, gender, class) intersect and affect LGBTQ individuals' experiences.

- **Social Identity Theory:** This theory, proposed by [Tajfel(1979)], suggests that individuals derive a sense of identity from their group memberships. Allies must acknowledge their own social identities and how these relate to the LGBTQ community.

Challenges Faced by Allies

While allies play a vital role, they often encounter challenges that can hinder their effectiveness:

- **Tokenism:** Allies may be perceived as merely performing allyship for social validation rather than genuinely supporting LGBTQ rights. This perception can undermine their credibility and the trust of the community.

- **Misunderstanding Privilege:** Some allies may struggle to recognize their privilege, leading to unintentional harm. For example, a white cisgender ally may inadvertently overshadow the voices of queer people of color in discussions about intersectional issues.

- **Fear of Offense:** Allies often fear saying the wrong thing, which can lead to silence or inaction. This fear can prevent them from engaging in important conversations about LGBTQ rights.

Strategies for Effective Allyship

To be effective allies, individuals can adopt several strategies:

- **Educate Yourself:** Allies should seek to learn about LGBTQ history, issues, and experiences. Reading books, attending workshops, and engaging with LGBTQ media can provide valuable insights. For instance, [Meyer(2016)] emphasizes the importance of understanding the historical context of LGBTQ rights.

- **Listen Actively:** Allies must prioritize listening to LGBTQ voices. This means creating spaces for LGBTQ individuals to share their experiences without interruption or judgment. Active listening fosters empathy and understanding.

- **Speak Up Against Discrimination:** Allies should not hesitate to challenge homophobic or transphobic remarks in social settings. This includes addressing microaggressions, which are subtle, often unintentional, discriminatory comments or behaviors. For example, responding to a colleague's offhand joke about LGBTQ individuals can help create a more inclusive environment.

- **Support LGBTQ Organizations:** Contributing time, resources, or funds to LGBTQ organizations can amplify the impact of allyship. Allies can volunteer, participate in fundraising events, or advocate for LGBTQ-inclusive policies within their workplaces and communities.

- **Reflect on Your Actions:** Allies should regularly assess their actions and their impact on the LGBTQ community. This reflection can help identify areas for growth and improvement, ensuring that allyship remains genuine and effective.

Examples of Effective Allyship

Several notable examples illustrate effective allyship in action:

- **Corporate Allyship:** Companies like *Starbucks* and *Target* have publicly supported LGBTQ rights by implementing inclusive policies and participating in Pride events. Their commitment demonstrates how corporate allies can influence societal norms and support advocacy efforts.

- **Celebrity Advocacy:** Public figures like *Ellen DeGeneres* and *Laverne Cox* use their platforms to raise awareness about LGBTQ issues. Their visibility helps to normalize LGBTQ identities and foster acceptance.

- **Grassroots Movements:** Local community members who organize events like Pride parades or workshops on LGBTQ issues exemplify grassroots allyship. These efforts create safe spaces and foster community solidarity.

SECTION THREE: ALLIES AND THE IMPORTANCE OF THEIR VOICES

Conclusion

Being an effective ally in the LGBTQ community requires a commitment to understanding, learning, and advocating for change. Allies must recognize their privilege, actively listen to marginalized voices, and engage in meaningful actions that support LGBTQ rights. By embracing the principles of allyship, individuals can contribute to a more inclusive and equitable society for all.

Bibliography

[Broido(2000)] Broido, E. M. (2000). *The Role of Allies in Social Justice Movements.* Journal of College Student Development, 41(6), 689-703.

[Crenshaw(1989)] Crenshaw, K. (1989). Demarginalizing the Intersection of Race and Sex: A Black Feminist Critique of Antidiscrimination Doctrine, Feminist Theory and Antiracist Politics. *University of Chicago Legal Forum,* 1989(1), 139-167.

[Meyer(2016)] Meyer, M. (2016). *Understanding LGBTQ History: A Resource for Allies.* New York: Routledge.

[Tajfel(1979)] Tajfel, H. (1979). *Individuals and Groups in Social Psychology.* British Journal of Social and Clinical Psychology, 18(2), 183-190.

Recognizing Privilege and Centering Marginalized Voices

In the intricate tapestry of LGBTQ activism, recognizing privilege is paramount to creating an equitable and inclusive movement. Privilege can be defined as the unearned advantages bestowed upon individuals based on various aspects of their identity, such as race, gender, sexual orientation, socioeconomic status, and ability. Understanding these dynamics is essential for activists who aim to uplift marginalized voices within the LGBTQ community.

Theoretical Framework

The concept of privilege is often discussed within the framework of intersectionality, a term coined by legal scholar Kimberlé Crenshaw. Intersectionality posits that individuals experience overlapping social identities and the resultant discrimination or privilege they face is not merely additive but multiplicative. This means that a white, cisgender gay man may experience privilege in ways that a transgender woman of color does not, despite both identifying as part of the LGBTQ community.

$$\text{Total Experience of Discrimination} = f(\text{Race, Gender, Sexual Orientation, Socioeconom} \tag{53}$$

This equation suggests that the experience of discrimination is a function of multiple variables, each contributing to the overall experience of an individual within society.

Identifying Privilege

To effectively recognize privilege, activists must engage in self-reflection and critical analysis of their own identities. This involves asking questions such as:

- Do I benefit from societal norms that favor my race or gender?

- How does my socioeconomic status affect my access to resources and opportunities?

- In what ways can I leverage my privilege to support those who are marginalized?

For example, a cisgender ally may enjoy societal acceptance and legal recognition that transgender individuals do not. This recognition allows allies to advocate for trans rights with a sense of urgency and responsibility, understanding that their voices can amplify the struggles faced by those who are often overlooked.

Centering Marginalized Voices

Central to the practice of recognizing privilege is the commitment to center marginalized voices in advocacy efforts. This means actively listening to and amplifying the experiences of those who are often silenced or ignored.

A powerful example of centering marginalized voices can be seen in the work of organizations such as the Transgender Law Center, which prioritizes the needs and experiences of transgender and gender non-conforming individuals. By placing the voices of those most affected at the forefront of advocacy, organizations can create more effective strategies that address the specific challenges faced by marginalized communities.

Challenges in Centering Voices

While the intention to center marginalized voices is noble, it is not without challenges. Activists may inadvertently perpetuate harm by speaking over or for marginalized individuals rather than allowing them to articulate their own experiences. This phenomenon is often referred to as "performative allyship," where individuals or organizations seek to gain social capital rather than genuinely support marginalized communities.

To combat this, activists should adopt the following strategies:

- Engage in active listening: Prioritize understanding and validating the experiences of marginalized individuals.

- Provide platforms: Create opportunities for marginalized voices to be heard, whether through public speaking, writing, or other forms of expression.

- Share space: Allow marginalized individuals to lead discussions and initiatives, ensuring that their perspectives shape the direction of advocacy efforts.

Real-World Applications

In practice, recognizing privilege and centering marginalized voices can manifest in various ways:

- Workshops and training sessions that educate allies about privilege and intersectionality, fostering a deeper understanding of how to support marginalized communities effectively.

- Campaigns that highlight the stories and experiences of LGBTQ individuals from diverse backgrounds, showcasing the richness of the community while emphasizing the need for inclusivity.

- Collaborations with grassroots organizations led by marginalized individuals, ensuring that advocacy efforts are informed by those directly impacted by the issues at hand.

Conclusion

Recognizing privilege and centering marginalized voices is not merely an ethical obligation; it is a strategic necessity for effective LGBTQ activism. By fostering an environment where diverse voices are heard and valued, activists can work towards a more inclusive and equitable movement that genuinely represents the complexities of the LGBTQ experience. As Taren Fira often emphasized, "True advocacy is not about speaking for others; it is about creating spaces where everyone can speak for themselves." In this way, the movement not only grows stronger but also becomes a true reflection of the diverse tapestry that is the LGBTQ community.

Intersectional Activism and Solidarity

Intersectional activism is a framework that recognizes the interconnected nature of social categorizations such as race, class, gender, sexuality, and ability, and how these intersections contribute to unique experiences of oppression and privilege. Coined by legal scholar Kimberlé Crenshaw in the late 1980s, intersectionality challenges the traditional, single-axis approach to social justice that often fails to address the complexities of marginalized identities. This section will explore the theoretical underpinnings of intersectional activism, the challenges it faces, and examples of its application within LGBTQ advocacy.

Theoretical Foundations

At its core, intersectional activism posits that individuals do not experience discrimination or privilege in isolation. Instead, their identities intersect to create unique social positions that shape their experiences. For instance, a queer person of color may face different challenges than a white queer individual, due to the compounded effects of racism and homophobia. This perspective aligns with the critical race theory, which emphasizes the importance of understanding how race and racism intersect with other forms of social stratification.

The mathematical representation of intersectionality can be expressed as follows:

$$O = f(I_1, I_2, I_3, \ldots, I_n) \tag{54}$$

where O represents the overall oppression experienced by an individual, and $I_1, I_2, I_3, \ldots, I_n$ represent various intersecting identities (e.g., race, gender, sexual orientation). This equation illustrates that oppression is not merely additive; rather, the interactions between identities can create unique forms of marginalization that require tailored responses.

Challenges in Intersectional Activism

Despite its importance, intersectional activism faces several challenges. One primary issue is the tendency for movements to prioritize certain identities over others, often sidelining those who do not fit neatly into mainstream narratives. For example, LGBTQ activism has historically centered on the experiences of white, cisgender gay men, frequently neglecting the voices of transgender individuals, people of color, and those from lower socioeconomic backgrounds.

Additionally, the complexity of intersectionality can lead to fragmentation within activist communities. Different groups may prioritize distinct issues, leading to tensions and misunderstandings. For instance, a focus on racial justice within LGBTQ spaces may be perceived as detracting from issues of sexual orientation, while some advocates for gender equality may overlook the specific challenges faced by non-binary and gender non-conforming individuals.

Examples of Intersectional Activism in Action

Despite these challenges, there are numerous examples of successful intersectional activism that highlight the power of solidarity among diverse communities. One prominent case is the Black Lives Matter (BLM) movement, which has actively included LGBTQ voices, particularly from Black trans women, in its advocacy efforts. The BLM movement's recognition of the unique struggles faced by Black LGBTQ individuals has fostered a more inclusive dialogue around racial and sexual justice.

Another significant example is the work of organizations like the Audre Lorde Project, which emphasizes the importance of community organizing for LGBTQ people of color. By centering the experiences of marginalized groups, the Audre Lorde Project has successfully mobilized individuals to address issues such as police violence, healthcare access, and housing insecurity, demonstrating the effectiveness of intersectional approaches in creating change.

Furthermore, the concept of "solidarity" plays a crucial role in intersectional activism. Solidarity involves recognizing shared struggles and supporting one another across different movements. This can be seen in the collaboration between LGBTQ activists and feminist organizations, which have united to advocate for comprehensive policies that address both gender and sexual orientation discrimination. Such alliances not only amplify marginalized voices but also foster a collective strength that is essential for enacting systemic change.

Conclusion

In conclusion, intersectional activism and solidarity are vital components of contemporary social justice movements. By acknowledging the complexities of identity and the interconnectedness of various forms of oppression, activists can work towards more inclusive and effective advocacy strategies. The ongoing challenge lies in ensuring that all voices are heard and valued within the movement, fostering a sense of unity that transcends individual differences. As Taren Fira exemplified in her advocacy, embracing intersectionality not only enriches the movement but also paves the way for a more equitable and just society for all individuals, regardless of their intersecting identities.

Allies as Catalysts for Change

Allies play a crucial role in the landscape of LGBTQ activism, acting as catalysts for change through their support, visibility, and advocacy. The concept of allyship transcends mere passive support; it embodies active engagement in the fight for equality and justice. This section explores the multifaceted role of allies in LGBTQ activism, the theoretical underpinnings of effective allyship, and the challenges they face in this endeavor.

Theoretical Foundations of Allyship

The theory of allyship can be traced back to the principles of social justice and intersectionality. *Intersectionality*, a term coined by Kimberlé Crenshaw, emphasizes that individuals experience overlapping systems of oppression based on their identities, such as race, gender, and sexual orientation. Allies must acknowledge their own privileges and understand how these intersecting identities affect their engagement in activism.

The *Ally Spectrum*, developed by various activists, categorizes individuals based on their level of engagement, from passive supporters to active advocates. This spectrum illustrates that allyship is not a static identity but a dynamic process that requires continuous learning, unlearning, and action.

The Role of Allies in LGBTQ Activism

Allies serve multiple functions within the LGBTQ movement:

- **Amplification of Marginalized Voices:** Allies can use their platforms to elevate the voices of LGBTQ individuals, ensuring that their stories and experiences are heard. For instance, public figures who identify as allies can share personal narratives from LGBTQ activists, thereby increasing visibility and fostering empathy among wider audiences.

- **Challenging Discrimination:** Allies possess the unique ability to confront discrimination within their own communities. When a straight ally speaks out against homophobic comments in a workplace setting, it not only challenges the discriminatory behavior but also sets a precedent for others to follow. This action can create a ripple effect, encouraging more individuals to stand against injustice.

- **Resource Mobilization:** Allies often have access to resources that can be mobilized for LGBTQ causes. This includes financial support, professional networks, and media exposure. For example, corporate allies can sponsor LGBTQ events, provide internships for queer youth, or implement inclusive policies within their organizations.

- **Education and Awareness:** Allies are instrumental in educating others about LGBTQ issues. Through workshops, panels, and community outreach, they can dispel myths and stereotypes, fostering understanding and acceptance. Educational initiatives that involve allies can significantly shift public opinion and reduce prejudice.

Challenges Faced by Allies

Despite their vital role, allies encounter several challenges:

- **Navigating Privilege:** Allies must continually reflect on their own privileges and how these affect their activism. This requires a commitment to understanding the complexities of power dynamics within the LGBTQ community and recognizing when to step back and allow marginalized voices to lead.

- **Resistance from Peers:** Allies may face backlash from friends, family, or colleagues when they advocate for LGBTQ rights. This resistance can manifest as social ostracism or accusations of being "too political." Navigating these relationships requires resilience and a steadfast commitment to the cause.

- **Burnout and Activist Fatigue:** Engaging in activism can be emotionally taxing. Allies may experience burnout, especially if they are not adequately supported within their own communities. It is essential for allies to practice self-care and seek support from fellow activists to sustain their efforts.

- **Misunderstanding of Allyship:** Some individuals may mistakenly believe that being an ally is a one-time act rather than a lifelong commitment. This misunderstanding can lead to superficial engagement, where allies may only participate during Pride Month or in response to high-profile incidents, rather than committing to ongoing advocacy.

Examples of Effective Allyship

Several examples illustrate the impact of effective allyship in LGBTQ activism:

- **Corporate Allies:** Companies like Ben & Jerry's and Nike have not only supported LGBTQ rights through financial contributions but have also integrated inclusive practices within their corporate structures. For instance, Ben & Jerry's has consistently used its platform to advocate for marriage equality and LGBTQ rights, demonstrating that corporate allyship can lead to tangible social change.

- **Celebrity Allies:** Celebrities such as Ellen DeGeneres and Laverne Cox have leveraged their visibility to advocate for LGBTQ rights. Their public support has helped normalize queer identities and foster acceptance in mainstream culture. Ellen's coming out in the 1990s was a pivotal moment that not only changed her career but also contributed to broader societal acceptance of LGBTQ individuals.

- **Grassroots Movements:** Local allies often play a critical role in grassroots movements. For example, during the Stonewall riots, many allies joined LGBTQ individuals in the fight against police brutality, demonstrating that solidarity can lead to significant societal shifts. This historical context underscores the importance of allyship in the ongoing struggle for LGBTQ rights.

Conclusion

Allies are indispensable in the fight for LGBTQ rights, serving as catalysts for change through their advocacy, education, and support. By recognizing the complexities of privilege and power dynamics, allies can engage more effectively in activism, amplifying marginalized voices and challenging discrimination. The journey of allyship is ongoing and requires a commitment to learning, unlearning,

BIBLIOGRAPHY 237

and acting in solidarity with the LGBTQ community. As we continue to navigate the challenges of advocacy, the role of allies will remain crucial in shaping a more inclusive and equitable society.

Elevating and Amplifying Ally Voices

In the ongoing struggle for LGBTQ rights, the role of allies cannot be overstated. Allies—those who do not identify as part of the LGBTQ community but actively support its members—play a critical role in amplifying voices that have historically been marginalized. This section explores the importance of allyship, the challenges allies face, and effective strategies for elevating and amplifying LGBTQ voices.

The Importance of Allyship

Allyship is rooted in the understanding that social justice is a collective endeavor. Allies possess the privilege of being able to navigate spaces that may be hostile to LGBTQ individuals. By using their privilege to advocate for equality, allies can help dismantle systemic barriers and challenge societal norms that perpetuate discrimination. The theory of intersectionality, coined by Kimberlé Crenshaw, highlights that individuals experience oppression differently based on their intersecting identities, including race, gender, and sexual orientation. Allies must recognize these complexities to effectively support LGBTQ individuals.

$$\text{Intersectionality} = \sum_{i=1}^{n} \text{Identity}_i \cdot \text{Oppression}_i \qquad (55)$$

This equation illustrates that the experience of oppression is multifaceted and cannot be understood through a singular lens. Allies must engage with this complexity to elevate the voices of those who face intersecting forms of discrimination.

Challenges Faced by Allies

Despite their good intentions, allies often encounter challenges that can hinder their effectiveness. One significant issue is the potential for performative allyship, where individuals engage in advocacy for social media clout rather than genuine support. This superficial engagement can undermine the very movements allies seek to support.

Moreover, allies may struggle with the discomfort of confronting their own privilege. Acknowledging one's privilege is essential for understanding how it can be used to uplift marginalized voices. For example, a white ally might have access to resources and platforms that a queer person of color does not. Failing to recognize this privilege can lead to a lack of genuine support and understanding.

Strategies for Elevating LGBTQ Voices

To be effective allies, individuals must adopt specific strategies that prioritize the voices of LGBTQ individuals. Here are some key approaches:

1. Listening and Learning Allies should prioritize listening to LGBTQ voices rather than speaking over them. This involves actively seeking out stories, experiences, and perspectives from LGBTQ individuals. Engaging with literature, documentaries, and art created by LGBTQ artists can provide valuable insights into their experiences. For example, reading works by authors such as Audre Lorde or James Baldwin can deepen understanding of the struggles faced by LGBTQ individuals.

2. Using Privilege to Advocate Allies must leverage their privilege to create space for LGBTQ voices. This can take various forms, such as using social media platforms to share LGBTQ stories, advocating for inclusive policies in workplaces, or participating in protests and demonstrations. For instance, during the Black Lives Matter protests, many allies took to the streets, amplifying the voices of Black LGBTQ individuals and ensuring their experiences were not overlooked.

3. Creating Inclusive Spaces Allies should work towards creating inclusive environments where LGBTQ individuals feel safe and valued. This involves implementing policies that protect against discrimination and harassment. For example, in educational settings, allies can advocate for comprehensive sex education that includes LGBTQ topics, ensuring that all students feel represented and supported.

4. Holding Others Accountable Allies have a responsibility to challenge homophobia and transphobia within their own circles. This includes addressing harmful jokes, stereotypes, or discriminatory comments. By holding friends, family, and colleagues accountable, allies can foster a culture of respect and understanding.

Examples of Effective Allyship

Several notable examples illustrate the power of allyship in elevating LGBTQ voices:

- **Corporate Allyship:** Companies like Ben & Jerry's have taken strong stances in support of LGBTQ rights, using their platform to advocate for marriage equality and LGBTQ-inclusive policies. Their campaigns not only raise awareness but also demonstrate how businesses can be allies in the fight for equality.

- **Celebrity Advocacy:** Celebrities such as Ellen DeGeneres and Laverne Cox have utilized their platforms to amplify LGBTQ voices. By sharing their stories and advocating for LGBTQ rights, they inspire millions and create a ripple effect of support.

- **Grassroots Movements:** Organizations like PFLAG (Parents, Families, and Friends of Lesbians and Gays) exemplify effective allyship. By providing support and resources for families of LGBTQ individuals, they foster acceptance and understanding within communities.

Conclusion

Elevating and amplifying ally voices is a vital aspect of the LGBTQ rights movement. Allies must engage with the complexities of intersectionality, confront their own privileges, and adopt strategies that prioritize the voices of LGBTQ individuals. By doing so, they can effectively contribute to a more inclusive and equitable society. As Taren Fira once said, "True change happens when we stand together, lifting each other up, and ensuring that every voice is heard." Through collective effort and genuine allyship, we can forge a path toward a brighter future for all.

Cultivating Empathy and Understanding

Empathy, defined as the capacity to understand or feel what another person is experiencing from within their frame of reference, is a cornerstone of effective allyship in the LGBTQ community. It is not merely an emotional response but a vital skill that fosters connection and drives advocacy forward. Understanding the complexities of LGBTQ experiences requires us to engage deeply with narratives that may differ significantly from our own.

Theoretical Frameworks of Empathy

Theories of empathy can be broadly categorized into two dimensions: cognitive empathy and affective empathy. Cognitive empathy involves understanding another person's perspective or mental state, while affective empathy encompasses the emotional resonance we feel in response to another's experiences. According to [?], cognitive empathy allows allies to grasp the social and political contexts that shape LGBTQ lives, while affective empathy enables them to connect on a human level, fostering genuine relationships.

This dual approach is crucial in activism, as it allows allies to not only advocate for policy changes but also to support individuals on a personal level. For example, a study by [?] indicates that individuals who engage in both forms of empathy are more likely to take action in support of marginalized groups. This intersection of understanding and emotional resonance can lead to more profound and lasting connections within the LGBTQ community.

Challenges in Cultivating Empathy

Despite its importance, cultivating empathy poses several challenges. One significant barrier is the prevalence of stereotypes and misconceptions surrounding LGBTQ identities. These misconceptions can lead to a lack of understanding and an unwillingness to engage with LGBTQ narratives. For instance, the stereotype that all LGBTQ individuals live a "glamorous" lifestyle can obscure the real struggles many face, including discrimination, mental health issues, and economic instability.

Moreover, privilege plays a critical role in the ability to empathize. Individuals who belong to dominant social groups may find it challenging to fully grasp the experiences of those who are marginalized. This disconnect can result in a form of empathy that is more performative than genuine, often referred to as "empathy fatigue," where individuals feel overwhelmed by the emotional weight of others' experiences without taking meaningful action [?].

Strategies for Cultivating Empathy

To effectively cultivate empathy and understanding, several strategies can be employed:

- **Active Listening:** Engaging in active listening is essential. This involves not only hearing the words spoken but also understanding the emotions behind them. Techniques such as paraphrasing and asking clarifying questions can enhance this process, allowing individuals to feel heard and validated.

- **Storytelling:** Sharing personal narratives is a powerful way to foster empathy. As highlighted by [?], stories can bridge gaps between different experiences, allowing individuals to see the world through another's eyes. Platforms such as social media have become vital in amplifying LGBTQ voices, creating spaces for storytelling that can challenge stereotypes and build understanding.

- **Education and Awareness:** Providing educational resources about LGBTQ history, rights, and experiences can help dismantle misconceptions. Workshops, seminars, and community discussions can serve as platforms for allies to learn from LGBTQ individuals directly, fostering a more nuanced understanding of their struggles and triumphs.

- **Engagement with Diverse Communities:** Actively engaging with diverse LGBTQ communities can broaden perspectives. Participating in events, volunteering, or collaborating with LGBTQ organizations can help allies gain firsthand experience of the challenges faced by these communities, enhancing both cognitive and affective empathy.

- **Reflexivity:** Encouraging allies to engage in reflexivity—reflecting on their own identities, privileges, and biases—can deepen their understanding of how these factors shape their perceptions of others. This practice can lead to more informed and compassionate advocacy efforts.

Examples of Empathy in Action

Empathy in action can be seen in various successful advocacy campaigns. For instance, the *It Gets Better Project* harnesses the power of personal storytelling to provide hope and support to LGBTQ youth facing bullying and discrimination. By sharing their own experiences, individuals from diverse backgrounds create a collective narrative that resonates with others, fostering a sense of belonging and understanding.

Another example is the rise of inclusive policies in workplaces that prioritize LGBTQ rights. Companies that engage their employees in training sessions on LGBTQ issues often report a significant increase in empathy and understanding among staff. These initiatives not only improve workplace culture but also empower employees to become advocates for their LGBTQ colleagues, creating a supportive environment.

Conclusion

Cultivating empathy and understanding is not a one-time effort but a continuous journey. It requires commitment, openness, and the willingness to confront uncomfortable truths about privilege and bias. As allies work to deepen their understanding of LGBTQ experiences, they not only enhance their advocacy efforts but also contribute to a more inclusive and compassionate society. By embracing empathy, allies can transform their relationships with LGBTQ individuals, fostering a community built on respect, understanding, and solidarity.

Taking Responsibility and Accountability

In the realm of LGBTQ activism, the concepts of responsibility and accountability are paramount. These principles not only guide individual actions but also shape the collective ethos of the movement. Taking responsibility means recognizing one's role in the ongoing struggle for equality, while accountability involves being answerable for one's actions and their impact on the community.

Theoretical Foundations

Theories of social responsibility suggest that individuals and organizations have an obligation to act in ways that benefit society. This is particularly relevant in the context of LGBTQ activism, where the stakes are high, and the consequences of inaction can be dire. Social Responsibility Theory posits that activists must engage in practices that promote the welfare of marginalized groups. This can be encapsulated in the following equation:

$$R = \frac{B}{C} \qquad (56)$$

where R represents the level of responsibility taken, B is the benefits accrued to the community, and C is the costs incurred by the activist. A higher ratio indicates a greater sense of responsibility.

Challenges of Accountability

Despite the clear importance of responsibility and accountability, numerous challenges persist. Activists often face backlash from both external opponents and internal factions. For instance, the rise of right-wing movements has led to increased scrutiny of LGBTQ organizations, necessitating a more robust approach to accountability. Activists must be prepared to address criticisms and defend their positions, which can strain resources and morale.

Moreover, the intersectionality of identities within the LGBTQ community complicates accountability. Different groups may have varying needs and perspectives, leading to potential conflicts. For example, a cisgender gay man may not fully understand the unique challenges faced by transgender individuals or queer people of color. This gap in understanding can result in actions that inadvertently harm marginalized voices within the community.

Examples of Accountability in Action

One notable example of accountability in LGBTQ activism is the response to the 2016 Pulse nightclub shooting in Orlando, Florida. The tragedy galvanized activists and organizations to reassess their strategies and ensure that they were inclusive of all members of the LGBTQ community, particularly those of color and those who are transgender. In the aftermath, many organizations issued public statements acknowledging their past shortcomings and committing to greater inclusivity in their advocacy efforts.

Another example can be seen in the #MeToo movement, which highlighted the importance of accountability in addressing sexual violence within all communities, including LGBTQ spaces. Activists began to recognize the need for safe reporting mechanisms and support systems for survivors, emphasizing that accountability must extend beyond public statements to actionable change.

Strategies for Enhancing Accountability

To foster a culture of responsibility and accountability, LGBTQ activists can employ several strategies:

- **Establish Clear Guidelines:** Creating a set of accountability guidelines can help clarify expectations for behavior and decision-making within organizations and movements.

- **Regular Reflection:** Engaging in regular reflection sessions allows activists to assess their actions and their impacts, fostering a culture of continuous improvement.

- **Community Feedback:** Soliciting feedback from community members can provide valuable insights into the effectiveness of advocacy efforts and highlight areas for improvement.

- **Training and Education:** Providing training on intersectionality and allyship can enhance understanding of diverse perspectives and promote more responsible activism.

Conclusion

Taking responsibility and accountability in LGBTQ activism is not merely a matter of ethical obligation; it is essential for the movement's integrity and effectiveness. By embracing these principles, activists can create a more inclusive and equitable society, ensuring that all voices are heard and valued. As Taren Fira often emphasized, the journey toward equality is a collective one, and it requires each of us to hold ourselves and each other accountable in the pursuit of justice and dignity for all.

Collaborative Advocacy for Lasting Change

Collaborative advocacy is a cornerstone of effective social movements, particularly in the realm of LGBTQ rights. This approach emphasizes the importance of partnerships among diverse groups, recognizing that unity can amplify voices and create a more substantial impact. In this section, we will explore the theories underpinning collaborative advocacy, the challenges faced, and notable examples that demonstrate its efficacy.

Theoretical Frameworks

At the heart of collaborative advocacy lies the theory of collective impact, which posits that large-scale social change requires a coordinated effort across multiple organizations and sectors. According to Kania and Kramer (2011), collective impact involves five key conditions:

1. **Common Agenda:** All participants must have a shared vision for change.

2. **Shared Measurement Systems:** Agreement on how success will be measured and reported.

3. **Mutually Reinforcing Activities:** Each participant must engage in activities that support the overall goals.

4. **Continuous Communication:** Open and frequent communication among stakeholders to build trust and alignment.

5. **Backbone Support:** A dedicated organization to coordinate the efforts of the various stakeholders.

These principles provide a framework for LGBTQ advocacy groups to collaborate effectively, ensuring that their efforts are not only aligned but also sustainable over time.

Challenges in Collaborative Advocacy

Despite its potential, collaborative advocacy is not without challenges. One of the primary obstacles is the issue of *power dynamics*. Different organizations may have varying levels of influence, resources, and recognition, which can lead to tensions and inequities in participation. For instance, larger, more established organizations may overshadow smaller grassroots groups, potentially stifling diverse voices within the movement.

Another significant challenge is *communication barriers*. Misunderstandings can arise when organizations have different cultures, terminologies, and operational styles. This can hinder the development of a common agenda and shared measurement systems, ultimately undermining the collaborative effort.

Furthermore, the lack of *funding and resources* for collaborative initiatives can impede progress. Many LGBTQ organizations operate on limited budgets, making it difficult to allocate resources for joint projects or initiatives. This scarcity can lead to competition rather than collaboration, as organizations vie for limited grants and funding opportunities.

Examples of Successful Collaborative Advocacy

Despite these challenges, there are numerous examples of successful collaborative advocacy within the LGBTQ movement. One notable instance is the **Equality Federation**, which brings together state-based LGBTQ advocacy organizations across the United States. By fostering collaboration among these groups, the Equality Federation has been able to amplify their collective voice, leading to significant legislative victories, such as the passage of non-discrimination laws in various states.

Another exemplary case is the **Global Equality Fund**, which supports collaborative projects aimed at advancing LGBTQ rights worldwide. This initiative exemplifies how international coalitions can address shared challenges, such as violence against LGBTQ individuals, by pooling resources and expertise. By working together, organizations can implement comprehensive strategies that consider local contexts while addressing global issues.

In addition to these large-scale collaborations, grassroots movements also exemplify the power of collective advocacy. The **Transgender Day of Visibility**, for instance, is a global event that encourages collaboration among various LGBTQ organizations, activists, and allies. By uniting for a common cause, participants can effectively raise awareness, share resources, and celebrate the contributions of transgender individuals within the broader LGBTQ community.

Strategies for Effective Collaborative Advocacy

To foster successful collaborative advocacy, organizations can adopt several strategies:

- **Establish Clear Goals:** Define specific, measurable objectives that all partners can agree upon. This clarity helps maintain focus and direction.

- **Foster Inclusivity:** Ensure that all voices, particularly those from marginalized communities, are included in the decision-making process. This practice not only enriches the collaboration but also strengthens the overall movement.

- **Invest in Relationship Building:** Prioritize trust-building activities among partners. Regular meetings, team-building exercises, and open communication can help establish a solid foundation for collaboration.

- **Leverage Technology:** Utilize digital tools to facilitate communication and coordination among partners. Platforms such as Slack or Trello can enhance collaboration, especially for geographically dispersed teams.

- **Celebrate Successes Together:** Recognizing and celebrating collective achievements can reinforce the partnership and motivate continued collaboration.

Conclusion

Collaborative advocacy is essential for achieving lasting change in the LGBTQ movement. By embracing the principles of collective impact and addressing the challenges that arise, organizations can work together to create a more inclusive and equitable society. The examples of successful collaborations illustrate the power of unity in advocacy, proving that when diverse voices come together, they can effect significant social change. Taren Fira's journey underscores the importance of collaboration in advocacy, inspiring future activists to prioritize collective efforts in their quest for equality.

The Power of Allyship in Shaping Society

Allyship plays a crucial role in the fight for LGBTQ rights and social justice. It embodies the idea that individuals who do not identify as part of a marginalized group can still actively support and advocate for that group's rights. This section delves into the theoretical underpinnings of allyship, the challenges faced by allies, and the tangible impacts they can have on society.

Theoretical Foundations of Allyship

Allyship is grounded in various social justice theories, including intersectionality and social identity theory. Intersectionality, a term coined by Kimberlé Crenshaw, emphasizes that individuals experience multiple, overlapping identities (e.g., race, gender, sexual orientation) that shape their experiences of oppression and privilege. Understanding intersectionality is vital for allies, as it encourages them to recognize the diverse experiences within the LGBTQ community and the specific challenges faced by individuals at these intersections.

Social identity theory posits that a person's self-concept is derived from their perceived membership in social groups. Allies must understand their own social identities and how they relate to the LGBTQ community. This awareness allows allies to leverage their privilege to advocate effectively, ensuring that they amplify marginalized voices rather than overshadow them.

Challenges Faced by Allies

While allyship is essential, it is not without its challenges. Allies may struggle with:

- **Recognizing Privilege:** Allies must confront their own privilege and understand how it affects their interactions with marginalized communities. This can lead to discomfort and defensiveness, which can hinder effective allyship.

- **Fear of Missteps:** Allies often fear making mistakes or offending the community they wish to support. This fear can lead to inaction, which ultimately perpetuates the status quo.

- **Tokenism:** Allies must be cautious not to engage in tokenism, where they superficially support LGBTQ issues without making meaningful contributions. True allyship requires sustained commitment and action.

- **Backlash:** Allies may face backlash from their own communities for supporting LGBTQ rights, especially in conservative environments. This can be a significant barrier to effective advocacy.

Examples of Effective Allyship

Effective allyship can take many forms, from individual actions to organized movements. Here are a few notable examples:

- **Corporate Allyship:** Many corporations have adopted inclusive policies and practices, such as gender-neutral bathrooms and LGBTQ-inclusive health benefits. Companies like Apple and Google have publicly supported LGBTQ rights, leveraging their platforms to advocate for equality. Their involvement has not only raised awareness but also influenced public opinion and policy.

- **Community Support:** Local organizations and community members can create safe spaces for LGBTQ individuals. For instance, allies can organize events that celebrate LGBTQ culture, such as Pride parades or community festivals. These events foster visibility and solidarity, showing that allies stand in support of LGBTQ rights.

- **Political Advocacy:** Allies can engage in political advocacy by lobbying for LGBTQ-inclusive legislation. For example, during the fight for marriage equality, many heterosexual allies participated in rallies, wrote to their representatives, and shared their support on social media. Their voices helped amplify the call for equality, making it harder for policymakers to ignore the demand for change.

The Impact of Allyship on Society

The power of allyship extends beyond individual actions; it can transform societal norms and attitudes. When allies actively support LGBTQ rights, they contribute to a culture of acceptance and inclusivity. This cultural shift can lead to:

- **Increased Visibility:** Allies help elevate LGBTQ voices and experiences, making them more visible in society. This visibility can challenge stereotypes and misconceptions, fostering greater understanding and acceptance.

- **Policy Change:** Allies can influence policymakers by demonstrating public support for LGBTQ rights. When allies advocate for change, they can help dismantle discriminatory laws and practices, leading to more equitable policies.

- **Cultural Change:** As allies engage in conversations about LGBTQ rights, they help shift societal attitudes. This cultural change can create a more inclusive environment where LGBTQ individuals feel safe and valued.

Conclusion

In conclusion, allyship is a powerful force in shaping society and advancing LGBTQ rights. By understanding the theoretical foundations of allyship, recognizing the challenges faced by allies, and engaging in effective advocacy, individuals can make a meaningful impact. The collective efforts of allies, combined with the resilience of the LGBTQ community, can create a more just and equitable society for all. As Taren Fira often emphasized, "True change comes not just from the voices of the oppressed but from those who stand beside them, lifting each other up in solidarity."

$$\text{Allyship Impact} = \text{Visibility} + \text{Policy Change} + \text{Cultural Change} \tag{57}$$

Chapter Four: Beyond Advocacy

Section One: Taren Fira's Legacy

Inspiring Future LGBTQ Activists

The legacy of Taren Fira serves as a beacon of hope and inspiration for future LGBTQ activists. Her journey, marked by resilience, creativity, and unwavering commitment to equality, provides a roadmap for those who dare to challenge the status quo. Taren's approach to activism was not merely about fighting for rights but about igniting a passion in others to join the movement. This section explores the ways in which Taren inspired future generations, the theoretical frameworks that underpin her impact, and the challenges that these emerging activists may face.

The Role of Mentorship

One of the most significant ways Taren Fira inspired future activists was through mentorship. The concept of mentorship in activism can be understood through various theoretical lenses, including social learning theory, which posits that individuals learn from observing others. Taren recognized the importance of guiding young activists, sharing her experiences, and offering practical advice. This mentorship created a ripple effect, empowering mentees to become advocates in their own right.

For example, during her tenure at the Alyndra LGBTQ Center, Taren developed a mentorship program that paired seasoned activists with newcomers. This initiative not only provided guidance but also fostered a sense of community and belonging. The success of this program can be quantified through increased participation in local activism, as evidenced by a 40% rise in volunteer sign-ups within the first year.

Storytelling as a Tool for Inspiration

Taren was a master storyteller, understanding that personal narratives could evoke empathy and inspire action. The theoretical framework of narrative identity suggests that individuals construct their identities through the stories they tell about themselves. Taren's ability to share her own journey—filled with both struggles and triumphs—allowed others to see themselves in her story.

In her speeches and writings, she often recounted her experiences of coming out, facing discrimination, and finding her voice. These stories resonated deeply with her audience, motivating many to engage in activism. For instance, after a particularly moving speech at the annual Alyndra Pride event, a group of young activists emerged, inspired to organize their own community initiatives. The power of storytelling in activism cannot be overstated; it serves as both a catalyst for change and a means of forging connections among diverse groups.

Utilizing Digital Platforms

In the digital age, Taren also recognized the importance of online platforms in inspiring future activists. The rise of social media has transformed the landscape of activism, allowing for greater visibility and engagement. Taren adeptly used platforms like Twitter and Instagram to share her message, mobilize supporters, and amplify marginalized voices.

The concept of digital activism is rooted in the theory of networked movements, which emphasizes the role of technology in facilitating collective action. Taren's online campaigns, such as the hashtag #QueerVoicesMatter, garnered widespread attention and encouraged countless individuals to share their stories. This online movement not only raised awareness but also fostered a sense of solidarity among LGBTQ individuals worldwide.

As a result of her efforts, a notable increase in youth engagement in LGBTQ issues was observed. Reports indicated that 60% of participants in online activism initiatives reported feeling more empowered to take action in their communities.

Addressing Challenges Faced by Future Activists

While Taren Fira's legacy is one of inspiration, it is essential to acknowledge the challenges that future LGBTQ activists may encounter. These include systemic discrimination, burnout, and the complexities of intersectionality. Taren often spoke candidly about her struggles with mental health and the importance of self-care in activism.

SECTION ONE: TAREN FIRA'S LEGACY   253

Theories of resilience suggest that individuals can develop coping strategies to navigate adversity. Taren's advocacy for mental health resources within the LGBTQ community laid the groundwork for future activists to prioritize their well-being. Her establishment of the "Activist Wellness Initiative" provided essential support services, including counseling and workshops on managing activist fatigue.

Moreover, the challenge of intersectionality cannot be ignored. Future activists must navigate the diverse identities within the LGBTQ spectrum and advocate for inclusivity. Taren's work highlighted the importance of centering marginalized voices, ensuring that the movement remained equitable and representative.

Creating Sustainable Change

Finally, Taren Fira's legacy emphasizes the importance of creating sustainable change. Future activists are encouraged to adopt a long-term perspective, understanding that meaningful progress requires perseverance and strategic planning. Theories of social change advocate for a combination of grassroots organizing and policy advocacy to achieve lasting impact.

Taren's establishment of the Taren Fira Foundation exemplified this approach. The foundation focuses on funding initiatives that empower LGBTQ youth, support mental health, and promote intersectional advocacy. By investing in future leaders, Taren ensured that her vision for a more equitable society would continue to thrive.

In conclusion, Taren Fira's inspiring legacy provides a blueprint for future LGBTQ activists. Through mentorship, storytelling, digital engagement, and a commitment to sustainable change, she ignited a passion for activism that will continue to influence generations to come. As future advocates carry forward her message, they do so with the knowledge that they are part of a larger movement—one that seeks to create a world where everyone can live authentically and without fear.

Establishing the Taren Fira Foundation

In the wake of Taren Fira's groundbreaking advocacy work, the establishment of the Taren Fira Foundation emerged as a pivotal moment in the ongoing struggle for LGBTQ rights and representation. Founded in 2025, the foundation aimed to create a sustainable infrastructure for activism, education, and community support, addressing the multifaceted challenges faced by LGBTQ individuals both locally and globally.

Vision and Mission

The vision of the Taren Fira Foundation was rooted in the belief that every individual deserves to live authentically, free from discrimination and prejudice. Its mission encompassed several key objectives:

- **Advocacy:** To promote and protect the rights of LGBTQ individuals through legislative efforts and public awareness campaigns.
- **Education:** To provide resources and training for activists, allies, and community members on LGBTQ issues, intersectionality, and effective advocacy strategies.
- **Support:** To create safe spaces and community centers that offer mental health resources, legal assistance, and social support for LGBTQ individuals.
- **Research:** To conduct and disseminate research on the challenges faced by LGBTQ communities, particularly focusing on marginalized groups within the community.

Theoretical Framework

The foundation's approach was informed by several theoretical frameworks that emphasized the importance of intersectionality, community empowerment, and grassroots activism. Drawing on the work of scholars such as Kimberlé Crenshaw, the foundation recognized that LGBTQ individuals do not experience oppression in isolation; rather, their identities intersect with race, class, gender, and other social categories, creating unique challenges that must be addressed holistically.

$$\text{Intersectionality} = \sum_{i=1}^{n} \text{Identity}_i \cdot \text{Oppression}_i$$

This equation illustrates how various identities contribute to an individual's overall experience of oppression, highlighting the need for tailored advocacy efforts that consider these intersections.

Addressing Problems and Challenges

Establishing the Taren Fira Foundation was not without its challenges. Initial funding was a significant barrier, as many philanthropic organizations were hesitant to invest in LGBTQ initiatives, particularly those that addressed

SECTION ONE: TAREN FIRA'S LEGACY

intersectional issues. To combat this, the foundation employed a multifaceted fundraising strategy that included:

- **Crowdfunding Campaigns:** Utilizing social media platforms to engage the community and raise awareness about the foundation's mission.

- **Corporate Partnerships:** Collaborating with businesses committed to diversity and inclusion, securing sponsorships for events and programs.

- **Grant Applications:** Applying for grants from organizations dedicated to social justice and LGBTQ rights, emphasizing the foundation's unique approach to intersectionality.

These efforts resulted in a robust financial foundation, allowing the Taren Fira Foundation to launch its inaugural programs.

Programs and Initiatives

The foundation's first initiative was the *Safe Spaces Project*, aimed at creating community centers in underserved areas where LGBTQ individuals could access resources and support. These centers provided:

- **Mental Health Services:** Offering counseling and support groups led by trained professionals who understood the unique challenges faced by LGBTQ individuals.

- **Legal Assistance:** Providing resources for individuals facing discrimination or legal challenges related to their sexual orientation or gender identity.

- **Educational Workshops:** Hosting events focused on topics such as health, safety, and advocacy skills, empowering community members to become active participants in their own rights.

The foundation also launched the *Advocacy Academy*, a training program designed to equip emerging activists with the skills needed to effectively advocate for LGBTQ rights. This program included modules on:

- **Grassroots Organizing:** Teaching participants how to mobilize their communities and create impactful campaigns.

- **Policy Advocacy:** Providing insights into navigating political landscapes and engaging with policymakers.

- **Digital Activism:** Leveraging social media and online platforms to amplify voices and foster global solidarity.

Impact and Legacy

By 2030, the Taren Fira Foundation had made significant strides in promoting LGBTQ rights and fostering community resilience. The establishment of the foundation not only honored Taren Fira's legacy but also created a lasting impact on future generations of activists. The foundation's emphasis on intersectionality and community empowerment served as a model for other organizations, inspiring a wave of advocacy efforts across the globe.

In conclusion, the Taren Fira Foundation stands as a testament to the power of collective action and the importance of creating inclusive spaces for marginalized voices. Through its innovative programs and unwavering commitment to social justice, the foundation continues to champion the rights of LGBTQ individuals, ensuring that Taren Fira's vision of a world free from discrimination lives on.

Creating Sustainable Change

Creating sustainable change in LGBTQ advocacy requires a multifaceted approach that integrates community engagement, policy reform, and continuous education. Taren Fira's journey exemplifies how to establish enduring impact through strategic initiatives that empower marginalized voices and foster inclusivity.

Theoretical Framework

At the core of sustainable change lies the theory of *social change*, which posits that lasting transformation occurs when communities are actively involved in the decision-making processes that affect their lives. This theory is complemented by *intersectionality*, a framework that emphasizes the interconnectedness of various social identities and the unique challenges faced by individuals at these intersections. Taren Fira championed these theories, advocating for a model of activism that recognizes and addresses the diverse needs of the LGBTQ community.

Challenges to Sustainable Change

Despite the progress made in LGBTQ rights, several challenges hinder the creation of sustainable change:

- **Political Resistance:** Many legislative bodies resist reforms that promote LGBTQ equality due to conservative ideologies. For instance, the backlash against marriage equality in various states illustrates how political climates can impede progress.

- **Funding Limitations:** Nonprofits and advocacy organizations often struggle with securing long-term funding, which is critical for sustaining programs and outreach efforts. The volatility of donor support can lead to project discontinuation, undermining the efforts of activists like Taren Fira.

- **Community Fragmentation:** The LGBTQ community is not monolithic; it encompasses a wide range of identities and experiences. This diversity can lead to fragmentation, making it difficult to unify efforts towards common goals. For example, the varying priorities between different subgroups (e.g., transgender rights versus marriage equality) can complicate coalition-building.

Strategies for Sustainable Change

To counter these challenges, Taren Fira implemented several strategies to create sustainable change:

1. Building Coalitions: Fira understood the power of collaboration. By forming coalitions with other social justice movements, she was able to amplify the voices of marginalized groups. An example of this is her partnership with feminist organizations to address the intersection of gender and sexual orientation in advocacy efforts.

2. Education and Awareness: Taren emphasized the importance of education in fostering understanding and acceptance. She launched campaigns that targeted schools and workplaces, promoting LGBTQ-inclusive curricula and training programs. These initiatives not only educated allies but also equipped LGBTQ individuals with the tools to advocate for themselves.

3. Policy Advocacy: Fira's approach included lobbying for comprehensive legislation that protects LGBTQ rights. By working with legislators to draft bills that address discrimination in housing, employment, and healthcare, she ensured that legal protections were in place to support sustainable change. For instance, her efforts were instrumental in passing the *Equality Act*, which aimed to extend civil rights protections to LGBTQ individuals nationwide.

4. **Grassroots Mobilization:** Taren recognized that true change begins at the grassroots level. She organized community forums and workshops to engage individuals in discussions about their rights and the importance of activism. This grassroots mobilization empowered community members to take action, leading to the establishment of local advocacy groups that continued her work.

Case Study: The Taren Fira Foundation

The establishment of the *Taren Fira Foundation* serves as a prime example of creating sustainable change. The foundation focuses on three key areas:

1. **Funding for Grassroots Organizations:** By providing grants to local LGBTQ groups, the foundation ensures that grassroots efforts receive the necessary resources to thrive. This approach addresses the funding limitations faced by many organizations.

2. **Education Programs:** The foundation develops educational materials and workshops aimed at schools, businesses, and community organizations to foster inclusivity. These programs are designed to create safe spaces for dialogue and understanding.

3. **Advocacy Training:** The foundation offers training sessions for aspiring activists, equipping them with the skills needed to navigate the political landscape effectively. This training emphasizes the importance of intersectionality and the need for a holistic approach to advocacy.

Conclusion

Creating sustainable change in LGBTQ advocacy is an ongoing journey that requires dedication, collaboration, and a commitment to inclusivity. Taren Fira's legacy demonstrates that by addressing systemic barriers, fostering community engagement, and prioritizing education, activists can create a lasting impact that transcends generations. The principles and strategies she championed continue to inspire new waves of advocates, ensuring that the fight for LGBTQ rights remains vibrant and resilient.

Continuing the Fight for LGBTQ Rights

The struggle for LGBTQ rights is far from over, and as Taren Fira's legacy illustrates, the fight must continue on multiple fronts. The ongoing battle

SECTION ONE: TAREN FIRA'S LEGACY

encompasses legal, social, and cultural dimensions, each requiring sustained effort and innovative strategies to address the myriad challenges that persist.

Legal Frameworks and Challenges

Despite significant progress in many countries, legal protections for LGBTQ individuals remain inconsistent. For instance, while marriage equality has been achieved in numerous nations, many regions still lack comprehensive anti-discrimination laws. According to the *Human Rights Campaign*, in 2021, only 22 countries worldwide recognized same-sex marriage, leaving millions without basic legal rights. The equation that emerges from this disparity is:

$$\text{Legal Rights} = \text{Marriage Equality} + \text{Anti-Discrimination Laws} + \text{Adoption Rights}$$

This formula highlights that marriage equality alone does not equate to full legal recognition and protection. Activists must advocate for a holistic approach that includes all aspects of legal rights.

Social Acceptance and Cultural Shifts

Social acceptance is equally crucial in the fight for LGBTQ rights. Cultural attitudes can significantly influence the legal landscape. For example, in countries where LGBTQ individuals face societal stigma, legal protections may be less robust. Taren Fira emphasized the importance of visibility and representation in media as a means of fostering understanding and acceptance. Research has shown that increased representation of LGBTQ characters in popular media correlates with greater public acceptance.

$$\text{Public Acceptance} \propto \text{Media Representation}$$

This relationship underlines the necessity of continued advocacy for inclusive representation in all forms of media. By challenging stereotypes and showcasing diverse narratives, activists can shift public perception and create a more supportive environment for LGBTQ individuals.

Intersectional Advocacy

The fight for LGBTQ rights cannot be separated from other social justice movements. Intersectionality, a term coined by scholar Kimberlé Crenshaw, emphasizes the interconnectedness of various forms of discrimination. Taren Fira's advocacy work often involved collaborating with movements focused on racial justice, gender equality, and economic equity. For instance, the Black Lives Matter movement has highlighted the unique challenges faced by queer people of color, showcasing the need for an intersectional approach to activism.

$$\text{Intersectional Advocacy} = \text{LGBTQ Rights} + \text{Racial Justice} + \text{Gender Equality}$$

This equation illustrates that the fight for LGBTQ rights is inextricably linked to broader social justice issues. By uniting with other movements, activists can amplify their voices and address the systemic inequalities that affect marginalized communities.

Grassroots Mobilization

Grassroots movements play a pivotal role in continuing the fight for LGBTQ rights. Taren Fira often highlighted the importance of community organizing and local activism. Effective grassroots strategies include organizing rallies, educational workshops, and community outreach programs. These initiatives not only raise awareness but also build solidarity among LGBTQ individuals and their allies.

One successful example is the annual Pride events held worldwide, which serve as both a celebration of identity and a platform for advocacy. These events mobilize thousands of individuals, creating a visible and powerful statement in support of LGBTQ rights. The impact of grassroots mobilization can be quantified through participation metrics:

$$\text{Impact} = \text{Number of Participants} \times \text{Media Coverage}$$

Higher participation rates, coupled with extensive media coverage, can lead to increased public support and pressure on policymakers to enact change.

Digital Activism

In the digital age, social media has become an essential tool for advocacy. Taren Fira recognized the power of platforms like Twitter, Instagram, and TikTok in mobilizing support and disseminating information. Digital activism allows for rapid dissemination of messages and can engage younger generations in the fight for LGBTQ rights.

The effectiveness of digital campaigns can be illustrated through the equation:

$$\text{Engagement} = \text{Shares} + \text{Likes} + \text{Comments}$$

A high level of engagement on social media can translate into real-world action, encouraging individuals to participate in protests, sign petitions, or contact their representatives.

Mental Health and Well-being

Continuing the fight for LGBTQ rights also involves addressing the mental health needs of activists and community members. The pressures of activism can lead to burnout and mental health challenges. Taren Fira advocated for self-care and community support as vital components of sustained activism.

$$\text{Activist Well-being} = \text{Self-Care} + \text{Community Support}$$

By prioritizing mental health, the LGBTQ community can foster resilience and maintain momentum in the ongoing struggle for rights.

Conclusion

In conclusion, the fight for LGBTQ rights is a multifaceted endeavor that requires ongoing commitment and innovation. Taren Fira's legacy serves as a reminder that while progress has been made, the journey is far from complete. By continuing to advocate for legal protections, promote social acceptance, engage in intersectional activism, mobilize grassroots efforts, harness digital tools, and prioritize mental health, the LGBTQ community can ensure that the fight for equality remains vibrant and impactful. The road ahead may be challenging, but as Taren Fira demonstrated, it is a road worth traveling.

Remembering Taren Fira's Impact

Taren Fira, a name that resonates deeply within the LGBTQ community and beyond, left a legacy that transcends the confines of traditional activism. Her impact is felt not only in the policies she fought for but also in the hearts and minds she inspired. To fully appreciate Taren's contributions, we must delve into the multifaceted nature of her influence, examining the theory behind her activism, the problems she addressed, and the examples that illustrate her profound effect on society.

Theoretical Foundations of Taren's Activism

At the core of Taren Fira's activism lies a robust theoretical framework rooted in intersectionality, a term coined by legal scholar Kimberlé Crenshaw.

Intersectionality posits that individuals experience oppression in varying configurations and degrees of intensity based on their overlapping social identities, such as race, gender, sexuality, and class. Taren understood that LGBTQ rights could not be viewed in isolation; rather, they were deeply intertwined with other social justice movements.

Taren's approach was informed by the works of theorists like Audre Lorde, who emphasized the importance of recognizing difference and using it as a source of strength. Taren often quoted Lorde's assertion that "there is no such thing as a single-issue struggle because we do not live single-issue lives." This philosophy guided her efforts to create an inclusive movement that acknowledged and celebrated diversity within the LGBTQ community.

Addressing Key Problems

Throughout her career, Taren confronted numerous problems that plagued the LGBTQ community, including systemic discrimination, lack of representation, and inadequate healthcare access. One of the most pressing issues she tackled was the criminalization of queer identities in various parts of the world. Taren's advocacy work highlighted the plight of LGBTQ individuals in countries where homosexuality remains illegal, often leading to violence and persecution.

Moreover, Taren recognized the significant health disparities faced by LGBTQ individuals, particularly among marginalized groups. According to the *National LGBTQ Health Education Center*, LGBTQ individuals are at a higher risk for mental health issues, substance abuse, and chronic illnesses. Taren championed for equitable healthcare access, emphasizing that "healthcare is a human right, not a privilege." She worked tirelessly to dismantle barriers that prevented marginalized LGBTQ individuals from receiving the care they deserved.

Examples of Impact

Taren's impact can be illustrated through various initiatives and campaigns that she spearheaded. One notable example is the establishment of the "Safe Haven" project, a community-driven initiative aimed at providing resources and support for LGBTQ youth experiencing homelessness. Through this project, Taren mobilized local organizations and community members to create safe spaces where young people could find shelter, mentorship, and access to mental health services.

Furthermore, Taren was instrumental in organizing the annual "Alyndra Pride Festival," which grew from a small gathering into a vibrant celebration of diversity and inclusion. The festival not only served as a platform for LGBTQ visibility but also raised funds for local charities that supported marginalized communities. Taren's ability to unite people from various backgrounds under a common cause exemplified her belief in the power of collective action.

Legacy and Continuing Influence

Taren Fira's legacy endures through the countless individuals she inspired to join the fight for LGBTQ rights. Her mentorship of young activists created a ripple effect, empowering a new generation to advocate for social justice. As noted by her mentee, Jamie Lee, "Taren taught us that our voices matter, and that change is possible when we stand together." This sentiment encapsulates the essence of Taren's impact—encouraging others to harness their power and work collectively towards a more equitable world.

In the wake of her passing, Taren's influence continues to shape LGBTQ advocacy efforts. The Taren Fira Foundation, established in her honor, remains dedicated to advancing LGBTQ rights and supporting grassroots activism. Through scholarships, grants, and community programs, the foundation embodies Taren's vision of a world where every individual can live authentically and without fear.

Conclusion

Remembering Taren Fira's impact is not merely an act of nostalgia; it is a call to action. As we reflect on her contributions, we are reminded of the ongoing struggles faced by the LGBTQ community and the importance of continuing the work she started. Taren's legacy serves as a beacon of hope, inspiring us to advocate for justice, equity, and inclusivity for all. In the words of Taren herself, "The fight is far from over, but together, we can create a world where love always wins."

Mentoring the Next Generation of Activists

Mentorship plays a pivotal role in the landscape of activism, particularly in the LGBTQ community, where the need for guidance, support, and knowledge transfer is paramount. Taren Fira, as a seasoned advocate, recognized the importance of nurturing budding activists and ensuring that the torch of advocacy continued to burn brightly. This section delves into the methods, theories, and challenges associated with mentoring the next generation of LGBTQ activists.

The Importance of Mentorship in Activism

Mentorship in activism is not merely a transfer of knowledge; it is a dynamic relationship that fosters growth, resilience, and empowerment. According to social learning theory, individuals learn behaviors and norms through observation and imitation of role models. This theory emphasizes the significance of mentors as role models who can shape the attitudes and behaviors of emerging activists.

In the context of LGBTQ activism, mentoring provides a safe space for young advocates to explore their identities, understand the complexities of social justice, and develop the skills necessary for effective advocacy. Taren often emphasized that mentorship was about creating a supportive environment where questions could be asked freely, and experiences could be shared without fear of judgment.

Challenges in Mentoring

While mentoring is crucial, it is not without its challenges. One of the primary issues faced by mentors in the LGBTQ community is the diversity of identities and experiences among mentees. Each individual comes with unique backgrounds, challenges, and perspectives, which can complicate the mentoring relationship.

For instance, a mentor may struggle to relate to a mentee who identifies as non-binary when the mentor's own experiences are rooted in a binary understanding of gender. This highlights the necessity for mentors to engage in continuous learning and self-reflection. Taren often advocated for a model of mentorship that was adaptive and responsive, encouraging mentors to actively listen and learn from their mentees' experiences.

Strategies for Effective Mentorship

To navigate the complexities of mentoring, Taren employed several strategies that proved effective in fostering meaningful relationships with young activists:

1. **Active Listening:** Taren believed that mentorship begins with listening. By creating an open dialogue, mentors could better understand the aspirations and concerns of their mentees. This approach not only builds trust but also empowers mentees to express their thoughts and feelings candidly.

2. **Skill Development Workshops:** Taren organized workshops focusing on various skills essential for activism, such as public speaking, organizing events, and understanding policy advocacy. These workshops provided a platform for hands-on learning and practical application of concepts discussed.

3. **Networking Opportunities:** Connecting mentees with a broader network of activists and organizations was another key strategy. Taren often facilitated introductions to established activists, allowing mentees to expand their horizons and gain insights from diverse experiences.

4. **Creating Safe Spaces:** Taren was committed to establishing safe spaces where young activists could gather, share their experiences, and discuss the challenges they faced. These spaces fostered a sense of community and belonging, crucial for the emotional well-being of mentees.

5. **Encouraging Intersectionality:** Recognizing the importance of intersectionality, Taren emphasized the need to address the unique challenges faced by LGBTQ individuals from marginalized backgrounds. Mentors were encouraged to incorporate discussions of race, class, and ability into their mentoring practices, fostering a more inclusive approach to activism.

Real-Life Examples of Successful Mentorship

Taren's commitment to mentorship yielded tangible results. One notable example is the story of Jamie, a young transgender activist who faced significant challenges in her community. Under Taren's mentorship, Jamie developed the confidence to organize a local pride event, which became a significant milestone for LGBTQ visibility in her town.

Through Taren's guidance, Jamie learned not only the logistical aspects of event planning but also the importance of building coalitions with local businesses and organizations. The success of the pride event inspired Jamie to pursue a career in advocacy, demonstrating the profound impact of mentorship on individual trajectories.

The Legacy of Mentorship

Taren Fira's legacy in mentoring the next generation of activists is a testament to the transformative power of guidance and support. By investing time and resources into nurturing young leaders, Taren ensured that the fight for LGBTQ rights would continue long into the future. The stories of mentees like Jamie serve as reminders of the rippling effects mentorship can have, shaping not just individual lives but entire communities.

In conclusion, mentoring the next generation of LGBTQ activists is not merely an act of guidance; it is a commitment to fostering resilience, inclusivity, and empowerment. Taren Fira's approach exemplifies how effective mentorship can cultivate a vibrant and diverse movement, ensuring that the voices of future advocates are heard and valued.

Supporting LGBTQ-inclusive Policies and Practices

Supporting LGBTQ-inclusive policies and practices is crucial in fostering an equitable society where individuals can live authentically without fear of discrimination. This section explores the theoretical frameworks, practical challenges, and successful examples of LGBTQ-inclusive policies that Taren Fira championed throughout her activism.

Theoretical Frameworks

The support for LGBTQ-inclusive policies is underpinned by several theoretical frameworks, including:

- **Social Justice Theory:** This framework emphasizes the importance of equity and fairness in societal structures. It advocates for policies that dismantle systemic barriers faced by marginalized communities, including LGBTQ individuals.

- **Intersectionality:** Coined by Kimberlé Crenshaw, intersectionality examines how various forms of discrimination overlap. Understanding that LGBTQ individuals may also face additional challenges based on race, gender, and socioeconomic status is crucial for developing comprehensive policies.

- **Human Rights Framework:** This approach posits that LGBTQ rights are human rights. It advocates for policies that protect individuals from discrimination based on sexual orientation or gender identity, aligning with international human rights standards.

Challenges in Implementing Inclusive Policies

Despite the theoretical support for LGBTQ-inclusive policies, several challenges persist:

- **Political Resistance:** In many regions, political leaders may resist LGBTQ-inclusive policies due to prevailing cultural norms or personal

SECTION ONE: TAREN FIRA'S LEGACY 267

beliefs. This resistance can manifest as legislative pushback against anti-discrimination laws or marriage equality initiatives.

- **Social Stigma:** Deep-rooted societal prejudices can hinder the acceptance of LGBTQ-inclusive policies. Public opinion often lags behind legislative changes, creating a climate where individuals may feel unsafe or unwelcome.

- **Lack of Awareness:** Many policymakers may lack an understanding of LGBTQ issues and the importance of inclusive policies. This gap in knowledge can lead to inadequate or ineffective policy measures.

Successful Examples of LGBTQ-inclusive Policies

Taren Fira's advocacy efforts contributed to several successful examples of LGBTQ-inclusive policies:

- **Marriage Equality:** One of the most significant victories in LGBTQ rights has been the legalization of same-sex marriage. In Alyndra, Taren played a pivotal role in advocating for marriage equality, which was achieved in 2015. This landmark legislation not only granted legal recognition to same-sex couples but also symbolized a broader acceptance of LGBTQ identities.

- **Anti-Discrimination Laws:** Taren's advocacy led to the implementation of comprehensive anti-discrimination laws that protect LGBTQ individuals in employment, housing, and public accommodations. These laws serve as a legal framework to combat discrimination and promote equal treatment.

- **Inclusive Education Policies:** Recognizing the importance of education, Taren worked with school districts to develop LGBTQ-inclusive curricula. These policies aim to create safe and supportive environments for LGBTQ students, ensuring they receive an education free from bias and discrimination.

Strategies for Supporting Inclusive Policies

To support the development and implementation of LGBTQ-inclusive policies, Taren Fira employed various strategies:

- **Grassroots Mobilization:** Taren understood the power of grassroots movements in influencing policy change. She organized community events, rallies, and workshops to raise awareness about LGBTQ issues and mobilize public support for inclusive policies.

- **Coalition Building:** Collaborating with other social justice movements was essential in amplifying the voice of LGBTQ advocacy. Taren formed coalitions with organizations focused on racial justice, gender equality, and disability rights, recognizing that an intersectional approach strengthens advocacy efforts.

- **Public Education Campaigns:** Taren initiated public education campaigns to inform the community about the importance of LGBTQ-inclusive policies. These campaigns utilized social media, public speaking engagements, and educational materials to dispel myths and promote understanding.

Conclusion

Supporting LGBTQ-inclusive policies and practices is not merely an act of charity; it is a fundamental necessity for the realization of a just society. Taren Fira's legacy exemplifies the impact of advocacy rooted in theory, informed by lived experiences, and driven by a commitment to social justice. By addressing the challenges, leveraging successful examples, and employing effective strategies, future activists can continue to push for meaningful change, ensuring that LGBTQ individuals are recognized, respected, and valued in all facets of society.

Leaving a Lasting Cultural and Social Impact

Taren Fira's journey as a queer advocate transcended mere activism; it became a cultural phenomenon that reshaped societal norms and values within Alyndra and beyond. This section delves into the multifaceted ways in which Taren's work left an indelible mark on both cultural and social landscapes, illustrating the profound implications of her advocacy.

Cultural Shifts through Representation

One of the most significant aspects of Taren's impact was her commitment to representation. By amplifying diverse queer voices through various forms of media—art, literature, and performance—Taren challenged the dominant narratives that often marginalized LGBTQ identities. The theory of representation posits that visibility in cultural contexts can lead to increased acceptance and understanding. This was evident in the way Taren organized art exhibitions that featured queer artists, showcasing their work in mainstream venues.

SECTION ONE: TAREN FIRA'S LEGACY

For instance, the *Queer Expressions* exhibition in 2023 not only highlighted the creativity of LGBTQ artists but also attracted a diverse audience, fostering dialogue around queer identity. Taren's emphasis on intersectionality ensured that the narratives of queer people of color, transgender individuals, and non-binary folks were included, thereby enriching the cultural tapestry of Alyndra.

Educational Initiatives and Community Engagement

Taren recognized that cultural impact is inextricably linked to education. She spearheaded initiatives aimed at educating the broader community about LGBTQ issues, employing workshops, seminars, and public discussions to dismantle stereotypes and promote understanding. The *Understanding Queerness* program, launched in 2022, became a cornerstone of community engagement, attracting participants from all walks of life.

The curriculum included discussions on the history of LGBTQ rights, the significance of language in shaping perceptions, and the importance of allyship. Feedback from participants indicated a marked increase in empathy and awareness, highlighting the program's effectiveness in fostering a more inclusive environment.

Media Advocacy and Public Discourse

Taren's influence extended into the realm of media, where she adeptly utilized platforms to advocate for LGBTQ rights. Her appearances on talk shows, podcasts, and social media campaigns played a crucial role in shifting public discourse. The concept of *framing theory* is particularly relevant here; by strategically framing LGBTQ issues in relatable terms, Taren was able to engage audiences who may have previously held prejudiced views.

For example, her viral campaign, *#QueerAndProud*, encouraged individuals to share their coming-out stories, creating a wave of solidarity and visibility. This campaign not only humanized LGBTQ experiences but also generated widespread media coverage, further normalizing queer identities in the public sphere.

Legislative Advocacy and Policy Change

Taren's cultural impact was also evident in her legislative advocacy. By mobilizing community support and engaging with political leaders, she played a pivotal role in the passage of several key pieces of legislation aimed at protecting LGBTQ rights in Alyndra. The *Equality Act of 2024*, which aimed to prohibit discrimination based on sexual orientation and gender identity, was a direct result of grassroots activism that Taren helped cultivate.

The sociological concept of *collective efficacy*—the shared belief in the ability to achieve goals through collective action—was exemplified in Taren's work. Her ability to rally community members and foster a sense of shared purpose was instrumental in creating a political climate conducive to change.

Legacy of Empowerment and Inspiration

Perhaps the most enduring aspect of Taren Fira's impact is the legacy of empowerment she instilled in future generations of activists. Through mentorship programs and the establishment of the Taren Fira Foundation, she ensured that the fight for LGBTQ rights continued long after her departure. The foundation's mission to support emerging queer leaders aligns with the theory of *social capital*, which emphasizes the importance of networks and relationships in fostering community resilience.

Taren's story became a source of inspiration, demonstrating that individual actions can lead to significant social change. Her life and work serve as a testament to the power of activism, encouraging others to embrace their identities and advocate for justice.

Conclusion: A Lasting Impact

In conclusion, Taren Fira's contributions to cultural and social impact were profound and multifaceted. Through representation, education, media advocacy, legislative change, and empowerment, she not only transformed the landscape of LGBTQ rights in Alyndra but also inspired a global movement. Her legacy serves as a reminder of the potential for individuals to effect change and the importance of ongoing advocacy in the quest for equality and acceptance.

Building LGBTQ Community Centers and Safe Spaces

In the journey toward equality and acceptance, the establishment of LGBTQ community centers and safe spaces plays a pivotal role in fostering a sense of belonging and security for individuals within the community. These centers serve as vital hubs for support, advocacy, and education, addressing the unique challenges faced by LGBTQ individuals in society.

Theoretical Framework

The theoretical underpinnings of community centers can be explored through the lens of *Social Identity Theory*, which posits that individuals derive a sense of self from their group memberships. For LGBTQ individuals, community centers provide a space where they can affirm their identities and connect with others who share similar experiences. Moreover, the *Minority Stress Theory* explains the elevated levels of stress experienced by marginalized groups due to discrimination and societal stigma. Community centers can mitigate this stress by offering resources, counseling, and a supportive environment.

Identifying Problems

Despite the crucial role of LGBTQ community centers, several challenges persist in their establishment and operation:

- **Funding Limitations:** Many centers struggle to secure adequate funding, which can limit their ability to offer comprehensive services. Reliance on grants, donations, and fundraising events can create instability.

- **Community Resistance:** In some areas, community centers face opposition from conservative groups or individuals who may not support LGBTQ rights. This resistance can manifest in protests, vandalism, or political challenges that hinder the establishment of safe spaces.

- **Inclusivity Issues:** While LGBTQ community centers aim to be inclusive, they must also address intersectionality. Centers must ensure they are welcoming to people of diverse races, ethnicities, abilities, and socioeconomic backgrounds, as well as those who identify as non-binary or transgender.

- **Resource Allocation:** Limited resources can lead to a lack of programming that addresses the specific needs of various subgroups within the LGBTQ community, such as youth, seniors, or those experiencing homelessness.

Examples of Successful Community Centers

Several LGBTQ community centers around the world exemplify how these spaces can thrive despite challenges:

- **The Stonewall Community Foundation (New York, USA):** This foundation supports LGBTQ organizations through grants and funding initiatives, helping to ensure that community centers can provide essential services such as mental health support, housing assistance, and educational programs.

- **The LGBT Center (Los Angeles, USA):** This center offers a wide range of services, including health care, legal assistance, and youth programs. It has successfully built partnerships with local businesses and organizations to enhance its resources and outreach.

- **The Queer Space (Melbourne, Australia):** A community-driven initiative that focuses on creating safe spaces for LGBTQ youth. The center provides workshops, support groups, and social events aimed at fostering connection and empowerment among young people.

- **The Rainbow Resource Center (Winnipeg, Canada):** This center serves as a hub for LGBTQ education and advocacy, offering training sessions for allies and community members to promote understanding and acceptance. It also provides resources for mental health support and crisis intervention.

Strategies for Building Effective Community Centers

To create and sustain effective LGBTQ community centers, the following strategies can be employed:

1. **Engagement with the Community:** Conducting needs assessments and engaging with community members to understand their specific needs and concerns is crucial for developing relevant programs and services.

2. **Diverse Programming:** Offering a variety of programs that cater to different age groups, identities, and interests can help attract a broader audience and foster inclusivity. This may include workshops, social events, health services, and educational initiatives.

3. **Partnerships and Collaborations:** Building alliances with local businesses, schools, and other organizations can enhance the center's visibility and resources. Collaborative efforts can lead to joint events, shared funding opportunities, and increased community support.

4. **Advocacy and Awareness Campaigns:** Community centers should actively engage in advocacy efforts to promote LGBTQ rights and raise awareness about the issues facing the community. This can include hosting events, participating in pride parades, and leveraging social media platforms for outreach.

5. **Safe Environment:** Ensuring that the center is a physically and emotionally safe space is paramount. This includes implementing anti-discrimination policies, providing training for staff on inclusivity, and creating a welcoming atmosphere for all individuals.

Conclusion

Building LGBTQ community centers and safe spaces is an essential endeavor in the fight for equality and acceptance. These centers not only provide critical resources and support but also foster a sense of belonging and community among LGBTQ individuals. By addressing the challenges they face and implementing effective strategies, advocates can ensure that these safe spaces thrive, empowering future generations to embrace their identities without fear. Taren Fira's legacy of activism underscores the importance of these centers in creating a world where everyone can live authentically and freely.

Celebrating Taren Fira's Legacy

Taren Fira's legacy stands as a vibrant testament to the power of advocacy and the relentless pursuit of equality within the LGBTQ community. Her journey, marked by both personal and collective struggles, illustrates the profound impact one individual can have on societal norms and policies. As we celebrate her contributions, it is essential to reflect on the multifaceted aspects of her legacy, which continue to inspire future generations of activists.

A Lasting Impact on LGBTQ Rights

Taren Fira's advocacy work fundamentally transformed the landscape of LGBTQ rights in Alyndra and beyond. Through her tireless efforts, she championed critical legislative changes that fostered inclusivity and protection for marginalized communities. The establishment of the Taren Fira Foundation is a pivotal aspect of her legacy, providing resources and support for LGBTQ individuals and organizations. The foundation's initiatives, such as scholarship programs and community outreach, ensure that her vision for a more equitable society endures.

Mentorship and Empowerment

One of the most significant elements of Taren Fira's legacy is her commitment to mentorship. By nurturing the next generation of LGBTQ activists, she created a ripple effect of empowerment. Taren believed that effective advocacy requires not only passion but also knowledge and strategy. She often conducted workshops and training sessions, equipping young activists with the tools necessary to navigate the complexities of social justice work. Her mentorship emphasized the importance of intersectionality, encouraging her mentees to consider the diverse experiences within the LGBTQ community.

Cultural and Social Transformation

Taren Fira's influence extended beyond policy changes; she played a crucial role in reshaping societal attitudes towards LGBTQ individuals. Through art, storytelling, and public speaking, she challenged stereotypes and fostered empathy. Her ability to articulate personal narratives and connect them to broader social issues made her a compelling advocate. Taren's work in the arts, particularly in organizing inclusive cultural events, helped to humanize LGBTQ experiences, encouraging society to embrace diversity.

Building Community and Safe Spaces

In her quest for equality, Taren prioritized the creation of safe spaces for LGBTQ individuals. She understood that advocacy is not solely about legislation; it is also about fostering a sense of belonging. Community centers established under her guidance became havens for individuals seeking support, resources, and connection. These spaces offered workshops, mental health services, and social events, reinforcing the idea that community is essential for resilience and empowerment.

Celebrating Diversity within the Movement

Taren Fira's legacy is also characterized by her commitment to celebrating diversity within the LGBTQ movement. She was an ardent advocate for the rights of queer people of color, transgender individuals, and those with non-binary identities. By amplifying marginalized voices, she ensured that the movement was inclusive and representative. Taren's efforts to engage with other social justice movements highlighted the interconnectedness of various struggles, fostering solidarity and collaboration.

Reflection and Commemoration

As we celebrate Taren Fira's legacy, it is vital to reflect on the lessons learned from her life and work. Her unwavering dedication to justice serves as a reminder that activism is a continuous journey requiring resilience, adaptability, and compassion. In honoring her memory, we commit to carrying forward her vision of a world where every individual, regardless of their identity, can live authentically and without fear.

Conclusion

In conclusion, Taren Fira's legacy is a mosaic of advocacy, mentorship, and community building that continues to inspire and empower. As we celebrate her contributions, let us remember that the fight for LGBTQ rights is ongoing. By embracing Taren's values and principles, we can ensure that her impact resonates for generations to come. The celebration of her life and work is not merely a retrospective; it is a call to action for all of us to continue the vital work of advocacy, inclusivity, and love.

$$\text{Legacy} = \text{Advocacy} + \text{Mentorship} + \text{Community Building} \qquad (58)$$

Section Two: Lessons Learned in LGBTQ Activism

Strategies for Effective Activism

In the realm of LGBTQ activism, effective strategies are paramount to creating meaningful change. Activism is not merely about raising awareness; it involves a multifaceted approach that combines advocacy, community engagement, and strategic planning. This section explores various strategies that have proven effective in LGBTQ activism, drawing upon historical examples, theoretical frameworks, and contemporary practices.

Understanding the Landscape

Before embarking on any activism campaign, it is essential to understand the socio-political landscape. This involves conducting a thorough analysis of the current laws, societal attitudes, and existing movements related to LGBTQ rights. The **SWOT analysis** (Strengths, Weaknesses, Opportunities, Threats) is a valuable tool in this regard. For instance, during the fight for marriage equality in the United States, activists conducted SWOT analyses to identify key allies in government, potential legal challenges, and public sentiment, which informed their strategies.

Building Coalitions

Coalition-building is a cornerstone of effective activism. By collaborating with other marginalized groups, activists can amplify their voices and broaden their impact. The **intersectionality theory**, as introduced by Kimberlé Crenshaw, highlights the importance of understanding how various forms of discrimination overlap. For example, the collaboration between LGBTQ activists and racial justice movements during the Black Lives Matter protests exemplifies how intersectional activism can lead to a more inclusive approach to social justice.

Utilizing Digital Platforms

In the digital age, social media has emerged as a powerful tool for activism. Platforms like Twitter, Instagram, and TikTok allow activists to reach a global audience quickly. The **hashtag activism** phenomenon, where specific hashtags such as #LoveIsLove and #TransRightsAreHumanRights trend worldwide, demonstrates the potential of digital campaigns to mobilize support and raise awareness. However, it is crucial to remember that digital activism should complement, not replace, on-the-ground efforts.

Engaging with Policy Makers

Effective activism often requires direct engagement with policymakers. Lobbying for legislative change is a critical strategy for achieving long-term goals. This involves not only advocating for specific policies, such as anti-discrimination laws, but also building relationships with lawmakers. For instance, the Human Rights Campaign (HRC) has successfully lobbied for various pieces of legislation by organizing meetings between constituents and their representatives, thereby putting a human face to the issues at stake.

Grassroots Mobilization

Grassroots movements are the backbone of effective activism. Mobilizing community members to participate in protests, rallies, and local events fosters a sense of ownership and empowerment. The Stonewall Riots of 1969 are a prime example of grassroots activism sparking a larger movement for LGBTQ rights. Organizing local events, such as pride parades and awareness campaigns, can galvanize community support and create a sense of solidarity.

Education and Awareness Campaigns

Education is a vital component of activism. Awareness campaigns that inform the public about LGBTQ issues can shift societal attitudes and reduce stigma. Programs in schools that promote LGBTQ inclusivity and understanding are essential in fostering acceptance from a young age. For example, the **It Gets Better Project** utilizes personal stories and educational resources to combat bullying and promote a more accepting society.

Evaluating Impact

Finally, evaluating the impact of activism is crucial for refining strategies and ensuring effectiveness. This can be done through qualitative and quantitative measures, such as surveys, interviews, and analysis of media coverage. Understanding what strategies worked, what did not, and why can inform future activism efforts. For instance, after the success of the marriage equality movement, activists conducted evaluations to assess the influence of various tactics, leading to improved approaches for subsequent campaigns.

Conclusion

In conclusion, effective activism requires a comprehensive understanding of the landscape, coalition-building, strategic engagement with policymakers, grassroots mobilization, educational initiatives, and ongoing evaluation of impact. By employing these strategies, LGBTQ activists can create lasting change and continue to advance the fight for equality. As Taren Fira often emphasized, "Activism is not a sprint; it's a marathon," highlighting the importance of sustained effort and adaptability in the face of challenges.

Overcoming Burnout and Activist Fatigue

In the realm of activism, particularly within the LGBTQ movement, the passionate pursuit of equality and justice can often lead to a phenomenon known as burnout. This state of emotional, physical, and mental exhaustion can result from prolonged stress and the relentless nature of advocacy work. Understanding how to navigate and overcome burnout is crucial not only for the individual activist but also for the broader movement's sustainability.

Understanding Burnout

Burnout is characterized by three primary dimensions: emotional exhaustion, depersonalization, and a diminished sense of personal accomplishment. According to Maslach and Leiter (2016), emotional exhaustion refers to feelings of being drained and depleted, while depersonalization manifests as a cynical attitude towards one's work and the people involved. Lastly, a diminished sense of personal accomplishment leads to feelings of ineffectiveness and lack of achievement.

The interplay of these dimensions can create a cycle of despair that hampers the effectiveness of activists. In a study by Lee et al. (2018), it was found that LGBTQ activists experience higher levels of burnout compared to their heterosexual counterparts, primarily due to the compounded stressors of discrimination, societal stigma, and the emotional toll of advocating for marginalized communities.

Identifying the Causes of Burnout

Several factors contribute to burnout in LGBTQ activism:
  1. **High Emotional Investment**: Activists often invest deeply in their causes, which can lead to emotional fatigue over time. 2. **Systemic Oppression**: Constant exposure to discrimination and hostility can be demoralizing, leading to feelings of helplessness. 3. **Lack of Resources**: Many activists work within underfunded organizations, which can increase workloads and decrease support. 4. **Isolation**: The nature of activism can be isolating, particularly for those who face rejection from their communities or families.

To combat these factors, it is essential to implement strategies that promote resilience and well-being.

Strategies for Overcoming Burnout

To effectively address burnout, activists can adopt a multi-faceted approach:

1. **Self-Care Practices** Self-care is vital for maintaining mental and emotional health. This includes:
  - **Physical Activity**: Engaging in regular exercise can significantly reduce stress levels. A study by Rebar et al. (2015) found that physical activity not only improves mood but also enhances overall well-being. - **Mindfulness and Meditation**: Mindfulness practices can help activists stay grounded and present, reducing anxiety and emotional fatigue. Research by Keng et al. (2011) indicates that mindfulness can lead to increased emotional regulation and resilience.

2. Building Support Networks Creating a strong support system is essential for combating feelings of isolation. Activists should:
   - **Seek Peer Support**: Connecting with fellow activists can provide a sense of community and understanding. Sharing experiences can alleviate feelings of loneliness and validate emotions. - **Engage in Group Activities**: Participating in social events or collaborative projects can foster camaraderie and reinforce a sense of belonging.

3. Setting Boundaries Establishing clear boundaries is crucial for maintaining balance. Activists should:
   - **Limit Engagement**: It is important to recognize personal limits and not overcommit to every cause. Setting realistic goals can prevent feelings of overwhelm. - **Take Breaks**: Regularly scheduled breaks away from activism allow for mental rejuvenation. This can involve short vacations or even brief moments of solitude during busy days.

4. Professional Help Seeking professional support from counselors or therapists can provide additional tools for coping with burnout. Mental health professionals can assist activists in developing coping strategies and processing the emotional toll of their work.

Examples of Resilience in Activism

Several prominent LGBTQ activists have publicly shared their struggles with burnout and the strategies they employed to overcome it. For instance, Taren Fira herself, during a particularly challenging period, took a sabbatical from activism to focus on personal well-being. She engaged in art therapy, which not only provided her with a creative outlet but also helped her process the emotional weight of her advocacy work.

Similarly, the organization *Queer Advocates for Change* implemented a wellness program that included weekly yoga sessions and mental health workshops. This initiative significantly reduced reported burnout levels among its members, demonstrating the effectiveness of proactive self-care measures.

Conclusion

Overcoming burnout and activist fatigue is an ongoing challenge in the field of LGBTQ advocacy. By understanding the causes of burnout and implementing effective coping strategies, activists can sustain their passion and commitment to the movement. It is crucial to prioritize mental health and well-being, not only for individual activists but for the entire community. As Taren Fira often emphasized, "We cannot pour from an empty cup." Therefore, nurturing oneself is as vital as the fight for justice, ensuring that the flame of activism continues to burn brightly for generations to come.

Bibliography

[1] Maslach, C., & Leiter, M. P. (2016). *Burnout: A Guide to Identifying Burnout and Pathways to Recovery*. Harvard Business Press.

[2] Lee, J., Lee, M., & Kim, S. (2018). Burnout among LGBTQ activists: The role of social support and coping strategies. *Journal of Social Issues*, 74(2), 275-293.

[3] Keng, S. L., Smoski, M. J., & Robins, C. J. (2011). Effects of mindfulness on psychological health: A review of empirical studies. *Clinical Psychology Review*, 31(6), 1041-1056.

[4] Rebar, A. L., Stanton, R., Geard, D., Short, C., Duncan, M. J., & Vandelanotte, C. (2015). A meta-meta-analysis of the relationship between physical activity and mental health. *Health Psychology Review*, 9(3), 367-411.

Collaborations and Building Alliances

In the realm of LGBTQ activism, collaborations and building alliances are not merely beneficial; they are essential for creating a robust movement capable of addressing the multifaceted challenges faced by the community. The synergy that arises from diverse groups working together can amplify voices, broaden perspectives, and foster innovative solutions to persistent issues. This section explores the theoretical underpinnings of collaboration, the challenges activists face in forming alliances, and practical examples of successful partnerships.

Theoretical Framework

At its core, collaboration in activism can be understood through the lens of *intersectionality*, a term coined by legal scholar Kimberlé Crenshaw. Intersectionality posits that individuals experience oppression and privilege differently based on various social identities, including race, gender, sexuality, and class. Activists must recognize these intersecting identities to build effective coalitions that address the unique challenges faced by marginalized groups within the LGBTQ community.

Additionally, the *Social Movement Theory* provides insight into how collective action can lead to social change. According to Charles Tilly, social movements are "sustained campaigns of claim-making" that rely on the mobilization of resources, the establishment of a supportive environment, and the development of a shared identity among participants. Collaborative efforts enhance these elements, allowing movements to pool resources and create a more inclusive platform for advocacy.

Challenges in Collaboration

Despite the clear benefits of collaboration, activists often encounter significant challenges when building alliances.

- **Differing Priorities:** Different organizations may have varying goals and priorities, leading to potential conflicts. For instance, a group focused on marriage equality may clash with another prioritizing transgender rights, as their immediate concerns might not align.

- **Power Dynamics:** Power imbalances can hinder collaboration, especially when larger, more established organizations overshadow smaller grassroots groups. This can lead to the marginalization of voices that are critical to the movement's diversity and inclusivity.

- **Communication Barriers:** Misunderstandings and miscommunications can arise from differing terminologies and cultural contexts. Activists must navigate these differences to foster effective dialogue and collaboration.

- **Resource Allocation:** Competing for limited funding and resources can create tension among organizations. This competition can detract from the collective mission and lead to fragmentation within the movement.

Successful Collaborations

Despite these challenges, numerous examples illustrate the power of collaboration in LGBTQ activism:

The Marriage Equality Movement One of the most notable examples of successful collaboration is the marriage equality movement in the United States. Organizations such as the Human Rights Campaign (HRC) and the American Civil Liberties Union (ACLU) joined forces with local grassroots organizations to create a unified front advocating for marriage rights. This collaboration not only pooled resources but also amplified the voices of individuals from diverse backgrounds, ensuring that the movement was inclusive and representative.

Transgender Rights Advocacy Another significant collaboration occurred in the fight for transgender rights. The Transgender Law Center partnered with various LGBTQ organizations and women's rights groups to address issues such as healthcare access, workplace discrimination, and legal recognition of gender identity. By forming alliances across different sectors, these organizations were able to develop comprehensive strategies that addressed the unique challenges faced by transgender individuals.

Global Solidarity Networks On an international scale, collaborations among LGBTQ organizations have proven vital in advocating for global human rights. The International Lesbian, Gay, Bisexual, Trans and Intersex Association (ILGA) works in coalition with local activists in countries where LGBTQ rights are severely restricted. These alliances have led to significant advancements in policy changes and greater visibility for LGBTQ issues worldwide.

Building Effective Alliances

To foster effective collaborations, activists should consider the following strategies:

- **Establish Common Goals:** Identifying shared objectives is critical for unifying diverse groups. This requires open dialogue and a willingness to understand each other's priorities and challenges.

- **Emphasize Inclusivity:** Alliances should actively seek to include marginalized voices within the LGBTQ community. This can be achieved through outreach efforts and creating spaces where all members feel valued and heard.

- **Foster Trust and Respect:** Building trust among collaborators is essential. This can be accomplished by acknowledging past grievances, respecting different perspectives, and committing to transparent communication.

- **Leverage Resources:** Organizations should share resources and expertise to strengthen their collective impact. This includes not only financial resources but also knowledge, networks, and skills.

- **Evaluate and Adapt:** Continuous evaluation of collaborative efforts can help identify areas for improvement. Activists should be open to adapting their strategies based on feedback and changing circumstances.

Conclusion

In conclusion, collaborations and alliances are indispensable for the success of LGBTQ activism. By understanding the theoretical frameworks that underpin these efforts, acknowledging the challenges, and drawing on successful examples, activists can forge stronger, more inclusive movements. As Taren Fira exemplified, the power of unity in diversity not only enriches the advocacy landscape but also paves the way for meaningful change. The legacy of collaboration will continue to inspire future generations of activists, ensuring that the fight for LGBTQ rights remains resilient and unwavering.

Celebrating Victories and Learning from Setbacks

In the realm of LGBTQ activism, the journey is often a tapestry woven with both triumphs and challenges. It is crucial to celebrate victories, no matter how small, as they serve as milestones that inspire and motivate continued efforts. Simultaneously, reflecting on setbacks provides valuable lessons that can shape future strategies and approaches.

The Importance of Celebrating Victories

Celebrating victories, whether legislative achievements, increased visibility, or community engagement, fosters a sense of accomplishment and reinforces the belief that change is possible. Each victory, no matter the scale, contributes to a larger narrative of progress. For instance, the legalization of same-sex marriage in Alyndra marked a significant milestone for LGBTQ rights, symbolizing acceptance and equality. This victory was not just a legal change; it was a cultural shift that encouraged many individuals to embrace their identities openly.

Psychological theories, such as Bandura's Social Learning Theory, suggest that observing others' successes can enhance motivation and self-efficacy among activists. When victories are celebrated publicly, they serve as models for what is achievable, encouraging others to engage in activism. Celebrations can take many forms, from community gatherings and pride parades to social media campaigns highlighting accomplishments.

Learning from Setbacks

While victories are essential, setbacks are inevitable in any activist movement. Understanding that setbacks are not failures, but rather opportunities for growth, is crucial for sustaining momentum. For instance, after the initial push for marriage equality, activists faced significant backlash and legal challenges, including attempts to roll back rights through referendums and discriminatory legislation.

Theories of resilience, such as the Resilience Theory proposed by Rutter (1987), emphasize the importance of adaptability in the face of adversity. Activists must cultivate resilience to navigate the emotional and strategic challenges posed by setbacks. This involves analyzing what went wrong, identifying areas for improvement, and adjusting strategies accordingly.

An example of this can be seen in the aftermath of the failed attempt to pass the Equality Act in Alyndra. Activists regrouped, conducted thorough analyses of the opposition's arguments, and developed new strategies that included broader coalition-building and targeted outreach to undecided legislators. This reflective process not only strengthened their advocacy but also fostered a sense of unity and purpose within the community.

The Role of Reflection in Activism

Reflection is a powerful tool for learning and growth. Activists are encouraged to maintain journals or engage in group discussions to process experiences, both positive and negative. By articulating their thoughts and feelings about victories and setbacks, activists can gain insights that inform future actions.

The concept of reflective practice, as articulated by Schön (1983), underscores the importance of thinking critically about one's experiences. This approach allows activists to understand the complexities of their work and recognize patterns that may emerge over time. For instance, after a successful pride event, activists might reflect on what strategies led to high attendance and engagement, while also considering aspects that could be improved for future events.

Case Studies: Celebrating and Learning

To illustrate the dual importance of celebrating victories and learning from setbacks, we can examine two case studies from Taren Fira's activism.

Case Study 1: The First Pride Parade The inaugural LGBTQ Pride Parade in Alyndra was a monumental victory, drawing thousands of participants and garnering significant media attention. This event not only celebrated LGBTQ identities but also served as a powerful statement against discrimination. The organizers celebrated the turnout with a post-parade gathering, where speeches highlighted the importance of visibility and community support.

However, the aftermath revealed challenges, including instances of harassment and negative reactions from certain community members. The organizers took these setbacks seriously, conducting surveys to gather feedback and engaging in discussions about safety and inclusivity for future events. This reflective process led to enhanced security measures and a more comprehensive outreach strategy for subsequent parades, ensuring that all participants felt safe and welcomed.

Case Study 2: Legislative Advocacy for Non-Binary Rights Another significant victory was the successful advocacy for the inclusion of non-binary gender options in official documents. This achievement was celebrated through social media campaigns and community forums, emphasizing the importance of recognizing diverse gender identities.

However, the victory was met with backlash from conservative groups, leading to attempts to repeal the new policy. Activists learned from this setback by conducting workshops on effective communication and countering misinformation. They also strengthened alliances with other marginalized groups, demonstrating solidarity and resilience in the face of opposition. This collaboration not only fortified their advocacy efforts but also expanded their reach and influence.

Conclusion

In conclusion, the journey of LGBTQ activism is characterized by a dynamic interplay of celebrating victories and learning from setbacks. Each victory reinforces the belief in the possibility of change, while each setback offers invaluable lessons that can inform future strategies. By embracing both aspects, activists like Taren Fira can cultivate a resilient and adaptive movement that continues to strive for equality and justice. Through reflection, collaboration, and a commitment to learning, the LGBTQ community can navigate the complexities of activism, ensuring that every step taken is a step toward a more inclusive and equitable society.

The Enduring Importance of Queer Advocacy

The enduring importance of queer advocacy cannot be overstated. It serves as a critical counterforce to systemic oppression, discrimination, and violence faced by LGBTQ+ individuals. At its core, queer advocacy seeks not only to secure rights and recognition but also to affirm the dignity and humanity of all individuals, regardless of their sexual orientation or gender identity. This section will explore the theoretical underpinnings of queer advocacy, the persistent challenges it addresses, and practical examples that illustrate its significance in contemporary society.

Theoretical Frameworks

Queer advocacy operates within several theoretical frameworks that highlight the complexities of identity and power dynamics. One such framework is Judith Butler's theory of gender performativity, which posits that gender is not an innate quality but rather a set of behaviors and performances that society expects of individuals. This challenges traditional binary notions of gender and emphasizes the fluidity of identity, making it essential for advocacy efforts to embrace non-binary and gender-nonconforming identities.

Another important theoretical contribution comes from intersectionality, a term coined by Kimberlé Crenshaw. Intersectionality examines how various social categorizations—such as race, class, gender, and sexuality—intersect to create overlapping systems of discrimination or disadvantage. Queer advocacy must therefore consider these intersections to effectively address the unique challenges faced by marginalized groups within the LGBTQ+ community, such as queer people of color, transgender individuals, and those with disabilities.

Persistent Challenges

Despite significant progress in LGBTQ+ rights, numerous challenges persist, necessitating ongoing advocacy. These challenges include:

- **Legal Inequality:** Many countries still lack comprehensive legal protections for LGBTQ+ individuals. For instance, in several regions, same-sex relationships are criminalized, and individuals may face severe penalties, including imprisonment or even death. Advocacy efforts are crucial in lobbying for legal reforms that ensure equality and justice.

- **Social Stigma:** Social attitudes toward LGBTQ+ individuals remain a significant barrier to acceptance. In many societies, individuals face ostracism, discrimination, and violence based on their sexual orientation or gender identity. Advocacy plays a vital role in changing public perceptions and fostering an environment of acceptance and understanding.

- **Mental Health Disparities:** LGBTQ+ individuals experience higher rates of mental health issues, including depression and anxiety, often stemming from societal rejection and discrimination. Advocacy efforts must address these disparities by promoting mental health resources and support systems tailored to the needs of queer individuals.

- **Healthcare Access:** Access to appropriate healthcare services, including gender-affirming care for transgender individuals, remains a critical issue. Advocacy is necessary to ensure that healthcare providers are educated about LGBTQ+ health needs and that policies are enacted to eliminate discrimination in healthcare settings.

Practical Examples of Queer Advocacy

The significance of queer advocacy is illustrated through various successful initiatives and movements that have made a lasting impact on society:

- **The Stonewall Riots:** Often cited as the catalyst for the modern LGBTQ+ rights movement, the Stonewall Riots of 1969 represented a turning point in queer advocacy. The riots were a response to police harassment and discrimination against LGBTQ+ individuals. They galvanized activists and led to the formation of organizations advocating for LGBTQ+ rights, highlighting the importance of grassroots activism.

- **Marriage Equality:** The fight for marriage equality in various countries serves as a powerful example of successful queer advocacy. In the United States, the landmark Supreme Court case Obergefell v. Hodges (2015) legalized same-sex marriage nationwide. This victory was the result of decades of advocacy, legal challenges, and public awareness campaigns that shifted societal attitudes toward marriage equality.

- **Trans Rights Advocacy:** Organizations such as the Transgender Law Center and GLAAD have been at the forefront of advocating for transgender rights, including access to healthcare and legal recognition of gender identity. Their efforts have led to increased visibility and support for transgender individuals, showcasing the importance of targeted advocacy for marginalized subgroups within the LGBTQ+ community.

- **Global LGBTQ+ Advocacy:** International organizations, such as ILGA (International Lesbian, Gay, Bisexual, Trans and Intersex Association), work tirelessly to promote LGBTQ+ rights globally. Their efforts include lobbying for policy changes, providing resources for grassroots movements, and fostering international solidarity among LGBTQ+ activists. This highlights the interconnectedness of queer advocacy across borders and cultures.

Conclusion

In conclusion, the enduring importance of queer advocacy lies in its ability to challenge systemic injustices, promote inclusivity, and empower marginalized voices. By drawing upon theoretical frameworks such as gender performativity and intersectionality, advocates can address the complex realities faced by LGBTQ+ individuals. The persistent challenges of legal inequality, social stigma, mental health disparities, and healthcare access necessitate ongoing advocacy efforts. Through practical examples, such as the Stonewall Riots and the fight for marriage equality, the transformative power of queer advocacy is evident. As society continues to evolve, the need for robust and inclusive advocacy remains critical in the pursuit of equality and justice for all.

Self-Care and Community Care in Activism

In the realm of activism, particularly within the LGBTQ community, the significance of self-care and community care cannot be overstated. Activists often find themselves navigating a landscape fraught with emotional challenges, societal pushback, and the weight of historical injustices. This section explores the theoretical foundations of self-care and community care, the problems activists face, and practical examples of how these concepts can be implemented effectively.

Theoretical Foundations

Self-care is defined as the practice of taking an active role in protecting one's own well-being and happiness, particularly during periods of stress. According to [?], self-care is not merely a luxury but an essential component of sustainable activism. Theories of self-care emphasize the importance of individual well-being as a precursor to effective advocacy.

Community care, on the other hand, extends the notion of self-care to the collective. It recognizes that the well-being of individuals is inextricably linked to the health of their communities. As articulated by [?], community care involves mutual support, shared resources, and collective healing, particularly for marginalized groups. This approach is vital in LGBTQ activism, where individuals often face systemic oppression that can lead to isolation and burnout.

Problems Faced by Activists

Despite the clear benefits of self-care and community care, activists frequently encounter several barriers that hinder their ability to practice these principles:

- **Burnout:** The emotional toll of activism can lead to burnout, characterized by exhaustion, cynicism, and a reduced sense of accomplishment. A study by [?] found that nearly 70% of LGBTQ activists reported experiencing burnout within their first five years of advocacy.

- **Stigma:** Many activists feel guilty for prioritizing self-care, fearing it may be perceived as self-indulgent or as a lack of commitment to the cause. This stigma can prevent individuals from seeking necessary rest and recuperation.

- **Resource Limitations:** Community organizations often operate on tight budgets, limiting their ability to provide adequate mental health resources and support systems for activists.

- **Isolation:** Activists may experience feelings of isolation, particularly when their identities or experiences are not represented within mainstream movements. This can exacerbate mental health struggles and hinder collective care efforts.

Practical Examples of Self-Care and Community Care

Implementing self-care and community care strategies can take various forms, ranging from individual practices to collective initiatives. Below are some effective examples:

1. **Mindfulness and Reflection:** Activists can benefit from mindfulness practices, such as meditation or journaling. These practices encourage individuals to reflect on their experiences, recognize their emotional needs, and cultivate resilience. A survey conducted by [?] indicated that activists who engaged in regular mindfulness practices reported higher levels of emotional well-being and lower levels of stress.

2. Peer Support Networks: Establishing peer support groups allows activists to share their experiences, challenges, and coping strategies. These groups can provide a safe space for individuals to express their feelings and receive validation. The *Queer Peer Support Network* is an example of a successful initiative that has fostered community care among LGBTQ activists.

3. Mental Health Resources: Organizations should prioritize mental health by providing access to counseling services, workshops, and training on self-care strategies. For instance, the *LGBTQ+ Wellness Initiative* offers free therapy sessions and workshops on managing stress and anxiety, demonstrating a commitment to both self-care and community care.

4. Collective Celebrations: Celebrating victories, no matter how small, can enhance community morale and foster a sense of belonging. Organizing events that acknowledge the hard work of activists, such as appreciation dinners or community awards, can help combat feelings of isolation and burnout.

5. Advocacy for Structural Change: Activists should advocate for policies that support mental health resources within their communities. This includes pushing for funding for mental health services that specifically cater to LGBTQ individuals, ensuring that community care is not an afterthought but a priority.

Conclusion

In conclusion, self-care and community care are essential components of sustainable activism within the LGBTQ community. By recognizing the interconnectedness of individual and collective well-being, activists can create a more supportive environment that fosters resilience and long-term commitment to the fight for equality. As Taren Fira often emphasized, "You cannot pour from an empty cup; take care of yourself so that you can take care of others." This philosophy serves as a guiding principle for activists seeking to balance their personal needs with the demands of advocacy.

The Intersection of Activism and Mental Health

Activism, while a powerful force for change, can often take a toll on mental health. This intersection of activism and mental health is crucial for understanding the well-being of activists, particularly within the LGBTQ community, where the struggle for rights and recognition is ongoing and often fraught with challenges.

This section explores the complexities of this intersection, discussing relevant theories, problems faced by activists, and examples that illustrate the need for mental health awareness in advocacy.

Theoretical Frameworks

One prominent theory that can be applied to the intersection of activism and mental health is the **Stress-Coping Theory**. This theory posits that stress arises when individuals perceive a discrepancy between the demands placed upon them and their resources to cope with those demands. Activists often face significant stressors, including societal discrimination, backlash from political entities, and personal sacrifices.

The equation that can summarize this relationship is:

$$\text{Stress} = \text{Demands} - \text{Resources}$$

Where: - **Demands** refer to the challenges and responsibilities associated with activism. - **Resources** encompass the support systems, coping strategies, and personal resilience available to the activist.

Another relevant framework is the **Trauma-Informed Care** approach, which emphasizes understanding, recognizing, and responding to the effects of all types of trauma. Given the historical and ongoing oppression faced by LGBTQ individuals, many activists may experience trauma that affects their mental health, making it essential for organizations to adopt trauma-informed practices.

Problems Faced by Activists

Activists often encounter several mental health challenges, including:

- **Burnout:** The emotional, physical, and mental exhaustion caused by prolonged and intense activism. Burnout can lead to reduced motivation and effectiveness, as well as feelings of helplessness.

- **Secondary Trauma:** Activists may experience vicarious trauma by witnessing the struggles of others within their community. This can lead to anxiety and depression.

- **Isolation:** The demanding nature of activism can lead to social isolation, as activists may find it challenging to maintain personal relationships outside of their advocacy work.

- **Imposter Syndrome:** Many activists struggle with feelings of inadequacy, questioning their impact and contributions to the movement, which can lead to decreased self-esteem and mental health issues.

Examples and Case Studies

A poignant example of the intersection of activism and mental health can be found in the case of **Marsha P. Johnson**, a prominent figure in the LGBTQ rights movement. Johnson, who played a crucial role in the Stonewall riots, faced immense personal struggles, including mental health challenges exacerbated by societal discrimination and violence. Her story highlights the necessity of mental health support within activist communities.

Another example is the **Trans Lifeline**, an organization that provides support and resources for transgender individuals, particularly in crisis situations. By recognizing the mental health challenges faced by the trans community, the organization emphasizes the importance of mental health resources in advocacy efforts. They offer peer support and crisis intervention, acknowledging that the fight for rights is deeply intertwined with the need for mental well-being.

Strategies for Supporting Mental Health in Activism

To address the mental health challenges faced by activists, several strategies can be implemented:

- **Self-Care Practices:** Encouraging activists to prioritize self-care through mindfulness, exercise, and hobbies can help mitigate burnout and promote mental well-being.

- **Peer Support Groups:** Creating safe spaces for activists to share their experiences and emotions can foster community and reduce feelings of isolation.

- **Mental Health Training:** Providing training for activists on recognizing signs of mental health issues and accessing resources can empower them to seek help when needed.

- **Institutional Support:** Organizations should integrate mental health resources into their advocacy efforts, ensuring that activists have access to counseling and support services.

Conclusion

The intersection of activism and mental health is a critical area of focus for advocates within the LGBTQ community. Recognizing the mental health challenges faced by activists is essential for fostering resilience and sustainability in the movement. By implementing supportive strategies and creating a culture that prioritizes mental well-being, the LGBTQ advocacy community can ensure that its advocates are not only fighting for rights but also taking care of their own mental health in the process. The future of activism depends on the well-being of its champions, making this intersection not just relevant but vital for the ongoing struggle for equality and justice.

Resilience and Perseverance in the Face of Challenges

Resilience and perseverance are two of the most vital traits that an activist can possess, particularly in the tumultuous world of LGBTQ advocacy. Activism often requires navigating a landscape fraught with obstacles, including societal pushback, discrimination, and emotional exhaustion. Taren Fira exemplified these qualities throughout her journey, demonstrating that while the path may be rocky, the commitment to the cause must remain steadfast.

Theoretical Framework

The concept of resilience in psychology refers to the ability to adapt and recover from adversity. According to Masten (2001), resilience is not merely a trait but a dynamic process that involves positive adaptation in the face of significant adversity. In the context of LGBTQ activism, this means that individuals must not only endure challenges but also emerge stronger and more committed to their cause.

Perseverance, on the other hand, is often defined as sustained effort and determination in the pursuit of a goal despite difficulties. Duckworth et al. (2007) emphasize that grit, a combination of passion and perseverance, is a critical predictor of success. In the realm of LGBTQ rights, perseverance manifests as the relentless pursuit of equality, often in the face of overwhelming odds.

Challenges Faced by LGBTQ Activists

Activists like Taren Fira encounter numerous challenges, ranging from systemic discrimination to personal attacks. For instance, during her advocacy for marriage equality, Taren faced significant backlash from conservative groups who opposed her efforts. This included public protests, hate mail, and even threats to her personal safety. Such experiences are not uncommon; a 2019 report by the Human Rights Campaign found that 70% of LGBTQ activists reported experiencing harassment or discrimination while advocating for their rights.

Additionally, activists often grapple with emotional and mental health challenges. The constant exposure to negativity and hostility can lead to burnout, a state of physical, emotional, and mental exhaustion caused by prolonged stress. According to the American Psychological Association (2020), burnout can significantly hinder an activist's ability to continue their work, making resilience and self-care crucial.

Examples of Resilience and Perseverance

Taren Fira's journey provides numerous examples of resilience and perseverance. One notable instance occurred during the organization of the first LGBTQ Pride event in Alyndra. Despite facing logistical challenges and opposition from local authorities, Taren rallied her community, emphasizing the importance of visibility and representation. Her mantra, "Visibility is our strength," became a rallying cry, inspiring many to join the movement.

Another significant example was during her international advocacy at the United Nations. Taren encountered bureaucratic hurdles that threatened to derail her efforts to address global LGBTQ rights. However, rather than succumbing to frustration, she employed a strategy of coalition-building, collaborating with other marginalized groups to amplify their collective voices. This approach not only highlighted the interconnectedness of various social justice movements but also showcased her resilience in the face of institutional barriers.

Strategies for Cultivating Resilience

Cultivating resilience requires intentional strategies. Taren often emphasized the importance of community support. Activists can bolster their resilience by surrounding themselves with like-minded individuals who provide encouragement and understanding. This sense of belonging fosters emotional strength and helps mitigate the effects of external negativity.

Moreover, self-care practices are essential in maintaining resilience. Taren advocated for regular mental health check-ins, mindfulness practices, and the importance of taking breaks when needed. Research by the National Institute of Mental Health (2019) supports this, indicating that self-care significantly reduces stress and enhances overall well-being, which is crucial for sustaining long-term activism.

The Role of Storytelling in Resilience

Storytelling has emerged as a powerful tool for resilience in LGBTQ activism. By sharing personal narratives, activists can transform their struggles into sources of strength and inspiration. Taren often utilized storytelling in her advocacy, illustrating how sharing her experiences of discrimination and triumph could resonate with others and foster a sense of solidarity.

A study by the Narrative Research Group (2021) found that storytelling not only helps individuals process their experiences but also cultivates empathy among listeners. This mutual understanding can create a supportive environment where resilience thrives.

Conclusion

In conclusion, resilience and perseverance are fundamental to the success of LGBTQ activists like Taren Fira. By embracing these qualities, activists can navigate the challenges they face, inspire others, and ultimately drive meaningful change. As Taren often said, "The fight for equality is not a sprint; it's a marathon." This perspective underscores the importance of resilience in sustaining the momentum necessary for long-term advocacy.

The journey may be fraught with challenges, but with resilience, activists can transform adversity into strength, ensuring that their voices continue to resonate in the ongoing struggle for LGBTQ rights.

Creating Sustainable and Lasting Change

Creating sustainable and lasting change within the LGBTQ advocacy landscape requires a multifaceted approach that integrates theory, practice, and community engagement. This section explores key theoretical frameworks, identifies prevalent challenges, and provides illustrative examples to underscore the importance of sustainability in activism.

Theoretical Frameworks

One of the foundational theories in social change is the **Social Movement Theory**, which posits that organized groups can effect social change through collective action. This theory emphasizes the importance of mobilization, resource mobilization, and framing processes. According to [?], movements must not only mobilize resources but also frame their issues in ways that resonate with broader societal values.

Another relevant framework is **Intersectionality**, introduced by [Crenshaw(1989)], which argues that individuals experience overlapping systems of oppression. This perspective is crucial for LGBTQ activism, as it highlights the need to address the unique challenges faced by marginalized subgroups within the community, such as queer people of color, transgender individuals, and those with disabilities. Sustainable change must consider these intersecting identities to ensure inclusivity and effectiveness.

Challenges to Sustainability

Despite the theoretical underpinnings that guide LGBTQ activism, several challenges hinder the creation of sustainable change:

- **Burnout and Activist Fatigue:** Activists often face emotional and physical exhaustion due to the relentless nature of their work. This phenomenon is exacerbated by the lack of adequate support systems within organizations, leading to high turnover rates and diminished effectiveness [?].

- **Funding Instability:** Many LGBTQ organizations rely on grants and donations, which can be unpredictable. A lack of consistent funding threatens the longevity of initiatives and programs designed to foster community support and advocacy [?].

- **Fragmentation of Efforts:** Without a cohesive strategy, LGBTQ advocacy can become fragmented, with groups working in silos rather than collaboratively. This fragmentation can dilute the impact of advocacy efforts and lead to missed opportunities for coalition-building [?].

Strategies for Sustainable Change

To overcome these challenges and foster sustainable change, LGBTQ activists can employ several strategies:

1. **Building Resilient Organizations:** Creating structures that prioritize mental health, self-care, and community support can combat burnout. For instance, organizations like *The Trevor Project* have implemented peer support programs that empower volunteers and staff to share their experiences and provide mutual support [?].

2. **Diversifying Funding Sources:** By developing diverse funding strategies, organizations can mitigate the risks associated with reliance on a single

source of income. This can include establishing partnerships with businesses, engaging in crowdfunding campaigns, and applying for a wide range of grants [?].

3. **Fostering Collaboration:** Encouraging collaboration among LGBTQ organizations can enhance resource sharing and amplify collective impact. Initiatives like *Pride at Work* exemplify successful partnerships that unite labor movements with LGBTQ advocacy, creating a stronger voice for workers' rights [?].

Examples of Successful Initiatives

Several initiatives exemplify the principles of sustainable and lasting change in LGBTQ advocacy:

- **The Human Rights Campaign (HRC):** HRC has implemented long-term strategies aimed at both legislative change and community education. Their efforts in lobbying for marriage equality culminated in a significant victory in 2015 with the Supreme Court's decision in *Obergefell v. Hodges*, illustrating how sustained advocacy can lead to landmark legal changes [?].

- **Trans Lifeline:** This organization provides direct support services for transgender individuals, including crisis intervention and resources. By centering the needs of the trans community, Trans Lifeline demonstrates how targeted initiatives can create lasting impact and foster resilience within marginalized populations [?].

- **The Queer Liberation March:** In 2019, this grassroots event emerged as a response to the corporatization of Pride. By emphasizing the original spirit of LGBTQ activism, the march seeks to reclaim visibility and advocate for the rights of all queer individuals, showcasing the power of community-led initiatives [?].

Conclusion

Creating sustainable and lasting change in LGBTQ advocacy is a complex but achievable goal. By integrating theoretical insights, addressing challenges, and implementing effective strategies, activists can foster a resilient movement that not only advocates for immediate rights but also lays the groundwork for future generations. The legacy of activists like Taren Fira serves as a reminder that sustainable change is possible when we prioritize inclusivity, collaboration, and community empowerment.

Reflections and Insights from Experienced Activists

In the realm of LGBTQ activism, the wisdom accumulated by seasoned advocates serves as a guiding light for new generations. These reflections and insights not only encapsulate the trials and triumphs of activism but also provide a framework for understanding the complexities of social change. Below, we explore key themes that emerge from the experiences of veteran activists, illustrating the nuanced landscape of LGBTQ advocacy.

The Importance of Intersectionality

One of the most profound insights from experienced activists is the necessity of intersectionality in advocacy. Kimberlé Crenshaw's theory of intersectionality posits that individuals experience overlapping systems of discrimination and privilege, which must be acknowledged to create effective and inclusive strategies. Activists emphasize that acknowledging intersections—such as race, gender, class, and sexuality—is crucial for building solidarity among diverse communities.

For instance, veteran activist Jordan Lee reflects on the early days of their advocacy work, stating, "I learned quickly that our fight for LGBTQ rights could not be separated from the fight against racism and sexism. If we wanted to create real change, we had to uplift all marginalized voices, not just our own." This sentiment underscores the importance of coalition-building and the need to center the experiences of those who are often left out of mainstream LGBTQ narratives.

The Role of Personal Narratives

Personal storytelling emerges as a powerful tool in the arsenal of activists. Experienced advocates highlight the impact that sharing personal experiences can have on changing hearts and minds. The narrative framework, as discussed by narrative theorists like Walter Fisher, posits that humans are natural storytellers, and through narratives, we construct meaning and identity.

Activist Maria Gonzalez shares, "When I came out publicly, I was terrified. But sharing my story of struggle and acceptance opened doors for conversations that I never thought possible. It humanized the issue for many who had never met someone like me." This exemplifies how personal narratives can serve to bridge gaps in understanding and foster empathy, ultimately leading to greater acceptance and support for LGBTQ rights.

Resilience in the Face of Adversity

Another recurring theme in the reflections of seasoned activists is the importance of resilience. The journey of advocating for LGBTQ rights is fraught with challenges, including legal setbacks, societal pushback, and personal sacrifices. Activists often recount moments of despair, yet they emphasize the necessity of perseverance.

"Every setback is a setup for a comeback," asserts veteran activist Alex Chen. "We faced countless defeats, but each one taught us valuable lessons about strategy and community mobilization." This sentiment aligns with the psychological concept of resilience, which refers to the ability to bounce back from adversity. Research indicates that resilience can be cultivated through supportive networks, self-care practices, and a strong sense of purpose.

The Significance of Mentorship

Mentorship plays a pivotal role in sustaining activist movements. Experienced advocates stress the importance of passing down knowledge and skills to the next generation. Mentorship not only fosters growth within individuals but also strengthens the collective movement.

As veteran activist Samira Patel notes, "When I mentor young activists, I'm not just sharing my knowledge; I'm investing in the future of our community. It's about building a legacy." This perspective echoes the findings of mentorship studies, which highlight the benefits of mentorship in enhancing leadership skills, increasing confidence, and promoting a sense of belonging within activist spaces.

Adapting to Changing Landscapes

The landscape of activism is constantly evolving, influenced by cultural shifts, technological advancements, and political climates. Experienced activists stress the need for adaptability in strategies and approaches. The rise of digital activism, for example, has transformed the way movements organize and mobilize.

"Social media has changed everything," reflects activist Tara Kim. "We can reach thousands in a matter of minutes, but we must also be mindful of the digital divide and ensure our strategies are inclusive." This highlights the importance of balancing traditional grassroots organizing with modern digital tactics, ensuring that all voices are heard, regardless of their access to technology.

Self-Care and Community Care

Lastly, the insights of seasoned activists underscore the critical need for self-care and community care within the movement. The emotional toll of activism can lead to burnout, and experienced advocates emphasize the importance of prioritizing mental health.

Activist and mental health advocate Jordan Rivera states, "We cannot pour from an empty cup. Taking care of ourselves and each other is not just a luxury; it's a necessity for sustainable activism." This perspective aligns with the emerging discourse on community care, which emphasizes collective responsibility for the well-being of all members within a movement.

In conclusion, the reflections and insights from experienced LGBTQ activists provide invaluable guidance for both current and future advocates. By embracing intersectionality, harnessing the power of personal narratives, cultivating resilience, fostering mentorship, adapting to change, and prioritizing self-care, activists can navigate the complexities of advocacy with greater effectiveness and compassion. These lessons serve as a beacon of hope and inspiration, reminding us that the fight for equality is not only a collective endeavor but also a deeply personal journey.

Section Three: Taren Fira's Final Message

Reflections on a Life of Activism

Taren Fira's journey through the vibrant yet tumultuous landscape of LGBTQ activism serves as a testament to the power of resilience, courage, and unwavering commitment to justice. Throughout her life, Taren faced myriad challenges that shaped her into a formidable advocate. In reflecting on her life of activism, several key themes emerge: the importance of intersectionality, the necessity of community, the role of personal narratives, and the enduring fight for equality.

The Importance of Intersectionality

Taren understood that LGBTQ rights do not exist in a vacuum. Her advocacy was deeply rooted in the recognition of intersectionality, a term coined by legal scholar Kimberlé Crenshaw, which describes how various forms of social stratification, such as race, gender, and class, overlap and affect individuals' experiences. Taren often articulated that the fight for LGBTQ rights must also encompass the struggles faced by marginalized communities, particularly queer people of color and those from lower socioeconomic backgrounds.

$$\text{Intersectionality} = f(\text{Race, Gender, Class, Sexual Orientation}) \quad (59)$$

This equation highlights that the experience of being LGBTQ is not uniform; rather, it is influenced by a multitude of factors. Taren's advocacy efforts were characterized by her commitment to amplifying the voices of those who often went unheard, ensuring that the LGBTQ movement was inclusive and representative of its diverse constituents.

The Necessity of Community

Throughout her activism, Taren emphasized the significance of community. She often stated, "We are stronger together than we could ever be alone." This belief manifested in her efforts to build coalitions among various social justice movements. By collaborating with groups focused on racial justice, women's rights, and disability rights, Taren fostered a sense of solidarity that transcended individual struggles.

One notable example of this was the annual Alyndra Pride Festival, which Taren helped organize. The festival not only celebrated LGBTQ identities but also featured workshops and panels on issues like racial equity and mental health. This holistic approach to activism underscored Taren's belief that true liberation could only be achieved through collective action.

The Role of Personal Narratives

Taren recognized the transformative power of storytelling. She believed that personal narratives could serve as catalysts for change, bridging gaps in understanding and fostering empathy. In her speeches and writings, she often shared her own experiences of discrimination and triumph, illustrating how vulnerability could inspire others to join the fight for equality.

The effectiveness of personal narratives in activism aligns with the concept of narrative ethics, which posits that storytelling is not merely a means of communication but a way to enact social change. By sharing her journey, Taren encouraged others to do the same, creating a tapestry of experiences that highlighted the richness and complexity of LGBTQ lives.

$$\text{Empathy} = \sum_{i=1}^{n} \text{Narrative}_i \quad (60)$$

Here, Narrative_i represents individual stories that contribute to a collective understanding of LGBTQ issues, emphasizing that empathy grows with each shared experience.

The Enduring Fight for Equality

Despite significant progress in LGBTQ rights, Taren remained acutely aware of the ongoing challenges. She often reflected on the backlash against LGBTQ rights and the rise of conservative movements that sought to undermine the hard-won gains. Taren's resilience in the face of such adversity was a defining characteristic of her activism.

In her final public address, she poignantly stated, "The fight for equality is a marathon, not a sprint. We must prepare for the long haul, for the road ahead is fraught with challenges." This metaphor encapsulated her understanding that activism requires sustained effort, adaptability, and an unwavering commitment to justice.

Taren's legacy is not merely the policies she influenced or the events she organized; it is the spirit of activism she instilled in others. Her reflections serve as a call to action for future generations, reminding them that the path to equality is paved with perseverance, solidarity, and love.

In conclusion, Taren Fira's life of activism was marked by a profound understanding of the complexities of social justice. Her reflections on intersectionality, community, storytelling, and the ongoing fight for equality continue to inspire and guide those who dare to dream of a more just world. As we honor her legacy, may we carry forward her message: that together, we can create a society where everyone, regardless of their identity, can thrive and be celebrated.

Hope for the Future of LGBTQ Equality

The future of LGBTQ equality shines with a spectrum of possibilities, each hue representing the collective hopes, dreams, and aspirations of countless individuals who have fought valiantly for their rights. The journey towards equality is akin to a grand tapestry, woven from the threads of resilience, courage, and unity. As we reflect on the progress made and the challenges that remain, it is essential to embrace an optimistic vision for what lies ahead.

At the heart of this hope is the recognition that societal attitudes toward LGBTQ individuals have shifted dramatically over the past few decades. Research indicates a growing acceptance of diverse sexual orientations and gender identities, particularly among younger generations. According to a study by the Williams

Institute, acceptance of same-sex relationships has increased from 27% in 1973 to over 70% in recent years. This shift in public opinion suggests that the groundwork for a more inclusive society is firmly established, paving the way for continued progress.

However, the path forward is not without its obstacles. The rise of anti-LGBTQ sentiment in various regions, often fueled by political rhetoric and misinformation, poses a significant challenge to the advancements made. For instance, the enactment of discriminatory laws, such as those restricting transgender individuals' access to healthcare and public facilities, threatens to undo years of hard-fought gains. The International Lesbian, Gay, Bisexual, Trans and Intersex Association (ILGA) reports that over 70 countries still criminalize same-sex relationships, highlighting the urgent need for global advocacy and solidarity.

To counteract these setbacks, it is crucial to foster a culture of allyship and intersectionality within the LGBTQ movement. This involves recognizing that the fight for equality is interconnected with other social justice movements, such as racial justice, gender equality, and economic justice. By embracing an intersectional framework, activists can better address the unique challenges faced by marginalized groups within the LGBTQ community, including people of color, transgender individuals, and those living in poverty. The concept of intersectionality, coined by scholar Kimberlé Crenshaw, emphasizes that individuals experience overlapping systems of oppression, which must be acknowledged and addressed in advocacy efforts.

Moreover, the power of storytelling cannot be underestimated in the quest for LGBTQ equality. Personal narratives have the ability to humanize issues, challenge stereotypes, and foster empathy among those who may not share similar experiences. The impact of storytelling is exemplified by campaigns such as the "It Gets Better Project," which has provided a platform for LGBTQ individuals to share their journeys and inspire hope in younger generations. As more people come forward with their stories, the collective narrative of the LGBTQ community becomes richer and more diverse, reinforcing the message that everyone deserves love, acceptance, and equality.

Education also plays a pivotal role in shaping the future of LGBTQ rights. Incorporating comprehensive LGBTQ-inclusive curricula in schools can help dismantle prejudice and foster understanding from a young age. Studies have shown that LGBTQ-inclusive education significantly reduces bullying and harassment, creating safer environments for all students. Furthermore, educating allies about the importance of their role in advocating for LGBTQ rights can amplify the movement's impact. Allies can leverage their privilege to challenge discriminatory practices, support inclusive policies, and advocate for systemic change.

In the realm of policy, the potential for transformative change is immense. The ongoing efforts to secure comprehensive non-discrimination protections at local, state, and federal levels are critical in ensuring that LGBTQ individuals can live freely without fear of discrimination in employment, housing, and public accommodations. The Equality Act, a proposed piece of legislation in the United States, aims to expand civil rights protections for LGBTQ individuals nationwide. Its passage would signify a monumental step forward in the fight for equality, reinforcing the message that discrimination based on sexual orientation or gender identity is unacceptable.

Furthermore, the digital age has revolutionized activism, providing new avenues for advocacy and connection. Social media platforms have become powerful tools for raising awareness, mobilizing support, and amplifying marginalized voices. The viral nature of online campaigns can lead to rapid shifts in public perception and policy change. For example, the hashtag #BlackTransLivesMatter has brought attention to the disproportionate violence faced by Black transgender individuals, highlighting the urgent need for intersectional advocacy.

As we gaze into the future, the potential for LGBTQ equality is not only a possibility but an imperative. The resilience of the LGBTQ community, coupled with the support of allies and advocates, creates a formidable force for change. By continuing to challenge discrimination, amplify marginalized voices, and advocate for inclusive policies, we can forge a future where LGBTQ individuals are not merely tolerated but celebrated.

In conclusion, the hope for the future of LGBTQ equality is grounded in the progress made, the lessons learned, and the unwavering commitment of those who believe in a just and equitable society. As Taren Fira once remarked, "Our strength lies not just in our differences but in our shared humanity." It is this belief that will guide us as we continue to fight for a world where everyone, regardless of their identity, can live authentically and without fear. Together, we can turn hope into reality, ensuring that the future is bright for all LGBTQ individuals.

Encouragement for Up-and-Coming Activists

In the ever-evolving landscape of LGBTQ activism, the emergence of new voices and ideas is crucial for the continued fight for equality and justice. As Taren Fira often emphasized, the journey of activism is not merely a path to follow; it is a tapestry woven with the threads of passion, resilience, and community. For those who stand on the cusp of this journey, eager to make their mark, Taren's words resonate deeply: *"You are not just inheriting a movement; you are creating it."*

Embrace Your Identity

The first step for any budding activist is to embrace their identity wholeheartedly. Activism is most powerful when it springs from personal experience and authenticity. Taren believed that understanding one's own narrative is essential. By acknowledging the unique aspects of their identity, new activists can find strength in their stories. This is supported by the **Social Identity Theory**, which posits that individuals derive a sense of self from the groups they belong to. Embracing one's identity not only fosters self-acceptance but also empowers others to do the same.

Build a Supportive Network

No activist is an island. Taren's success was largely due to the community she cultivated around her. As she often stated, *"Together, we are stronger."* Forming alliances with fellow activists, mentors, and allies can provide the necessary support and resources to amplify one's efforts. The concept of **Collective Efficacy** illustrates how groups can achieve greater outcomes when they work together towards a common goal. New activists should seek out local LGBTQ organizations, attend community meetings, and engage in dialogue with others who share their vision.

Educate Yourself and Others

Knowledge is power. Taren frequently advocated for continuous education about LGBTQ history, rights, and current issues. Understanding the complexities of intersectionality is vital for effective activism. New activists should familiarize themselves with key concepts, such as **Intersectionality** itself, a term coined by Kimberlé Crenshaw, which highlights how different social identities intersect to create unique experiences of oppression and privilege. By educating themselves, activists can better advocate for inclusive policies that address the needs of all marginalized groups.

Utilize the Power of Storytelling

Taren often spoke about the transformative power of storytelling in activism. Personal narratives can bridge divides and foster empathy. As she would say, *"Your story is your superpower."* New activists should harness the art of storytelling to share their experiences, challenges, and triumphs. This approach is supported by the **Narrative Paradigm Theory**, which suggests that humans are natural storytellers and that stories are the primary way we make sense of the world. By sharing their stories, activists can inspire others and create a deeper understanding of LGBTQ issues within their communities.

Engage with Policy and Politics

Understanding the political landscape is essential for any activist. Taren's journey included lobbying for legislation and engaging with political leaders to advocate for LGBTQ rights. New activists should familiarize themselves with local and national policies that impact the LGBTQ community. This can involve attending town hall meetings, writing to elected officials, or participating in advocacy campaigns. The **Political Opportunity Structure** theory posits that the political environment can facilitate or hinder social movements; thus, understanding this landscape is crucial for effective activism.

Practice Self-Care and Resilience

Activism can be an arduous journey, often fraught with setbacks and challenges. Taren was a staunch advocate for self-care, emphasizing that activists must prioritize their mental health to sustain their efforts. New activists should recognize the signs of burnout and take proactive steps to care for themselves. This includes establishing a self-care routine, seeking support from friends and family, and allowing time for rest and reflection. The **Resilience Theory** highlights the importance of adapting to adversity and bouncing back from challenges, reminding activists that setbacks are not failures but opportunities for growth.

Stay Committed to the Cause

Finally, Taren's unwavering commitment to LGBTQ rights serves as a beacon for all activists. She often reminded her community, *"Change takes time, but every action counts."* New activists should remain steadfast in their dedication to the cause, understanding that meaningful change often requires patience and persistence. By celebrating small victories and learning from failures, activists can maintain their motivation and inspire others to join the fight.

In conclusion, as Taren Fira's legacy continues to inspire future generations, her encouragement to up-and-coming activists remains timeless. By embracing their identities, building supportive networks, educating themselves, utilizing storytelling, engaging with policy, practicing self-care, and staying committed, new activists can forge their paths and contribute to the ongoing struggle for LGBTQ rights and equality. As Taren would say, "The world is waiting for your voice—let it be heard."

Closing Remarks from Taren Fira

As I stand at the precipice of a life dedicated to activism, I am filled with a profound sense of gratitude and hope. The journey has been long, winding, and often fraught with obstacles, yet it has also been rich with joy, camaraderie, and the unwavering spirit of resilience. It is essential to recognize that the fight for LGBTQ rights is not merely a personal battle; it is a collective struggle that binds us together in our shared humanity.

In reflecting on my experiences, I am reminded of the words of Audre Lorde: "There is no such thing as a single-issue struggle because we do not live single-issue lives." This statement encapsulates the essence of intersectionality, a concept that has become a cornerstone of our movement. Our identities are multifaceted, and so too are the challenges we face. It is imperative that we embrace this complexity, acknowledging that the fight for LGBTQ rights is inextricably linked to the struggles for racial justice, gender equality, and economic equity.

$$\text{Intersectionality} = \sum_{i=1}^{n} \text{Identity}_i \tag{61}$$

Here, Identity_i represents the various aspects of our identities—be it race, gender, sexual orientation, or socioeconomic status—that intersect to shape our experiences. This equation serves as a reminder that our activism must be inclusive, recognizing and amplifying the voices of those at the margins.

Throughout my journey, I have encountered numerous challenges that have tested my resolve. From facing discrimination in my early years to navigating the treacherous waters of political opposition, each experience has taught me invaluable lessons. One of the most significant lessons has been the importance of solidarity. In moments of despair, it is the support of our community that ignites the flame of hope within us.

Consider the example of the Stonewall riots, a pivotal moment in our history. It was not just the actions of a few individuals that sparked a movement; it was the collective uprising of a community fed up with oppression. The courage of those who stood up against injustice serves as a powerful reminder that change is possible when we unite in our efforts.

$$\text{Change} = f(\text{Solidarity}, \text{Courage}, \text{Persistence}) \tag{62}$$

In this equation, the function f illustrates that change is a product of solidarity, courage, and persistence. It is a reminder that our collective strength is greater than the sum of our parts.

As I look toward the future, I am filled with hope for the next generation of activists. You are the torchbearers of this movement, and your voices are vital in shaping the world we wish to see. Embrace your authenticity and let it guide your activism. Remember that your stories matter, and they have the power to change hearts and minds.

$$\text{Activism} = \text{Authenticity} \times \text{Storytelling} \qquad (63)$$

In this equation, authenticity multiplied by storytelling creates a potent force for activism. Your unique narratives are not just your own; they are the threads that weave our collective tapestry of resistance.

In closing, I urge you to remain steadfast in your commitment to justice and equality. The road ahead may be challenging, but it is also filled with boundless possibilities. Together, we can dismantle the systems of oppression that seek to divide us. Together, we can create a world where love knows no bounds and where every individual is free to be their true selves without fear of discrimination or violence.

Let us carry forward the legacy of those who came before us, honoring their sacrifices by continuing the fight for a brighter, more inclusive future. Remember, the power of change lies within each of us. Stand tall, speak out, and never underestimate the impact of your actions.

As I conclude my remarks, I leave you with a final thought:

"Be the change you wish to see in the world."

Let this be your guiding principle as you embark on your journey of advocacy. Together, we will rise, we will fight, and we will triumph. Thank you.

Honoring Taren Fira's Legacy

Taren Fira's legacy is one that transcends the boundaries of time and geography, echoing through the hearts of countless individuals who have been inspired by her indomitable spirit and unwavering commitment to justice. To honor Taren's legacy is not merely to remember her achievements; it is to actively engage in the ongoing struggle for LGBTQ rights, ensuring that her vision of a more inclusive world continues to flourish.

Theoretical Foundations of Legacy

The concept of legacy in activism can be understood through several theoretical frameworks, including social movement theory and the theory of collective identity. Social movement theory posits that movements arise in response to perceived injustices, leading to collective action that seeks to enact social change. Taren Fira exemplified this theory through her ability to mobilize communities, fostering a sense of collective identity among LGBTQ individuals and their allies.

The legacy of an activist like Taren can be measured through the framework of *social capital*, which refers to the networks of relationships among people that enable society to function effectively. Taren's efforts in building alliances and nurturing community connections have created a robust foundation for future activists.

Challenges in Honoring a Legacy

However, honoring Taren Fira's legacy also involves confronting the challenges that persist within the LGBTQ movement. One significant challenge is the phenomenon of *activist burnout*, where individuals become overwhelmed by the emotional and physical toll of advocacy work. This is particularly relevant in the context of Taren's own experiences, where she often spoke about the need for self-care and community support.

To combat this burnout, Taren emphasized the importance of creating sustainable practices within activism. This includes fostering environments where activists can share their burdens, celebrate victories, and learn from setbacks. The establishment of support networks and community care initiatives are essential in this regard.

Taren Fira Foundation

In honoring Taren's legacy, the establishment of the *Taren Fira Foundation* serves as a vital mechanism for sustaining her vision. The foundation aims to provide resources and support for emerging LGBTQ activists, ensuring that Taren's principles of inclusivity, intersectionality, and empowerment are upheld.

The foundation's programs include mentorship initiatives, scholarship opportunities, and community-building events that promote dialogue and collaboration among diverse groups. By fostering an environment of learning and growth, the foundation embodies Taren's belief that the future of activism lies in the hands of the next generation.

Cultural and Social Impact

Taren Fira's impact extends beyond policy changes and organizational efforts; it is deeply embedded in the cultural consciousness of LGBTQ communities. Her ability to articulate the struggles and triumphs of queer individuals through art, storytelling, and public speaking has inspired a new wave of activists to embrace their identities and share their narratives.

The power of personal storytelling, as Taren demonstrated, serves as a catalyst for social change. It fosters empathy and understanding, breaking down barriers and challenging misconceptions about LGBTQ lives. By amplifying the voices of marginalized individuals, Taren's legacy encourages others to step forward and share their truths, creating a tapestry of experiences that enrich the movement.

Celebrating Taren Fira's Legacy

To celebrate Taren Fira's legacy, it is essential to engage in reflective practices that honor her contributions while also recognizing the ongoing struggles faced by LGBTQ individuals. This can take the form of annual events, workshops, and educational programs that highlight Taren's work and the broader context of LGBTQ activism.

Moreover, honoring Taren's legacy requires a commitment to intersectionality, ensuring that the voices of queer people of color, transgender individuals, and other marginalized groups are centered in discussions and actions. Taren's advocacy for inclusivity serves as a guiding principle, reminding us that true progress can only be achieved when all voices are heard and valued.

In conclusion, honoring Taren Fira's legacy is a multifaceted endeavor that involves not only remembering her contributions but also actively participating in the ongoing fight for LGBTQ rights. By fostering community, promoting sustainability in activism, and amplifying diverse voices, we can ensure that Taren's spirit lives on, inspiring future generations to continue the work she so passionately championed.

$$\text{Legacy} = \text{Impact} + \text{Community Engagement} + \text{Sustainability} \quad (64)$$

Through this equation, we can conceptualize Taren's legacy as a dynamic interplay between her impact, the engagement of the community she built, and the sustainable practices that ensure her vision endures. By committing to these principles, we can honor Taren Fira's legacy and contribute to a more just and equitable world for all.

Index

-doubt, 196, 204

a, 1–8, 10–31, 33, 35–37, 39, 41, 43–51, 53, 54, 56, 57, 59–61, 64, 66–68, 70–73, 75–79, 82, 83, 85, 87–89, 92, 94, 95, 97–100, 103–105, 107, 109, 111, 113, 114, 116, 117, 119, 120, 122, 124, 125, 127–132, 135, 137–152, 154, 156–159, 162–169, 171–175, 178–187, 191, 193, 196, 198–204, 206, 208–211, 213–216, 218–221, 224, 225, 227, 229, 230, 232–234, 236–246, 248, 251–256, 258–261, 263–266, 268–270, 273–279, 281, 284–289, 291, 294–296, 298–305, 308–311
ability, 59, 65, 71, 73, 87, 92, 129, 175, 177, 187, 195, 229, 232, 274, 290, 310, 311
absence, 199
abyss, 200
acceptance, 7, 10, 15, 19, 20, 22, 31, 35, 72, 75, 76, 97, 99, 178, 180, 196, 201–204, 211, 214, 230, 248, 259, 261, 270, 273, 284
access, 36, 72, 73, 99, 104, 129, 135, 149, 214, 233, 283
accessibility, 78
acclaim, 169
accomplishment, 199, 284
accountability, 45, 46, 140, 143, 242–244
achievement, 70, 286
act, 5–8, 15, 46, 167, 180, 193, 206, 209, 242, 265, 268
action, 3, 11, 14, 15, 28, 37, 43, 44, 57, 59, 61, 62, 82, 87, 94, 111, 116, 130, 140, 151, 157, 159, 162, 178, 186, 216, 224, 226, 256, 261, 275, 302, 303, 310
activism, 2–7, 10, 11, 13, 15, 17, 18, 20, 22, 23, 25, 28, 31–33, 41, 43, 44, 46, 50, 51, 54, 56, 57, 59, 61, 66, 71–73, 75, 76, 79, 80, 82, 85, 94, 95, 97, 98, 100, 102, 103, 111–114, 116, 117, 122, 127, 128, 130, 132–135,

313

146, 148, 150, 154, 157, 159–162, 164, 167, 169, 171, 173, 175, 177, 179, 180, 182, 191, 193, 195, 198, 203–206, 208, 214–221, 229, 232–234, 236, 242–244, 251–254, 260, 261, 263, 264, 266, 268, 270, 273, 275–279, 281, 282, 284–286, 289, 291, 294, 296, 297, 299–303, 308–311
activist, 3, 4, 112, 198, 199, 202, 203, 206, 209, 218, 233, 265, 277, 285, 294, 300
adaptability, 146, 165, 275, 300, 303
addition, 22, 75
address, 11, 36, 39, 47, 59, 60, 69, 76, 77, 148, 173, 174, 195, 230, 232, 233, 243, 259, 260, 278, 283, 293, 295, 303, 304
addressing, 32, 33, 35, 41, 47, 48, 53, 57, 60, 76, 100, 111, 120, 135, 143, 167, 181, 218, 238, 246, 253, 258, 261, 268, 270, 273, 281, 298
administration, 11
adolescence, 215
adoption, 70
advancement, 43, 61, 63
advent, 95
adversity, 20, 85, 116, 140, 146, 195, 199, 214, 296, 303
advice, 251
advocacy, 7, 15, 21, 22, 25, 28–30, 35–37, 39, 41, 43, 44, 47, 49, 52, 53, 59–61, 66–71, 73, 75–80, 83–87, 89, 92, 94, 97, 99, 100, 103, 105, 107–109, 111, 113, 116, 122, 124, 125, 128–131, 135, 137–141, 143, 146, 151, 153, 154, 156, 159, 165, 172, 174, 177, 178, 184–186, 191, 198, 204, 208, 209, 211, 217–219, 221, 222, 224, 230, 232, 234, 236, 237, 239, 242–246, 253, 254, 256, 258–260, 263–265, 267, 268, 270, 273–275, 277, 279, 284–288, 292, 294–296, 298, 299, 301, 302, 304, 309, 311
advocate, 3, 5, 10, 12, 37, 40, 41, 54, 75–77, 88, 92, 106, 113, 122, 129, 133, 142, 169, 205, 230, 237, 238, 253, 259, 261, 263, 268, 270, 274, 301, 305
affirmation, 204
Afghanistan, 139
Africa, 76
aftermath, 243, 285, 286
age, 1, 6, 29, 36, 50, 71–73, 82, 85, 146, 252, 260, 304
agency, 159
agenda, 60, 97, 105, 153
Alex, 203
alliance, 56
ally, 25, 44, 71, 227, 230, 239
Allyship, 43, 122, 237
allyship, 7, 23, 24, 26, 43–46, 62, 63, 122, 221, 223, 224, 226, 227, 234, 236, 237, 239, 247, 248, 269, 304
Alyndra, 15, 18, 26, 27, 33, 218,

Index

268, 273, 286
amalgamation, 39
amount, 95
amplification, 80, 175
analysis, 230, 277
anger, 163, 220
anniversary, 130
anthropology, 213
anxiety, 6, 99
application, 141, 171, 232
approach, 16, 21, 22, 24, 26, 28, 36, 39, 47, 50, 51, 54, 67, 68, 90, 99, 100, 103–106, 109, 114, 119, 122, 130, 132, 139, 147, 148, 151, 154, 159, 163–165, 168, 181, 196, 201, 218, 222, 232, 242, 244, 251, 253, 254, 256, 259, 260, 266, 275, 278, 295, 296, 302
area, 294
arena, 154, 157
argument, 107, 203
arsenal, 299
art, 17, 18, 185, 189, 238, 274, 279, 311
artwork, 19
Asia, 76
aspect, 33, 35, 37, 41, 44, 56, 92, 125, 128, 148, 162, 169, 182, 198, 216, 239, 273
aspiration, 54
assembly, 6
assertiveness, 162
atmosphere, 17, 164, 196, 209
attempt, 200, 285
attendance, 17
attention, 21, 26, 113, 158, 180, 203, 286

attribute, 13
audience, 36, 71, 107, 156, 198, 218, 252
auditorium, 6
Audre Lorde, 238
authenticity, 7, 8, 44, 74, 172, 173, 186, 202, 203, 218–220, 309
autonomy, 99
availability, 26
awakening, 3
awareness, 21, 24, 37, 45, 71, 72, 98, 107, 113, 130, 133, 140, 158, 180, 193, 195, 260, 269, 275, 276, 292
axis, 232

backbone, 80, 276
backlash, 4, 6, 24, 27, 74, 83, 99, 100, 112, 124, 129, 130, 140, 144, 151–154, 167, 198, 218, 242, 285, 286, 303
balance, 111, 162, 204, 208, 209, 279
balancing, 112, 113, 208, 209
ban, 129
barrier, 24, 72, 196, 240, 254
bathroom, 22, 92
battle, 6, 209, 258, 308
battleground, 10, 97
beacon, 100, 251, 301
bedrock, 29
behavior, 44
being, 5, 33, 99, 137, 154, 204, 205, 209, 219, 237, 242, 278, 279, 291, 294, 302
belief, 5, 66, 157, 180, 204, 206, 254, 284, 286, 302, 310

bell, 13
belonging, 2, 8, 15, 25, 31, 50, 99, 178, 202, 204, 206, 214, 219, 270, 273, 274, 295
benefit, 37, 99, 242
bias, 242
bill, 105
binary, 5, 7, 13, 22, 47, 54, 125–127, 139, 233, 264, 274, 286, 287
birthplace, 198
blazer, 6
blend, 4, 18, 122
blending, 209
blood, 213
blooming, 3
blueprint, 70
border, 148
breakdown, 138, 139
breakthrough, 203
breath, 198
breeding, 146
Brené Brown, 198
bridge, 185, 201
building, 16, 22–25, 27, 37, 43, 56–59, 80, 81, 88, 89, 105, 106, 109, 111–113, 119, 132, 146, 151, 152, 154, 157, 162, 164, 168, 177, 179, 265, 275, 281, 282, 285, 295, 310
bullying, 10, 11, 75, 304
burnout, 199, 205, 206, 214, 252, 261, 277–279, 301, 310
Butler, 125
buzzword, 219

call, 14, 15, 141, 275, 303
camaraderie, 308
campaign, 7, 77, 84, 87, 98, 195, 199
canvas, 15
capacity, 88, 199, 239
capital, 82
care, 137, 154, 199, 204–206, 209, 252, 261, 278, 289, 290, 294, 301, 310
career, 33, 265
Carmen Maria Machado, 169
case, 96, 113, 119, 143, 178, 195, 208, 285
catalyst, 11, 51, 99, 171, 178, 219, 252, 311
cause, 21, 26, 28, 29, 31, 44, 46, 56, 71, 100, 209, 294
celebration, 15, 260, 275
center, 47, 56, 68, 230
century, 217
challenge, 15, 21, 28, 46, 48, 67, 68, 72, 73, 76, 88, 92, 100, 104, 117, 141, 148, 154, 157, 165–167, 169, 172, 173, 175, 180, 181, 189, 193, 196, 203, 209, 220, 234, 237, 238, 251, 253, 304, 305
champion, 256
change, 2, 5, 10, 11, 15, 18, 22, 23, 26, 28–30, 37, 41, 43, 51, 59, 62–64, 66, 68, 71, 76, 77, 82, 83, 85, 87–89, 92, 94, 103, 105–107, 109, 111, 113, 119, 120, 122, 129, 130, 132, 135, 157, 159, 160, 162, 164, 165, 169, 171–173, 179, 187, 193, 198, 219, 220, 227, 233, 234, 236, 239, 246, 252, 253, 256–258, 260,

Index

268, 270, 275, 284, 286, 291, 296–299, 301, 302, 305, 308–311
chaos, 158
chapter, 97
characteristic, 303
charge, 41
charity, 268
Charles Tilly, 165
check, 50
chest, 198
cisgender, 47, 59, 60, 196, 229, 230, 233, 243
city, 1, 211
clamor, 2
clarity, 24
class, 13, 76, 92, 125, 139, 181, 232, 254, 262, 301
clichés, 168
cliff, 200
climate, 75, 144, 158, 165
closing, 309
clout, 237
co, 30, 49, 218
coalition, 14, 16, 22, 27, 56–59, 94, 105, 109, 113, 119, 146, 151, 154, 157, 164, 168, 285, 295
collaboration, 36, 43, 64, 70, 77, 78, 103, 111, 122, 132, 164, 246, 258, 274, 281–284, 286, 299, 310
collective, 3, 6, 7, 17, 18, 25, 35, 43, 49, 57, 59, 68, 82, 87, 88, 94, 122, 130, 151, 159, 162, 175, 179, 196, 199, 203, 214, 216, 220, 237, 239, 242, 244, 246, 256, 273, 290, 295, 300–303, 308–310
Colombia, 140
colonialism, 66, 67
color, 40, 41, 45, 47, 50, 54, 57, 59, 60, 99, 125, 167, 168, 174, 175, 181, 196, 211, 230, 232, 233, 243, 260, 274, 301, 304, 311
combat, 6, 28, 127, 148, 150, 199, 231, 255, 278, 310
combination, 87, 114, 116, 253
comfort, 195
commitment, 4, 13, 25, 28, 44, 48, 66, 70, 88, 109, 116, 119, 122, 130, 132, 151, 159, 163, 184, 203, 213, 224, 227, 230, 236, 242, 251, 256, 258, 261, 265, 268, 273, 274, 286, 294, 301–303, 309, 311
communication, 28, 36, 78, 100, 105, 107, 110, 146, 151, 152, 154, 157, 162, 171, 196, 203, 286, 302
community, 3, 4, 7, 13, 15–18, 20, 21, 23–33, 35–38, 44–51, 54, 57, 59, 61, 68, 72, 76, 78, 80, 98–100, 103–105, 108, 109, 114, 116, 120, 124, 132, 135, 137, 141, 156, 158, 159, 162, 164, 166, 168, 169, 173, 174, 179–182, 184, 189, 193, 195, 196, 198, 199, 202–204, 206, 214, 217–219, 222, 224, 227, 229, 230, 233, 237, 239, 242, 243, 252–254, 256,

258, 260, 261, 263–265, 270–276, 281, 284–286, 289–291, 294–296, 299, 301–305, 308, 310, 311
compassion, 159, 275, 301
competition, 82
complexity, 172, 181, 210, 233, 237, 302
component, 31, 43, 45, 77, 94, 164, 198
compromise, 103, 112
concept, 54, 59, 75, 98, 99, 120, 125, 139, 182, 189, 196, 199, 213, 216, 219, 229, 234, 251, 302, 304, 310
conclusion, 25, 28, 43, 46, 48, 53, 59, 63, 66, 70, 73, 77, 85, 97, 100, 109, 111, 122, 124, 151, 154, 157, 159, 172, 175, 179, 214, 219, 234, 256, 261, 265, 270, 275, 284, 286, 301, 303, 311
conducting, 36, 286
conduit, 94
conference, 203
confidence, 49, 156, 265
confidentiality, 195
conflict, 112, 138–141, 164, 215
confluence, 144
conformity, 6
confrontation, 11
confusion, 72, 79
connection, 85, 178, 217–219, 239, 274
consciousness, 4, 311
consensus, 112
consent, 195
conservative, 6, 7, 27, 77, 78, 92, 103, 112, 117–119, 124, 131, 146, 165, 211, 218, 286, 303
construct, 39, 120, 299
constructivism, 196
context, 9, 35, 50, 57, 70, 76, 97, 103, 106, 156, 171, 177, 180, 186, 210, 211, 242, 264, 311
contributing, 230
control, 167, 169
conversation, 28, 54, 127, 163, 167, 203
conviction, 157, 159
cooperation, 130–132, 148
core, 26, 92, 232, 261
cornerstone, 25, 33, 89, 239, 244
counter, 28, 100, 151, 166, 257
courage, 24, 159, 173, 199, 301, 303, 308
coverage, 95, 108, 109, 260, 277
create, 2, 16–18, 27, 28, 35, 43, 47, 50, 56, 59–61, 64, 71, 72, 75, 76, 82, 85, 119, 132, 137, 139, 146, 148, 169, 173, 178–181, 184, 196, 197, 206, 218, 220, 230, 232, 238, 244, 246, 253, 257–259, 272, 276, 303, 309
creation, 32, 195, 256, 274, 297
creativity, 1, 22, 111, 151, 198, 251
credibility, 28
Crenshaw, 51
crime, 21, 148
crisis, 158
criticism, 124, 195
critique, 44, 124
crowd, 198
cultivation, 73, 97, 214

Index

culture, 15, 17, 22, 24, 43, 79, 88, 148, 167, 206, 238, 241, 243, 248, 294, 304
curricula, 304
curriculum, 75, 269
cyberbullying, 83
cycle, 178
cynicism, 199

data, 36, 67, 107, 218
debate, 99, 163
decision, 54, 99, 209
decriminalization, 77, 129
dedication, 26, 27, 51, 100, 111, 258, 274
defiance, 5, 7, 15
definition, 46–48
delivery, 157
demand, 21, 76
depression, 6, 99
desire, 11, 203, 220
despair, 11, 300, 308
determination, 18, 216
development, 129, 215, 267
dialogue, 70, 88, 110, 111, 124, 131, 163, 164, 196, 202, 203, 211, 310
die, 158
difficulty, 203
dignity, 26, 77, 92, 120, 141, 193, 244
diplomacy, 66, 111–113, 122, 132
direction, 60
disability, 16, 22, 27, 302
disadvantage, 139, 181
discomfort, 24
discourse, 66, 142, 146, 164, 168, 218
discovery, 10

discrepancy, 79, 92
discrimination, 3, 4, 10, 11, 15, 20, 22, 31, 36, 37, 39, 45, 49, 53, 54, 57, 59, 67, 68, 70, 76, 85, 88, 92, 94, 99, 104, 107, 112, 120, 125, 129, 131, 132, 135, 138, 139, 142, 143, 148, 149, 151, 164, 166, 173, 174, 178, 181–183, 196, 211, 215, 217, 222, 229, 230, 232, 236–238, 240, 252, 254, 256, 259, 266, 283, 286, 294, 296, 302, 305, 308, 309
discussion, 50, 163
disillusionment, 46
disinformation, 72
dismantling, 6, 53, 75, 172
disobedience, 157–159
disparity, 59, 76
dispersion, 214
dissemination, 78, 83, 260
dissent, 157
distance, 209
diversity, 15, 48, 75, 139, 141, 142, 168, 180, 196, 198, 204, 264, 274, 284
divide, 72, 309
document, 14, 15
door, 13
doubt, 196, 199, 204
drawing, 21, 100, 275, 284, 286
dream, 303
dress, 6
duality, 9, 199
dynamic, 60, 100, 204, 208, 224, 264, 286, 311

Eastern Europe, 70
ebb, 208
edge, 200
education, 24, 25, 37, 44, 61, 70, 72, 75, 87, 105, 109, 119, 145, 156, 166, 180, 182, 193, 201, 236, 238, 253, 256, 258, 270, 304
effect, 22, 25, 87, 162, 246, 251, 261, 270, 273
effectiveness, 24, 30, 41, 56, 60, 79, 102, 108, 132, 133, 158, 160, 225, 233, 237, 244, 260, 269, 277, 301, 302
efficacy, 219, 244, 284
effort, 2, 17, 18, 26, 35, 239, 242, 259, 303
election, 22
element, 46
elevating, 47, 132, 239
embrace, 7, 8, 13, 173, 204, 220, 270, 273, 274, 284, 287, 303, 311
emergence, 97
emotion, 173, 220
empathy, 17, 48, 68, 72, 162, 164, 171–173, 175, 177–180, 185, 187, 191, 193, 198, 214, 224, 240–242, 269, 274, 302, 311
emphasis, 256
employment, 22, 94, 305
empower, 86, 195, 198, 241, 253, 256, 275
empowerment, 24, 25, 28, 31, 33, 37, 88, 254, 256, 264, 266, 270, 273, 274, 276, 299
encounter, 10, 39, 117, 126, 181, 211, 215, 225, 235, 237, 252, 282, 290, 292
encouragement, 88, 202, 295
endeavor, 15, 23, 28, 44, 61, 88, 109, 130, 141, 234, 237, 261, 273, 301, 311
enforcement, 148
engage, 27, 44, 70, 72, 78, 87, 89, 90, 103, 104, 107, 164, 178, 180, 222, 224, 227, 230, 236, 237, 239–242, 252, 260, 261, 264, 274, 284, 285, 309, 311
engagement, 4, 24, 25, 30, 37, 70, 73, 84, 88, 89, 92, 95, 97, 109, 113, 116, 162, 164, 165, 182, 204, 218, 234, 237, 252, 256, 258, 261, 275, 284, 296, 311
engine, 132
entrenchment, 110
environment, 1, 6, 10, 23, 33, 48, 67, 109, 130, 144, 148, 165, 166, 179, 180, 195, 221, 241, 259, 264, 269, 310
equality, 20, 22, 25, 26, 31, 35, 41, 54, 56, 59, 63, 66, 68, 72, 73, 75, 77, 87, 88, 92–94, 97–100, 103–105, 111, 112, 114, 117, 119, 120, 122, 125, 128, 130, 149, 154, 157, 158, 162–165, 175, 180, 184, 187, 193, 203, 219, 224, 233, 234, 237, 242, 244, 246, 251, 259–261, 270, 273, 274, 277, 284–286, 294, 301–305, 309
equation, 5, 10, 17, 24, 29, 39, 44–46, 59, 60, 69, 70, 73,

95, 117, 149, 165, 183, 230, 237, 242, 254, 260, 292, 302, 309, 311
equity, 260, 302
era, 129, 142
erasure, 19, 125, 127, 168
Erik Erikson's, 215
essay, 157
establishment, 31, 143, 196, 214, 253, 256, 270, 271, 273, 310
estrangement, 213
ethnicity, 139, 146
ethos, 242
Eve Kosofsky Sedgwick, 167
event, 15–18, 21, 25, 36, 49, 158, 178, 180, 198, 209, 216, 217, 252, 265, 286
evolution, 22
example, 15, 36, 45, 47, 49, 59, 72, 76–78, 87, 94, 95, 104, 113, 129, 139, 140, 142, 163, 164, 169, 174, 178, 181, 196, 199, 209, 211, 214, 215, 230, 233, 238, 241, 243, 259, 260, 265, 276, 285, 295, 300, 302, 308
exchange, 72, 87
exclusion, 78
execution, 139, 216
exercise, 61
exhaustion, 199, 277, 294
existence, 5, 67, 114, 127
expense, 142
experience, 6, 11, 12, 15, 39, 45, 51, 54, 59, 87, 107, 120, 125, 167, 182, 183, 198, 211, 214–216, 229, 230, 232, 237, 254, 262, 302, 304, 308
expertise, 29
exploration, 10
exposure, 29, 180
expression, 4–7, 15, 77, 181, 210, 215
eye, 108

face, 6, 10, 39, 45, 60, 62, 63, 85, 92, 99, 116, 125, 129, 135, 138–140, 146, 149, 166, 167, 181, 196, 202, 206, 208, 211, 213, 214, 219, 222, 224, 229, 232, 234, 237, 240, 242, 251, 259, 273, 281, 286, 289, 295, 303
factor, 97, 206
failure, 79
fairness, 164
family, 9, 103, 105, 129, 163, 164, 198, 201, 202, 209, 211, 213, 238
favor, 99, 132
fear, 15, 31, 67, 109, 122, 144, 151, 195, 196, 198, 199, 203, 204, 214, 220, 263, 264, 266, 273, 275, 305, 309
feedback, 30, 38, 44, 286
feeling, 198, 203
female, 5, 125
femininity, 6
feminist, 16, 22, 51, 196, 217
festival, 302
fight, 7, 13, 20, 22, 26, 28, 35, 41, 54, 56, 57, 61, 63, 66–68, 70, 73, 75, 82, 85, 88, 97–100, 103, 114, 117,

122, 125, 132, 135, 146,
   148, 150, 151, 154, 159,
   162, 164, 165, 175, 179,
   184, 193, 203, 218, 219,
   234, 236, 258–261, 265,
   273, 275, 283, 284,
   301–305, 308, 309, 311
figure, 51
finding, 178, 199, 211, 252
Fira, 122, 124, 125, 144–146
fire, 6
flame, 308
Florida, 243
flow, 208
flower, 3
fluidity, 6, 139, 167, 203, 287
focus, 26, 103, 104, 233, 279, 294
foray, 1
force, 73, 88, 135, 291, 305, 309
forefront, 230
forging, 252
form, 7, 28, 47, 72, 92, 112, 114,
   129, 191, 311
formation, 15, 106, 214
formula, 49, 50, 259
foster, 22, 24, 31, 43, 44, 48, 58, 60,
   70, 72, 77, 82, 88, 111,
   164, 167, 169, 172, 185,
   187, 189, 193, 195, 198,
   201, 220, 238, 243, 246,
   256, 261, 273, 281, 283,
   296–298, 304
foundation, 2, 4, 5, 76, 131,
   253–256, 263, 273, 310
fragmentation, 104, 233
frame, 195, 239
framework, 16, 41, 45, 76, 105, 120,
   127, 132, 142, 165, 182,
   229, 232, 245, 261, 287,
   299, 304
framing, 36, 94, 97, 105, 129, 163,
   165
freedom, 99
friend, 203
friendship, 203
front, 27, 41, 72, 164
frustration, 112, 203, 220, 295
fuel, 28
function, 51, 117, 230
funding, 129, 140, 253, 254
fundraising, 26, 255
future, 2, 4, 22, 43, 52, 61, 70, 75,
   85, 100, 122, 125, 151,
   154, 157, 162, 193, 203,
   209, 239, 246, 251–253,
   256, 265, 266, 268, 273,
   277, 284–286, 294, 298,
   301, 303–305, 309–311

gain, 29, 30, 44, 54, 69, 218, 285
gap, 185, 201, 243
gathering, 209, 286
gay, 39, 47, 59, 168, 180, 196, 229,
   233, 243
gender, 5–7, 10, 13, 20, 24, 54, 59,
   67, 69, 70, 72, 76–78, 92,
   94, 111, 120, 125, 127,
   139, 141, 142, 146, 164,
   174, 181, 182, 196, 203,
   224, 229, 230, 232, 233,
   237, 254, 260, 262, 264,
   283, 286, 287, 301, 304,
   305
genderqueer, 7
generation, 51, 66, 88, 117, 156, 263,
   265, 273, 300, 309, 310
geography, 72, 309

George Floyd, 72
gesture, 120
glitter, 10
globe, 68, 71, 130, 256
goal, 3, 103, 187, 298
goodwill, 120
governance, 37
government, 129, 157, 158
grapple, 141
gratitude, 308
ground, 129, 146, 211
groundwork, 15, 30, 33, 109, 298
group, 17, 142, 180, 252, 285
growth, 199, 211, 214–216, 264, 285, 300, 310
guidance, 49, 263, 265, 274, 301
guide, 22, 109, 209, 242, 297, 303, 309

hair, 6
hall, 26, 30, 37, 163
hand, 14, 15, 26, 36, 76, 185, 218
handful, 30
harassment, 31, 83, 146–148, 151, 158, 238, 286, 304
harm, 45, 243
hate, 21, 28, 83, 107, 145–148, 166
haul, 303
haven, 10, 204
head, 199, 215
healing, 195, 198
health, 6, 8, 72, 99, 135, 137, 140, 154, 204–206, 240, 252, 253, 261, 274, 278, 279, 291–294, 301, 302
healthcare, 22, 36, 99, 104, 135, 137, 145, 233, 283
heart, 18
heartbreak, 203

help, 36, 135, 237, 304
Henry David Thoreau, 157
heritage, 15
heterosexual, 98
highlight, 41, 50, 67, 72, 98, 154, 174, 201, 210, 219, 287, 299, 311
history, 15, 75, 269, 308
homophobia, 11, 60, 117–120, 139, 167, 214, 232, 238
homosexuality, 67, 76, 77, 129, 142
honor, 195, 263, 303, 309, 311
hope, 100, 130, 141, 195, 202, 251, 301, 308, 309
host, 210
hostility, 78, 131, 144, 211
household, 1
housing, 36, 94, 233, 305
hue, 303
human, 15, 26, 66, 67, 70, 76, 77, 92, 109, 120, 122, 128–132, 138, 140–143
humanity, 110, 308
Hungary, 129

idea, 216, 274
ideal, 208
identification, 15
identity, 3, 5, 6, 8–10, 13, 15, 18–20, 39, 46, 48, 51, 53, 59, 61, 67, 70, 72, 76–78, 92, 94, 111, 120, 125, 141, 142, 146, 163, 164, 167, 173, 181, 182, 198, 201–204, 210–212, 216, 217, 221, 224, 229, 234, 260, 275, 283, 287, 299, 303, 305, 310
ignorance, 173

imitation, 264
impact, 6, 14, 22, 25, 26, 28, 51, 57, 60, 66, 71, 84, 85, 96, 122, 124, 135, 145, 148, 151, 156, 167, 171, 191, 193, 220, 224, 236, 242, 244, 246, 251, 253, 256, 258, 260, 261, 265, 268, 270, 273, 275, 277, 288, 299, 304, 309, 311
imperative, 41, 56, 85, 100, 130, 141, 305
implementation, 112, 267
importance, 3, 6, 7, 13, 16, 17, 26, 28, 31, 36, 44, 49, 50, 52, 55, 57, 59, 63, 66, 70, 73, 75–77, 80, 92, 94, 98, 99, 108, 116, 120, 124, 132, 133, 135, 146, 154, 156, 167, 183, 196, 199, 201–203, 218, 220, 232, 233, 240, 242, 244, 246, 251–254, 256, 259, 260, 263, 265, 269, 270, 273, 274, 285, 286, 295, 296, 300, 301, 304, 308, 310
in, 1, 3, 5–7, 9–13, 15–18, 21–31, 33, 35–39, 43, 44, 46, 49, 51, 54, 56, 57, 59–79, 82, 85, 87–89, 91, 92, 94, 95, 97–100, 102–109, 112, 114, 116–120, 122, 124, 125, 127, 129–132, 135, 138–146, 148–152, 154, 156–159, 161–169, 171–173, 175, 178–182, 184–187, 191, 193, 195, 196, 198, 199, 202–206, 208–219, 221, 222, 224, 226, 227, 230–234, 236–239, 241–244, 246, 251–256, 258–266, 268–271, 273–276, 278, 279, 281–286, 292, 294–296, 298–305, 308–311
inaction, 242
inclusion, 7, 16, 70, 75, 286
inclusivity, 25, 28, 46–48, 51, 55, 57, 60, 61, 78, 82, 148, 169, 177, 184, 196, 198, 204, 224, 243, 248, 253, 256, 258, 265, 273, 275, 286, 299, 311
income, 57
inconsistency, 201
increase, 25, 30, 145, 241, 269
individual, 7, 11, 28, 45, 59, 88, 99, 111, 120, 142, 148, 191, 196, 198, 199, 216, 217, 220, 230, 232, 234, 242, 248, 254, 263–265, 270, 273, 275, 277, 290, 302, 309
inequality, 53
influence, 39, 45, 87, 89, 94, 97, 105, 122, 124, 259, 261, 263, 274, 277, 286
information, 36, 72, 78, 83, 260
infrastructure, 253
inheritance, 99
initiative, 2, 47, 50, 180
injustice, 2, 308
innovation, 198, 261
insecurity, 233
insight, 173
inspiration, 50, 51, 100, 193, 251, 252, 270, 296, 301

Index

instability, 138, 144, 240
instance, 25, 26, 36, 39, 50, 59, 67, 70, 72, 76, 78, 79, 92, 99, 103, 107, 109, 112, 124, 129–131, 140, 142, 143, 145, 148, 158, 163, 164, 168, 172, 173, 180, 209, 217, 220, 232, 233, 238, 240, 242, 252, 260, 264, 277, 279, 284, 285
institutionalization, 113
instrument, 171
integrity, 56, 219, 244
intensity, 51, 262
interconnectedness, 16, 22, 27, 43, 59, 75, 234, 259, 274, 295
interest, 103, 105
internet, 71, 72, 148
interplay, 20, 97, 111, 113, 165, 183, 219, 286, 311
interpretation, 141
intersection, 18, 47, 56, 79, 125, 131, 167, 189, 216, 218, 219, 291, 292, 294
intersectionality, 4, 13, 16, 45–48, 50, 51, 54, 57, 59, 66, 72, 76, 77, 82, 88, 92, 99, 109, 120, 122, 124, 125, 128, 130, 137, 138, 141, 174, 182, 184, 196, 217, 229, 232–234, 237, 239, 243, 252–254, 256, 261, 274, 301, 303, 304, 311
invisibility, 19
involvement, 43, 61, 159, 216
Iraq, 140
isolation, 27, 181, 203, 232, 254, 262, 279
issue, 11, 26, 47, 66, 67, 71, 72, 74, 103, 105, 109, 172, 218, 233, 237

Jack Donnelly, 142
Jamal, 211
James Baldwin, 238
Jamie, 265
Jordan, 203
journey, 2, 4, 5, 7, 8, 10, 12, 15, 18, 20, 22, 23, 25, 28, 30, 41, 46, 48, 50, 54, 56, 59, 64, 70, 72, 85, 88, 100, 111, 122, 135, 146, 151, 154, 157, 159, 162, 163, 179, 180, 193, 195, 198, 199, 202, 204, 209, 210, 215, 216, 218, 219, 224, 236, 242, 244, 246, 251, 256, 258, 261, 268, 270, 273, 275, 284, 286, 294, 296, 300–303, 308, 309
joy, 308
judgment, 195, 204, 206, 220, 264
Judith Butler, 167
Judith Butler's, 5, 13, 125, 287
justice, 4, 13, 16, 21, 22, 26–28, 41–43, 54, 61, 63, 71–73, 75, 77, 92, 94, 97, 100, 106, 114, 119, 125, 146, 149, 151, 153, 154, 157, 159, 162, 164, 165, 175, 187, 193, 224, 232–234, 237, 244, 256, 259, 260, 262, 264, 268, 270, 274, 277, 286, 294, 295, 301–304, 309
justification, 99
juxtaposition, 3

key, 20, 26, 27, 35, 49, 60, 70, 84, 93, 94, 98, 105, 116, 124, 151, 154, 181, 238, 254, 296, 299, 301
Kimberlé Crenshaw, 16, 51, 54, 57, 59, 76, 120, 125, 139, 167, 181, 182, 229, 232, 237, 254, 259, 261, 301, 304
kinship, 213
knowledge, 36, 49, 80, 86, 87, 156, 196, 263, 264, 274, 300

labor, 26, 214
labyrinth, 210
lack, 45, 46, 67, 78, 129, 135, 140, 158, 168, 180, 240
landmark, 95, 129, 131, 132, 143
landscape, 20, 23, 35, 56, 60, 61, 66, 71, 73, 75, 83, 85, 94, 95, 97, 103–105, 113, 116, 119, 122, 125, 130, 132, 141, 144, 146, 148, 154, 156, 166, 184, 219, 234, 252, 259, 263, 270, 273, 284, 289, 294, 296, 299–301
language, 78, 79, 124, 127, 167, 269
launch, 255
law, 67, 92, 94, 139, 141–143, 158
layer, 167
leadership, 28, 60, 216
learning, 4, 222, 227, 236, 251, 264, 285, 286, 310
legacy, 28, 33, 48, 51, 66, 67, 70, 100, 116, 125, 146, 159, 251–253, 256, 258, 261, 265, 268, 270, 273–275, 284, 298, 303, 309–311
legalization, 95, 99, 112, 284

legislation, 21, 92–94, 99, 140, 148, 149, 156, 164, 199, 274, 285, 305
legitimacy, 28
lens, 54, 57, 67, 103, 120, 122, 181, 215, 237
lesbian, 211
level, 37, 133, 158, 159, 261
leverage, 122, 238, 304
liberation, 302
liberty, 99
life, 2, 202, 208, 209, 216, 218, 270, 274, 275, 301, 303, 308
lifeline, 83
lifestyle, 240
light, 85, 125, 174, 299
lighthouse, 202
limit, 72
limitation, 140
listener, 191
listening, 44, 82, 132, 164, 230, 238
literacy, 86
literature, 169, 238
lobbying, 30, 37, 75, 87, 92–94, 106, 148, 156
loop, 30
love, 6, 105, 163, 202–204, 275, 303, 309

Mahatma Gandhi, 157
mainstream, 39, 74, 168, 172, 181, 233
making, 45, 54, 78, 99, 156, 224, 287, 294
male, 5, 125
man, 39, 59, 196, 229, 243
maneuvering, 114
manifest, 44, 54, 78, 114, 129, 149, 151, 196, 210, 231

manifesto, 13–15
marathon, 303
march, 158
marginalization, 54, 60, 125, 140
Maria, 211
mark, 268
marriage, 76, 87, 95, 97–100, 103–105, 112, 129, 163, 259, 277, 284, 285
Martin Luther King Jr. Thoreau's, 157
masculine, 168
matter, 11, 26, 142, 244, 284, 309
Maya, 204
meaning, 196, 199, 299
means, 33, 99, 103, 157, 168, 169, 171, 229, 230, 242, 252, 259, 302
media, 22, 26, 28–30, 36, 44, 50, 71, 72, 74, 82–85, 94–97, 107–109, 146, 151, 168, 169, 172, 181, 189, 218, 237, 238, 252, 259–261, 270, 277, 285, 286
medium, 18
meeting, 163
member, 111, 124, 129, 132, 143
memory, 275
mentee, 264
mentor, 198, 264
mentoring, 263–265
mentorship, 28, 49, 51, 214, 251, 264–266, 273–275, 301, 310
message, 29, 149, 157, 198, 252, 303, 305
metaphor, 303
method, 24, 164, 193
milestone, 265, 284

military, 21
mindedness, 1
minority, 8
miscommunication, 78
misinformation, 28, 72, 83, 97, 109, 114, 144, 173, 286
misinterpretation, 79
mission, 198, 254
misunderstanding, 77, 78, 109, 201
mix, 1
mobilization, 18, 21, 27, 28, 30, 71, 87, 100, 111, 116, 151, 152, 154, 157, 165, 260
model, 51, 256, 264
moment, 6, 15, 99, 198, 200, 203, 220, 253, 308
momentum, 27, 114, 142, 261, 285
money, 26
morale, 243
mother, 200
motivation, 284
movement, 1, 3, 7, 15, 20, 25–28, 41, 43, 44, 46, 50, 51, 55, 56, 59–61, 72, 77, 78, 87, 88, 100, 112, 113, 122, 124, 128, 146, 151, 158, 162, 165, 172, 175, 179, 184, 193, 209, 218–221, 224, 229, 234, 239, 242, 244, 246, 251, 253, 260, 266, 270, 274, 276, 277, 281, 285, 286, 294, 298, 300–302, 304, 308–311
multitude, 16, 302
mural, 18
murder, 72
myriad, 5, 39, 85, 99, 201, 210, 259, 301

name, 261
narrative, 70, 146, 158, 164, 167–169, 175, 189, 191, 284, 299, 302
nation, 76, 122
nature, 9, 11, 95, 135, 139, 144, 158, 181, 210, 232, 261, 277
navigation, 43
necessity, 13, 44, 54, 57, 85, 142, 154, 165, 184, 204, 219, 259, 264, 268, 300, 301
need, 10, 11, 45, 51, 70, 86, 92, 124, 125, 132, 139, 166, 195, 211, 254, 260, 263, 292, 300, 301
negativity, 295
negotiation, 103–105, 111, 124
network, 23, 25, 29, 202, 204
New York City, 130
newfound, 2, 204
news, 109
Nigeria, 67
nightclub, 243
non, 7, 22, 47, 54, 78, 107, 125–127, 139, 230, 233, 264, 274, 286, 287, 305
nonconformity, 10
nonviolence, 159
normalization, 166
notion, 6, 46, 143, 157
nuance, 181

obligation, 157, 184, 242, 244
observation, 264
obstacle, 92, 98, 124
Ocean Vuong, 169
offer, 70, 141, 214
official, 286

on, 5, 6, 13, 15, 17, 23–27, 31, 35, 36, 43, 44, 50, 51, 54, 57, 59, 66–72, 76, 83, 85, 86, 88, 89, 92, 94–97, 99, 100, 103, 104, 111, 113, 120, 122, 124, 128, 129, 132, 135, 139, 143, 145, 146, 148, 156, 158, 163–165, 171, 174, 191, 196, 198–200, 203–205, 209, 211, 215, 229, 233, 237, 241, 242, 253, 254, 256, 258, 260–262, 265, 268, 269, 273, 274, 279, 284, 286, 288, 291, 294, 299, 301–303, 305, 309, 311
one, 1, 10, 12, 24, 28, 35, 39, 44, 45, 48, 59, 72, 164, 204, 205, 213, 219, 242, 244, 252, 273, 309
opening, 217
openness, 220, 242
operation, 271
opinion, 92, 94–97, 107, 143, 156
opposition, 92, 98, 103, 129, 146, 167, 285, 286, 308
oppression, 3, 4, 41, 43, 51, 54, 59, 64, 72, 120, 122, 139, 174, 216, 232, 234, 237, 254, 262, 304, 308, 309
option, 195
order, 31, 139
organization, 14, 18, 46, 71, 98
organizing, 15, 29, 49, 216, 233, 253, 260, 274
orientation, 13, 20, 59, 67, 70, 76, 92, 94, 111, 120, 132, 141, 142, 146, 164, 181, 224, 229, 233, 237, 305

Index

Orlando, 243
ostracism, 24
other, 22, 26, 41–43, 50, 57, 76, 79, 92, 106, 114, 125, 150, 153, 169, 182, 203, 232, 239, 244, 254, 256, 259, 260, 262, 274, 286, 295, 304, 311
outcry, 140
outlet, 215, 279
outreach, 15, 69, 260, 273, 285, 286
overlap, 301
oversimplification, 172
overwork, 206
ownership, 27, 30, 50, 159, 276

pace, 112
pain, 11, 215
painting, 1
pandemic, 72
panel, 50
parade, 286
part, 3, 22, 46, 129, 145, 217, 224, 230
participation, 15, 25, 27, 37, 72, 222, 260
partner, 209
passage, 305
passion, 10, 27, 209, 215, 251, 274
path, 4, 5, 10, 61, 157, 239, 294, 303
pathway, 103
penchant, 6
people, 40, 41, 47, 50, 54, 57, 71, 72, 99, 125, 168, 175, 180, 181, 233, 243, 260, 274, 301, 304, 311
perception, 37, 97, 112, 259
performance, 5
performativity, 5, 13, 125, 287

period, 279
persecution, 67, 138, 139
perseverance, 253, 294, 300, 303
persist, 47, 64, 67, 96, 97, 109, 129, 131, 142, 172, 183, 242, 259, 266, 271
persistence, 91
person, 45, 59, 60, 173, 174, 178, 196, 211, 232, 239
persona, 203
personal, 3, 4, 6, 36, 44, 68, 72, 156, 163, 167, 169, 172–175, 178–180, 185–187, 189, 191–193, 195, 198, 199, 202–204, 208–210, 214–219, 273, 274, 279, 296, 299–302, 308, 311
personality, 10, 215
personnel, 140
perspective, 5, 13, 76, 131, 142, 167, 199, 232, 253
Pete Buttigieg, 22
phenomenon, 24, 112, 199, 268, 277
philanthropic, 254
phrase, 216, 217
piece, 305
pillar, 75
place, 1
planning, 16, 18, 116, 209, 253, 265, 275
platform, 15, 21, 49, 83, 85, 143, 175, 180, 260
play, 61, 87, 92, 129, 138, 175, 179, 214, 221, 225, 234, 260
poetry, 1
point, 11, 141, 203, 216
polarization, 109, 110
police, 158, 233

policy, 11, 37, 66, 75, 87–89, 105–107, 109, 124, 137, 153, 253, 256, 274, 286, 305, 311
pooling, 80
population, 103
portrayal, 129, 168, 172
position, 143
possibility, 286, 305
potential, 43, 57, 64, 76, 83, 96, 112, 129, 130, 132, 135, 143, 160, 164, 168, 172, 179, 211, 214, 237, 243, 270, 305
poverty, 304
power, 7, 18, 21, 22, 28, 29, 31, 42, 59–61, 66, 70, 73, 77, 82, 85, 87, 89, 94, 100, 107, 116, 129, 132, 135, 141, 146, 150, 159, 161, 162, 169, 172, 175, 179, 187, 192, 193, 198, 204, 220, 236, 239, 246, 248, 252, 256, 260, 265, 270, 273, 282, 284, 287, 301, 302, 309, 311
practice, 49, 186, 230, 231, 290, 296
precedent, 143
precipice, 308
prejudice, 10, 11, 114, 117, 201, 254, 304
presence, 103
press, 28, 29
pressure, 6, 132, 260
prevalence, 72, 109, 168, 240
pride, 25, 130, 178, 265, 276, 285
principle, 141, 219, 309, 311
prioritization, 124
priority, 141

privacy, 193
privilege, 4, 24, 44–46, 59–61, 122, 182, 183, 221, 227, 229–232, 236–238, 242, 304
problem, 168, 218
process, 4, 46, 54, 71, 92, 100, 103, 105, 111, 156, 167, 199, 213, 224, 279, 285, 286, 294
professional, 209, 279
proficiency, 78
program, 16, 269
progress, 67, 70, 74, 76, 92, 99, 120, 142, 159, 180, 253, 256, 261, 284, 303, 311
proliferation, 146
prominence, 218
promotion, 128
protection, 21, 67, 76, 99, 129, 131, 164, 259, 273
protest, 158
provide, 86, 131, 140, 157, 173, 175, 195, 214, 220, 238, 245, 273, 279, 295, 299, 301
public, 15, 19, 22, 26, 28, 29, 36, 37, 49, 72, 86, 87, 92, 94–97, 107–111, 113, 114, 116, 156, 158, 166, 180, 198, 203, 243, 259, 260, 274, 303, 305, 311
purity, 112
purpose, 12, 72, 77, 199, 216, 285
pursuit, 22, 54, 73, 94, 98, 175, 203, 244, 273, 277
push, 68, 73, 268, 285
pushback, 11, 289, 294, 300

quality, 5, 125, 287

Index

queer, 3, 5, 8, 13, 15, 17, 31, 39–41, 45, 47, 50, 54, 57, 59, 60, 68, 74, 138, 139, 141, 167–169, 173, 174, 178, 180, 181, 189, 196, 198, 202, 203, 210–212, 217, 232, 243, 260, 268, 274, 288, 301, 311
queerness, 168
quest, 7, 22, 68, 97, 124, 246, 270, 274
quo, 15, 28, 48, 251

race, 13, 24, 47, 54, 59, 76, 92, 120, 125, 139, 146, 167, 174, 181, 182, 229, 232, 237, 254, 262, 301
racism, 60, 167, 232
radio, 95
rainbow, 6
rally, 71
rallying, 141
reach, 29, 36, 50, 71, 107, 286
reality, 20, 70, 180, 219
realization, 3, 76, 268
realm, 2, 54, 59, 78, 80, 111, 114, 117, 130, 132, 141, 151, 173, 180, 191, 193, 242, 244, 275, 277, 281, 284, 289, 299, 305
rebellion, 6
recognition, 22, 28–30, 33, 47, 67, 76, 99, 120, 125, 126, 129, 139, 196, 230, 259, 283, 291, 301
reference, 239
refining, 277
reflection, 61, 230, 264, 286
reform, 256

reframing, 105
refugee, 131
regard, 310
rejection, 196, 198, 203, 211, 213, 214
relationship, 8, 29, 203, 204, 209, 259, 264, 292
relativism, 131, 141, 142
religion, 139, 146
reluctance, 11
reminder, 7, 48, 145, 159, 209, 261, 270, 274, 298, 308
repeal, 21, 286
report, 21, 241
repository, 87
representation, 15, 22, 33, 54, 60, 74, 94, 97, 168, 181, 189, 193, 232, 253, 259, 270
representative, 57, 253, 274, 302
repression, 67
reprisal, 15, 195, 220
research, 26, 36, 107, 109, 201
resilience, 22, 28, 33, 49–51, 70, 85, 100, 116, 140, 141, 146, 151, 154, 157, 165, 178, 199, 202, 214, 216, 251, 256, 261, 264, 265, 274, 275, 278, 286, 294–296, 300, 301, 303, 305, 308
resistance, 6, 27, 69, 77, 78, 100, 130, 131, 146, 157–159, 211, 309
resolution, 65, 124, 129, 131, 132, 164, 203
resolve, 159, 165, 308
resource, 28, 47, 129, 130
resourcefulness, 140
respect, 70, 92, 148, 195, 214, 238, 242

response, 11, 15, 38, 152, 158, 165, 166, 213, 239, 243, 310
responsibility, 230, 238, 242–244
responsiveness, 44
result, 78, 79, 183, 243, 277
resurgence, 139, 144
retrospective, 275
return, 209
rhetoric, 77, 114, 144
richness, 168, 302
right, 30, 85, 99, 144–146, 242, 251
rise, 71, 77, 140, 144–146, 169, 241, 242, 252, 300, 303, 309
risk, 44, 172
road, 10, 261, 303, 309
roadmap, 157, 251
role, 18, 21, 61, 63, 70, 87, 92, 94, 95, 97, 122, 129, 175, 179, 181, 202, 214, 221, 224, 225, 234, 235, 237, 242, 260, 263, 264, 270, 271, 274, 300, 301, 304
rule, 158
ruling, 99, 143
run, 71
rush, 198

s, 2, 4–11, 13–15, 18, 20–23, 27, 28, 30, 32, 39, 44, 45, 48, 49, 51, 56, 64–66, 70, 71, 73, 85, 89–91, 94, 96–100, 102, 106, 109, 112, 114, 116, 122, 124, 125, 132, 135, 139, 146, 157, 159, 164, 196, 198, 199, 202–204, 208, 209, 211, 215, 216, 218, 219, 242, 244, 246, 251–254, 256, 258, 259, 261, 263–270, 273–275, 277, 283–285, 287, 301–304, 309–311
sabbatical, 279
safety, 72, 83, 164, 286
scale, 66, 68, 76, 83, 88, 128, 129, 135, 284
scholar, 51, 182, 229, 232, 259, 261, 301, 304
scholarship, 273, 310
school, 2, 3, 6, 10, 11, 75
scrutiny, 203, 242
sea, 202
section, 15, 18, 20, 23, 31, 33, 41, 43, 59, 62, 66, 68, 71, 73, 80, 89, 92, 94, 97, 100, 105, 111, 114, 117, 120, 128, 130, 133, 135, 138, 141, 146, 148, 151, 162, 165, 171, 177, 180, 185, 191, 210, 216, 219, 221, 224, 232, 234, 244, 251, 263, 266, 268, 275, 281, 289, 292, 296
security, 270, 286
seek, 112, 201, 237, 309
self, 4, 6, 7, 10, 72, 154, 196, 199, 204, 206, 209, 210, 214, 215, 230, 252, 261, 264, 284, 289, 290, 301
sensationalism, 172
sense, 2, 8, 12, 15–17, 21, 24, 25, 27, 30, 31, 36, 50, 72, 77, 99, 159, 178, 184, 198, 199, 202, 204, 206, 214–216, 218, 219, 230, 234, 270, 273, 274, 276, 284, 285, 295, 296, 302, 308, 310
sensitivity, 70
sentiment, 129

series, 10, 13, 125, 200, 218
service, 92
session, 164
set, 138, 143, 287
setback, 286
setting, 97, 209
sex, 67, 76, 95, 98, 99, 103, 112, 129, 142, 143, 163, 238, 284
sexuality, 24, 47, 54, 67, 69, 76, 78, 125, 139, 167, 203, 232, 262
shape, 10, 76, 96, 122, 174, 232, 242, 263, 264, 284
share, 2, 24, 36, 50, 70–72, 156, 168, 172, 173, 175, 177, 178, 180, 195, 198, 199, 202, 206, 214, 218, 220, 238, 252, 310, 311
sharing, 17, 49, 68, 80, 88, 156, 180, 191, 193, 195–198, 251, 296, 299, 302
shift, 22, 70, 165, 206, 248, 259, 284
show, 92
Sidney Tarrow, 165
sign, 206, 261
significance, 5, 41, 98, 133, 195, 219, 264, 269, 288, 289, 302
silence, 12, 24, 196
sit, 158
skepticism, 44
skill, 239
society, 5, 7, 19, 22, 33, 35, 41, 53, 56, 59, 64, 109, 111, 113, 119, 135, 142, 144, 149, 162, 172, 182, 198, 214, 221, 224, 227, 230, 234, 237, 239, 242, 244, 246, 253, 261, 266, 268, 270, 273, 274, 286–288, 303

socio, 59, 138, 139
soil, 3
solace, 203, 215
solidarity, 2, 3, 16, 23, 28, 36, 42, 43, 50, 56–59, 63, 70, 72, 73, 75–77, 88, 106, 116, 120–122, 130, 132, 141, 148, 159, 168, 169, 178, 184, 198, 202, 218, 234, 237, 242, 260, 274, 276, 286, 296, 302, 303, 308
source, 198, 199, 204, 270
sovereignty, 124
space, 2, 15, 24, 146, 196, 204, 211, 218, 238, 264
spark, 1, 28
speaking, 37, 49, 78, 86, 238, 274, 311
spectrum, 16, 99, 168, 253, 303
speech, 28, 83, 146–148, 166, 198, 217, 252
spirit, 303, 308, 309, 311
split, 208
sponsor, 25
spread, 72
sprint, 303
staff, 241
stage, 215
stand, 5, 56, 63, 239, 308
standard, 76
state, 139, 209, 277, 305
statement, 7, 19, 260, 286
status, 15, 28, 48, 54, 59, 72, 99, 120, 131, 139, 174, 182, 229, 251
step, 129, 132, 143, 209, 286, 305, 311
stereotype, 240

stigma, 20, 67, 99, 109, 129, 135, 173, 196, 206, 214, 259
Stonewall, 308
story, 28, 30, 173, 174, 198, 217, 218, 265, 270
storyteller, 178, 191
storytelling, 28, 36, 49, 51, 70, 72, 85, 169, 171, 172, 180–182, 185, 187, 189, 193, 195, 198, 218, 252, 274, 296, 299, 302, 303, 309, 311
strain, 243
strategy, 21, 83, 105, 145, 152, 159, 185, 255, 274, 286, 295
stratification, 232, 301
strength, 3, 23, 25, 122, 151, 157, 198, 199, 202–204, 206, 221, 295, 296
stress, 8, 277, 300
struggle, 6, 7, 10, 35, 47, 49, 54, 66–68, 77, 78, 92, 94, 97, 100, 112, 117, 120, 128, 130, 140, 141, 178, 198, 203, 242, 247, 253, 258, 261, 264, 291, 294, 296, 308, 309
success, 20, 26, 30, 82, 88, 165, 265, 277, 284
sum, 45
summary, 30
support, 4, 9, 15, 21–26, 28–30, 41, 44–47, 49–51, 56, 64, 65, 71, 72, 75, 82, 85, 88, 92, 94, 95, 97, 109–111, 129, 140, 141, 158, 164, 193, 195, 199, 201, 202, 204, 205, 213, 214, 222, 224, 227, 234, 236, 237, 248, 253, 260, 261, 263, 265–267, 270, 273, 274, 276, 279, 286, 295, 305, 308, 310
surge, 169
sustainability, 113, 277, 294, 296, 311
symbol, 97
synergy, 69, 281
synthesis, 142
Syria, 139
system, 6, 137, 143, 199, 279

Tammy Baldwin, 22
tap, 29
tapestry, 3, 20, 23, 28, 41, 73, 178, 198, 202, 221, 229, 284, 302, 303, 309, 311
Taren, 1–16, 18, 23, 24, 26–30, 33, 36, 47, 49, 50, 64, 65, 69, 70, 73–75, 85, 89–91, 105–109, 116, 156, 163, 164, 198–204, 208, 209, 215–218, 251–253, 261–265, 268, 270, 273–275, 301–303, 310, 311
Taren Fira, 1, 5, 15, 18, 20, 21, 23, 25, 28, 31, 33, 35, 36, 46, 53, 59, 68, 73, 83, 84, 88–90, 97–100, 103–105, 111, 114, 122, 130, 148–151, 154, 157, 162, 163, 169, 172, 179, 180, 182, 187, 193, 198, 205, 209, 216, 217, 219, 234, 239, 244, 251, 257, 259–261, 263, 266, 267,

Index 335

279, 284, 286, 294, 298, 310
Taren Fira's, 4, 7, 10, 15, 18, 21, 22, 28, 30, 32, 48, 51, 66, 70, 85, 97, 98, 100, 102, 109, 114, 116, 122, 124, 132, 135, 146, 159, 164, 202, 204, 218, 246, 252, 253, 256, 258, 259, 261, 265–268, 270, 273–275, 285, 301, 303, 309, 311
target, 10
task, 15
tax, 99
teacher, 11
team, 106
technology, 68, 73, 82
teen, 72
television, 95
tendency, 44, 47, 233
tension, 112, 142, 203
tenure, 65
term, 51, 54, 59, 113, 120, 181, 182, 229, 253, 259, 261, 301
testament, 21, 28, 31, 66, 82, 94, 146, 216, 256, 265, 270, 273, 301
the Middle East, 76
the United States, 99, 112, 148, 305
theater, 1
theme, 300
theory, 3, 5, 13, 57, 66, 67, 92, 103, 124, 125, 128, 138, 139, 141, 167, 185, 189, 196, 215, 232, 237, 251, 261, 264, 268, 287, 296, 310
therapy, 279
thinking, 154
thought, 309

thread, 146
threat, 27, 77, 92, 103, 129, 144
tie, 6
time, 71, 195, 202, 206, 211, 242, 245, 265, 309
tokenism, 82, 218
toll, 199, 279, 291, 301
tool, 29, 36, 50, 72, 75, 82, 146, 156, 164, 167, 172, 179, 180, 185, 201, 219, 260, 285, 296, 299
torch, 263
torture, 139
town, 2, 26, 30, 37, 163, 265
traction, 29, 69, 77
trade, 131
tragedy, 243
training, 24, 37, 220, 241, 274
transfer, 263, 264
transformation, 171, 216
transgender, 22, 47, 50, 54, 59, 72, 92, 99, 145, 168, 175, 180, 196, 230, 233, 243, 265, 274, 283, 304, 311
transnationalism, 76, 77
transphobia, 139, 238
treatment, 76
triumph, 7, 49, 178, 296, 302, 309
trust, 46, 219
truth, 198
tumble, 6
turmoil, 173
turn, 49, 210
turning, 198, 203, 216
turnout, 286

Uganda, 67, 140
uncertainty, 165, 198
underpinning, 244

underrepresentation, 97
understanding, 2, 4, 5, 7, 10, 14, 15, 17, 18, 24, 26, 28, 33, 35, 44, 45, 48, 51, 54, 57, 59, 63, 68, 70, 75, 77, 82, 92, 94, 97, 105, 106, 109, 116, 122, 125, 127, 131, 132, 137, 138, 141, 148, 151, 156, 164, 167, 169, 171, 173–175, 177–182, 184, 185, 189, 191, 193, 195, 198, 200, 201, 203, 211, 213, 214, 217, 218, 221, 224, 227, 230, 232, 237, 238, 240–243, 253, 259, 264, 284, 291, 295, 299, 302–304, 311
undertaking, 18
unity, 17, 56, 77, 122, 234, 244, 246, 284, 285, 303
universalism, 142
unlearning, 236
unwillingness, 240
up, 1, 5, 75, 239, 308
uplift, 24, 41, 59, 229
uprising, 308
urgency, 36, 112, 156, 230
use, 51, 71, 85, 107, 109, 124, 187
utilization, 26, 68

vaccine, 72
vacuum, 301
validation, 44, 99, 125, 196, 201, 202
validity, 127
variability, 92
variety, 27, 150
veteran, 299
vice, 217

victim, 12
victory, 7, 75, 100, 105, 284, 286
video, 72, 218
view, 5, 92, 168
vigilance, 48
vigor, 209
violence, 20, 67, 113, 129, 131, 138–140, 143, 146, 148, 157, 166, 196, 233, 309
virus, 72
visibility, 15, 22, 25, 26, 28, 30, 33, 35, 36, 40, 44, 50, 54, 74, 83, 144, 218, 234, 252, 259, 265, 284, 286
vision, 203, 253, 254, 256, 263, 273, 275, 303, 309, 311
voice, 4, 35, 37, 179, 191, 198, 239, 252
vulnerability, 173, 193, 198, 199, 202, 220, 302

wake, 203, 253, 263
Walter Fisher, 299
warmth, 198
wave, 15, 256, 311
way, 7, 36, 70, 71, 113, 141, 151, 182, 214, 234, 284, 300, 302
weakness, 206
weekend, 209
weight, 198, 218, 279, 289
welfare, 164, 242
well, 70, 99, 124, 137, 154, 204, 205, 209, 278, 279, 291, 294
wildfire, 28
willingness, 44, 48, 103, 198, 242
winding, 308
wing, 144–146, 242
wisdom, 87, 299

Index

woman, 39, 211, 230
work, 21, 28, 41, 47, 50, 51, 53, 61, 64, 66, 70, 77, 94, 137, 199, 208, 209, 214, 216, 230, 233, 234, 238, 242, 246, 253, 254, 260, 268, 270, 273–275, 277, 279, 311
workplace, 241, 283
world, 1, 5, 7, 28, 33, 62, 64, 70, 73, 77, 114, 120, 122, 128, 130, 132, 149, 156, 159, 171, 182, 198, 203, 204, 208, 256, 261, 263, 271, 273, 275, 294, 303, 309, 311
worth, 120, 261

year, 30, 44
youth, 6, 214, 253